Contents

1	Introduction	1
2	Refusing to 'Buy a Pig in a Poke': Saying 'no' to M. Schuman	6
3	The Durham Miners Won't Have It: Domestic Sovereignty and the Schuman Plan	28
4	At the Intersection of Three Circles: External Sovereignty and the Schuman Plan	62
5	Not Beyond the Point of No Return: National Security and the Schuman Plan	95
6	With but not Of: Britain and the Schuman Negotiations, 1950-2	121
7	Conclusion	157
	Bibliography	167
	Index	171

ABSENT AT THE CREATION: BRITAIN AND THE FORMATION
OF THE EUROPEAN COMMUNITY, 1950-2

To Michel Passeleur
In acknowledgement of many helpful suggestions.

Absent at the Creation: Britain and the Formation of the European Community, 1950-2

CHRISTOPHER LORD
Jean Monnet Chair in European Studies and Senior Lecturer in Politics, University of Leeds

Dartmouth

Aldershot • Brookfield USA • Singapore • Sydney

Published by
Dartmouth Publishing Company Limited
Gower House
Croft Road
Aldershot
Hants GU11 3HR
England

Dartmouth Publishing Company
Old Post Road
Brookfield
Vermont 05036
USA

British Library Cataloguing in Publication Data
Lord, Christopher
  Absent at the Creation:Britain and the
  Formation of the European Community, 1950-2
  I. Title
  341.2422

Library of Congress Cataloging-in-Publication Data
  Absent at the creation : Britain and the formation of the European
  community, 1950-1952 / Christopher Lord.
      p.   cm.
  Includes bibliographical references and index.
  ISBN 1-85521-520-9
  1. European Economic Community–Great Britain. 2. Great Britain-
-Economic policy–1945- 3. Great Britain–Politics and
government–1945- 4. Great Britain–Foreign relations–Europe.
5. Europe–Foreign relations–Great Britain. I. Title.
HC241.25.G7L669   1996
337.4041–dc20   95-25910
                                                                    CIP

ISBN 1 85521 520 9

Printed in Great Britain by the Ipswich Book Company, Suffolk

1 Introduction

This is the story of why Britain remained aloof from what was to become the first stage in the development of the European Community. The argument of the book is that abstention was grounded in a set of attitudes that regarded the British state as in some way unique; as fundamentally different from its continental counterparts in its constitutional characteristics, its relationship with its domestic society and its roles in the world system. Moreover, this was an analysis shared by Governments of both main parties, Labour and Conservative, over the two years of 1950-2, during which the decision on Britain's relationship with the Schuman Plan, or European Coal and Steel Community remained open.

The Schuman Plan, a turning point for Britain and Europe?

On 9 May 1950, French Foreign Minister, Robert Schuman, announced a plan to 'pool' French and German coal and steel production. Other countries were welcome to join if they wished. The key feature of the Plan was that it would be managed by a supranational High Authority, strictly independent of member governments. This would then aim to modernize production; ensure that coal and steel were available to member countries on equal terms; develop common trading practices with outside countries; and level up working conditions in the coal and steel industries, this to include the equalization of wages. At first sight, the Plan was ambivalent in its means between dirigisme and market liberalization. On the one hand, Schuman referred to a plan for production and investment. On the other, he rejected the interwar experience of cartels in the coal and steel industries for the fusion of markets. It was predicted that the removal of nationalistic restrictions to

1

cross-border transactions would spontaneously produce the most rational rearrangement of the West European coal and steel industries, thus anticipating that the main work would be done by markets and not by administrative direction.[1]

Two years before the Schuman Plan, the Labour Foreign Secretary, Ernest Bevin, had described plans for an elected European Assembly as a 'Pandora's Box' full of 'Trojan Horses' (Bullock, 1983, p.659), his infamous mixed metaphor somehow only serving to emphasize the discomfort that British Governments would feel at plans to construct an integrated Europe. Four years after the Schuman Plan, Sir Gladwyn Jebb, Permanent Secretary at the Foreign Office, would scribble the advice 'embrace destructively' when confronted with the proposal that would ultimately lead to the establishment of a Common Market under the Treaty of Rome (Horne, 1988, p.363). Throughout these years, a constant refrain of both politicians and officials was that Britain should attempt to deal with the dilemmas presented to itself by European integration by retaining a political lead in West Europe, in order to channel the politics of unification into safe channels that would not conflict with UK policy priorities.

Yet the initiative was lost and quickly lost. From about 1950, British Governments faced a steady decline in their ability to take the lead, to embrace destructively or to keep Pandora's box closed. The decision not to become a full member of the Schuman Plan is often taken to have been a turning point. This was the first time that the UK had failed to take part in the plurality of international organizations that was springing up in postwar Western Europe. The Organization of Economic Co-operation and Development (1948), the Council of Europe (1948), the North Atlantic Treaty Organization (1949) and the European Payments Union (1950) were all more or less products of the same era as the Schuman Plan, but, unlike the latter, they included Britain. Nonetheless, the single act of abstention was as significant as the many of participation, for the Schuman Plan was, of course, the first of the European Economic Communities that would eventually evolve into the modern European Union.

The Schuman Plan as 'Copernican Revolution'

The dramatic impact of the Schuman Plan was maximized by the secrecy of its preparation and the surprise of its announcement. But its more euphoric supporters were not unreasonable in claiming it as a Copernican revolution in the practice of European politics that would require a reworking of settled assumptions, a reordering of central relationships and a change in the very character of dominant political entities. The Schuman Plan would be built around Franco-German reconciliation, where conflict between these two countries had previously set the biorhythms of European politics and defined the foreign policy roles of states other than the two protagonists. Franco-German frictions had also set a low ceiling on the possibilities of European unification. By contrast, the Schuman Plan suggested that the reconciliation of the two main continental states would only be possible with a supranational approach to institution building.

Indeed, the proposal to institutionalize a European Coal and Steel Community through the construction of a supranational authority was a further radical feature of the Schuman Plan, representing, as it did, the first major break with a convention of constructing international organizations in Europe along intergovernmental lines in which all decisions would need the approval of each participating government. Nonetheless, lack of consensus about the supranational principle meant that the Schuman Plan always had the capacity to produce a 'nuclear Europe': a relatively small group of states, committed to a faster track to integration than the rest. The eventual character of Schuman's radicalism would depend on whether it ended by dividing West Europe permanently, or unleashing a dynamic in which integration was more effectively achieved by proceeding in two phases: a first phase in which the defining frameworks of a unifying Europe were all the more coherently constructed because of the restriction of the membership to an inner core of the most committed; a second phase in which other, initially reluctant, countries were successively reassured, converted and attracted by the successes of an inner core that assumed all the risks of political experimentation.

Supranationalism: friend or foe?

That supranationalism should have been seen as a threat in the UK, where many on the continent saw it as an opportunity, was, of course, a product of the different attitudes and values of governing elites in Britain and the Six countries which joined the Coal and Steel Community. In his book, *Swords into Ploughshares*, Innis Claude argues that International Organizations may be constructed for either a) state substituting roles or b) state supplementing roles (Claude, 1956, pp.14-17). At a more abstract level, Jurgen Habermas distinguishes between 'life worlds' and 'steering mechanisms'. Life worlds include the collective identities that we would like to cultivate and, inter alia, the political units to which we would like to belong. Steering mechanisms consist of the functional or instrumental dimension to social life: the institutions we need to achieve our objectives (Habermas, 1988). European integration might, therefore, occur because it represents an attractive identity, or because it improves the capacity of component groups and societies to achieve important objectives. It may conversely be rejected because it conflicts with powerful senses of identity, or because there is little that it can contribute to the effectiveness of public policy-making that cannot already be delivered by national institutions.

What distinguished British elites in the early 1950's from those of the Six was that they saw little role for supranational European processes as either substitutes or supplements for the activities of their own state. They felt little attraction for the 'life world' of European integration and saw no great need for collective European mechanisms to 'steer' themselves towards their objectives. Participation seemed to offer little to British Governments who considered themselves to be largely self-sufficient in their ability to deliver successful foreign and domestic policy. Nor was there any discernable dissatisfaction with British national identity or institutions. But to return to our opening theme that the British state was seen as fundamentally different from its neighbours in its domestic and external characteristics, many in Britain were prepared to concede that the Schuman Plan made eminent sense for governments other than their own; and, in particular, for those continental countries whose national identities had been discredited by occupation or defeat in war and whose states lacked the capacity for international influence, or for ambitious economic and welfare policies at home. Indeed, a supranational Community, limited to just a few countries, was in some ways useful to the construction of new political coalitions that the British Government sought to build in West Europe.

A belief in the exceptionalism of the British state was also responsible for another major theme of this book - that the UK could, uniquely amongst West European countries, afford the luxury of influence over the new European Community without full membership. British Governments of the period 1950-2 anticipated that their economic and strategic importance to West Europe would give them a sufficient purchase over the decision-making of any continental grouping for some kind of association short of membership to be negotiable on British terms. This would at least be enough to protect UK interests and, at most, a basis for Britain to continue to lead the new Europe from outside. A consequence of this was that British Governments in the early 1950's did not see themselves as flatly rejecting the Coal and Steel Community, or being fully excluded from the Six. To the extent that things turned out differently, they were making a very different decision to that they thought they were making.

Organization of the book

Chapters 2 and 6 will be concerned with the dynamics of decision-making and negotiation that surrounded British reactions to the Schuman Plan. Chapter 2 will show how, in the three weeks between 9 May and 1 June 1950, the British Cabinet decided that neither full participation nor complete detachment would satisfy its interests and that it was, therefore, best to seek some associate membership of the new Community. Chapter 6 will discuss the attempts that were made to operationalize this policy of being 'with, but not of' Europe, and examine the criticism that the British Government was seeking some elusive middle way.

Chapters 3-5 will provide a thematic study of British government attitudes towards the Schuman Plan. Each chapter will attempt to evaluate contemporary assessments of what supranational European institutions would mean for the British state: for the British state as a carrier of political identity and for its capacity to deliver domestic policy objectives (chapter 3); for the British state as an international actor and maker of effective foreign policy (chapter 4); and for the UK as a military power, readying itself to contribute to collective security arrangements at the beginning of the cold war (chapter 5). The period over which this will be examined will be mainly concentrated on 1950-2, as this will allow us to encompass the ideas of both Labour and Conservative Governments and to follow the entire span from the announcement of the Schuman Plan on 9 May 1950 to its final ratification on 17 June 1952. However, some material from 1948-50 will also help to illustrate the main themes of the book and a brief extension of the story into the mid 1950's will have to be made to complete the chronology of the UK's relationship with the new Coal and Steel Community.

Notes

1. Note from the French Ambassador in London to M. Monnet, 9 May 1950, PRO [CE 2318/2141/181].

2   Refusing to 'Buy a Pig in a Poke': Saying 'no' to M. Schuman

As with many historically seminal happenings, the introduction of the Schuman Plan was accompanied by accident, misunderstanding and even comedy. While the American Secretary of State, Dean Acheson, and the German Chancellor, Konrad Adenauer, were tipped off a few hours in advance of the French initiative on 9 May 1950, the British Government was taken by surprise, Acheson apparently having to feign innocence when a lunch in Downing Street was interrupted with news that the French Ambassador had an urgent message. An atmosphere of confusion even within the French Government had been evident a few days before when the Prime Minister, Georges Bidault, had berated the main originator of the Plan, Jean Monnet, for first offering the idea to Schuman, only to find that a draft lay unread on his desk and that he had only missed the opportunity to give his own name to the beginnings of the European Community through slovenly reading of his mail (Monnet, 1978).

Although Bevin told Schuman that his announcement of the Plan without prior consultation meant that relations between their countries would never be the same again, pique was no substitute for policy, and over the next three weeks in which an invitation to join the Schuman negotiations remained open, the implications of full participation were carefully sifted by Whitehall. The British Government machine immediately slipped into gear with an impressive committee and reporting structure, linking the Economic Policy Committee of the Cabinet with the assessments of the Treasury, Foreign Office, Ministry of Defence, Board of Trade, Ministry of Fuel and Power and Ministry of Supply (Bullen and Pelly, 1986, xiv). In addition, submissions were received from both the Coal and Steel industries. One problem was, of course, that the full effects of joining could not be known until a Treaty had been negotiated in detail. Another was that the British

Government was only likely to take part if the constitution of the Authority could be made substantially less supranational than anticipated in Schuman's original announcement. One response to these concerns would have been to take part in the talks, to seek allies both inside and outside France for alternatives to the scheme as originally presented by Schuman, to wait and see what terms eventually emerged and, *only then*, take a decision on whether Britain would put its own coal and steel industry into the pool.

However, it was precisely this approach that was repeatedly blocked by Schuman. The French Government insisted that a precondition of entering talks at all was that the agenda should be limited to the supranational principle. This did not mean that governments had to subscribe to supranationalism from the start, only that they had to agree that the only constitution that would be discussed would be a supranational one. If, at the end of the talks, a government remained unconvinced of this approach to institution building, it would be free to withdraw. What it should not be able to do was to introduce counterproposals during the talks for an Authority that would be obliged to receive directions from governments. Not only was there no room for compromise on this point, there was no scope for prevarication either. By the beginning of June, the British Government was forced up against a deadline to indicate whether it would participate in talks on the terms laid down, an invitation that was finally declined by the Cabinet on 1 June 1950. The British Government was unconvinced by French reassurances that it would be perfectly free to reject a supranational authority, once it had indicated its willingness to talk about such a constitution. Given possible difficulties in leaving talks at a later date, it was also unwilling to start negotiations on its two core industries on the basis of only scant detail about the way in which the proposed Coal and Steel Community would work. In Bevin's inimitable words, there was no question of 'buying a pig in a poke'.

One view of these events was that there was nothing inevitable to Britain's exclusion at the first hurdle from the Coal and Steel Community. It was the result of weaknesses of decision-making and diplomacy within and between the British and French Governments. The US Ambassador to Paris, David Bruce, felt that the British Government demonstrated 'a vacuum of comprehension and an ineptitude of diplomatic discourse'.[1] On the other hand, the French Ambassador to London, René Massigli, described Monnet and his friends as 'éléphants dans un magasin de porcelaine' (Massigli, 1978, p.199)

A second interpretation is that the Plan was handled with ruthless efficiency by Schuman and his associates; that they wanted to exclude Britain all along and, to this end, designed and executed the perfect diplomatic trap by devising a plan that London was bound to reject, while attracting to itself the blame for a falling out that, in fact, originated in Paris. Both views need to be rejected as simplifications, though, paradoxically, a detailed examination of each yields some partial truths that advance our understanding of the UK and the origins of the European Community.

1.   The charge of ineptitude

The French deadline was imposed on a British Cabinet that was depleted of three of its senior members. Attlee, Bevin and the Chancellor of the Exchequer, Stafford Cripps, were all in varying states of ill-health. In fact, of the four Cabinet Ministers without whom Kenneth Morgan claims no major decision was usually taken by the 1945-51 Government only Herbert Morrison would be available to preside over the decisive Cabinet meeting on 1 June; and of the four, Morrison, at that stage, had least experience of foreign affairs (Morgan, 1985, p.59). Indeed, his remark before the meeting that the 'Durham Miners won't have it' is generally taken as an indication of the parochialism of the group that met on 1 June 1950. The French must have known about the condition of the British Cabinet, and on the British side, a failure of Cabinet Government can be seen as failing to do justice to much of the impressive spade-work that had been done in the previous few days by the Whitehall machine. Against this, it can be argued that Attlee, Bevin and Cripps all had opportunities to express their views before and after 1 June 1950 and that the eventual cabinet decision was broadly consonant with their known views about European integration.

On the other hand, a closer examination of the evidence shows that there were moments during May 1950 when both Attlee and Cripps were prepared to think the unthinkable about the Schuman process. Cripps concluded as early as 15 May that the UK 'should accept at once to negotiate *on the basis proposed by the French*' primarily because it would be extremely hard to admit Britain at a later date to a scheme that had been devised by France, Germany and Benelux on their own[2]. Attlee likewise told Massigli, 'that we must be in from the beginning'. As these comments suggest, there was no necessary connection between the undeniably strong views of the British Government on sovereignty and any one set of negotiating tactics. Indeed, the argument for remaining in the process was that this could even be the 'sovereignty maximizing course', for the UK could otherwise be exposed to the danger of the Six forming an 'alternative coalition', in which they would establish their own preferred trade-off between sovereignty and integration and then force the UK into the grouping at some later date if it was not to suffer damage to its economic interests.[3]

Between 15 May and 23 May, Cripps and Attlee made three key distinctions, which if taken further, might have allowed the Government to finesse the sovereignty issue. First, there was a difference between acceptance of a supranational authority in a defined area of policy competence, such as the management of two specific industries, and full political federation. The latter might be the eventual consequence of the Schuman Plan, but it was by no means the immediate issue on which a decision was required. Second, Cripps asked for clarification to be sought from the French Government on whether the final sanction of the supranational authority was to be from the Council of Europe, or from a Treaty that was both intergovernmental and revocable, the implication being that in the latter case Britain's coal and steel industries might be subject to a supranational authority, but only so long as Parliament chose not to recall the powers conferred. The formality of national sovereignty would be preserved and the legal position would not be dissimilar to the procedure of delegated legislation whereby the national executive could make laws on its own on the strength of powers conferred upon it by Parliament. Third, national sovereignty and democratic accountability were separate problems and, in the conversations of May 1950, it appeared that the second and not the first was the main problem that the Schuman model presented to the senior members of the Cabinet.[4]

By contrast to this admittedly limited evidence of brainstorming by the Prime Minister and Chancellor, the problem with the rump Cabinet that made the fateful decision on 1 June was precisely that it lacked the authority to do anything else than register the broad operating assumptions of European policy as they had developed before summer 1950. If such assumptions were not to continue under an inertia of their own, blind to such radical developments as the proposal of the Schuman Plan, they needed to be critically reappraised by precisely those senior members of Government who were absent at the end of May 1950. Even if the prospect of reappraisal was slim before 1 June - and the remarks of Attlee and Cripps mere obiter dicta - fresh thinking was even more improbable afterwards. By then a high profile decision not to participate in the Schuman talks had been taken and it had to be publicly justified. The arteriosclerosis of assumptions about Britain and supranational Europe had begun.

Another possibility is that the Government did not do all it could to improve its position at the interface of domestic and foreign policy: to prevent itself from being squeezed between an intractable French negotiating position and an implacable Labour Party. Bevin would have been a key figure in such an operation, perhaps insisting on another meeting with Schuman before the French deadline, or using his authority with the Labour Party to back any formula for keeping Britain in the game. Yet in the days leading up to 1 June, sickness and pain seem to have brought out the bluff and peremptory sides of Bevin's character at the expense of the complex and creative. His recorded comments consist of little more than a string of clichés about not being 'pushed around'.

Further currency is given to the idea that the British Government missed a trick by the formula under which the Netherlands entered the talks. The Dutch only agreed to discuss a supranational constitution for a new Authority on the understanding that they had severe reservations about such a model and might not, therefore, find it possible to sign up at the end of the day. Indeed, Massigli claims that *all* governments entered the talks with the possibility of ultimate withdrawal fully reserved. What is more, within two weeks of accepting that discussions should be confined to the supranational model, the Dutch were making the intergovernmentalist counter-proposal that the High Authority should, in effect, be subordinated to a Council of Ministers (Schwabe, 1988, p.223). Doubts about the supranational principle were widespread and even those who were attracted by it were unclear which they would prefer in the event of having to choose: an independent High Authority or British participation. By calling the French bluff and remaining inside the negotiations, so the argument goes, the British Government could have put itself at the head of a very powerful coalition in favour of a more intergovernmental Coal and Steel Community, and even without the UK, there was some drift in this direction during the course of the detailed bargaining.

A suggestion that the British Government could have used the Dutch formula to prevent an irreparable breach on the issue of sovereignty is encouraged by Churchill's claim that the Conservatives would have supported UK entry to the talks on a like basis. The full significance of this can only be understood in conjunction with two observations. First, Conservative-Labour bipartisanship was a powerful feature of contemporary British foreign policy-making, in fact the only strain in bipartisanship in the early 1950s was presented by the opportunity to attack the Government that was opened by the decision not to join in the Schuman talks. There was a clear basis for unity in British politics on the Schuman question to a degree that, paradoxically, did not exist, for example, in French politics. Under close questioning in the House of Commons it became apparent that in substance Churchill's position was identical to the Government's: join the Schuman Plan if intergovernmental, associate if supranational. The sole difference between the parties was the tactical one of whether the UK should have entered the talks under the Dutch reserve. Second, the Cabinet had, by 1950, had considerable success in asserting its foreign policy authority over its own party. As Morgan explains, this was a period when the Labour Party was probably more manageable than at any time before or since in its history. It was presided over by a harmonious Cabinet with a clear leadership structure. Rebellions in the parliamentary party had run their course or been accommodated by 1950. The party conference was as 'dead as a dodo', in the words of backbencher, Ian Mikardo and party discipline was assured by an intimate relationship between the Cabinet and TUC leadership (Morgan, 1984, pp.45-79). In another context, that of the Atlantic Alliance, the Labour Party had shown that it could accept innovative principles of international organization that might have seemed improbable to any student of Labour politics a few years earlier. As with NATO, there was scope for the Cabinet to exercise a lead by associating the success of the Schuman Plan with western unity, thereby capitalizing on the contemporary state of cold war crisis to secure domestic consent for international institution building that would otherwise constitute an unacceptable compromise of core values.

On the other hand, even it had been able to ease its party into the Schuman talks on the Dutch formula, the British Government argued, not without reason, that its international position set it apart from the Netherlands. The loss of colonies in the East made it all the more important to the Netherlands that the German economy should be revived and open to Dutch business. This meant that the Netherlands had little choice but to go along with France and Germany in key initiatives in European economic integration - and everyone knew this. The Dutch were able to enter the negotiations with a face saving reserve, preserving their right of ultimate withdrawal, precisely because it was meaningless and known to be so. By contrast, as the Permanent Under Secretary at the Foreign Office, William Strang, made clear, Britain really was in a position to wreck the Schuman Plan by staying in the negotiations only to leave them at some later date.[5]

The consensus view in the British Government was that it was better to stay out from the start than to take the risk that at the end of the negotiations the supranational principle would have been inadequately diluted, or the UK insufficiently converted to its merits. Although Britain could quite reasonably refuse to sign the Treaty under all the understandings that the French had offered prior to 1 June 1950, the practical politics might well be that a British rejection would lead to a complete collapse of the initiative. As this could have serious repercussions for Franco-German reconciliation, the stability of the domestic politics of any of the Six, or even the smooth construction of NATO, the retribution of the United States, in particular, was expected to be savage in the event of a failure that could be blamed on Britain. In a sense the UK was still sufficiently different from other European states, such as the Netherlands, to be circumscribed by its own strength. Even though few in Britain wanted key sectors of continental opinion to stop believing that Europe could integrate without the UK - indeed, many hoped that they would carry on believing this - it was preferable that the probability of its non-participation should be known from the start. This would avoid sustaining false expectations of Britain's ability to join only to puncture them dangerously close to the moment at which the parliaments of the Six would have to ratify any Treaty. This was made doubly important by a perceptive understanding within the British Government that although the supranational model might be qualified during the course of the negotiations, there were limits to what was possible here, for the principle was fundamental to Franco-German reconciliation and heavily underwritten by the increasingly prominent role of the United States in the talks.

Nor was the prospect of entering a major international negotiation, only to quit them again, perhaps with the impression of failure, attractive to a government with a small majority. The Attlee Government was under pressure to conserve every scrap of governing credibility for a general election that seemed almost certain in the immediate future. To that extent the domestic political conjuncture was less than propitious to Britain's participation in the Schuman Plan.

The charge of incompetence against the French Government is mainly to be found in Raymond Massigli's book, *Une Comédie des erreurs*. Massigli argues that the received wisdom in the French Foreign Ministry, the Quai D'Orsay, remained that Franco-German reconciliation should only proceed within the context of wider European initiatives that included Britain. This had apparently been confirmed by a decision of the Government as a whole as recently as 22 March 1950 (Massigli, 1978, p.192). However, French policy was, in Massigli's view, then hijacked when the formal diplomatic machine was by-passed by a small, ad hoc team of technocrats and European integrationists, led by Jean Monnet, who put the Schuman Plan together in just 9 days. As with the criticisms that would later be made against Henry Kissinger's private diplomacy, Massigli saw this as breaking logjams with dramatic results but also many unanticipated costs that would later be disingenuously rationalized as a far sighted strategy. Thus Monnet claimed always to have anticipated a progression in which Franco-German reconciliation would first be secured, the success of the Community and supranationalism would then be demonstrated to Britain, encouraging it to join at some later date.

Massigli sees four problems with Monnet's account. First, Monnet was, apparently, genuinely taken aback by Massigli's own exposition of the extent to which the Schuman Plan was likely to drive French and British policy apart (Massigli, 1978, p.199). Second, the Monnet group steamed on without any consideration of how an intergovernmental Community could be used both to incorporate Britain and bind the German Prometheus quite as efficaciously as a supranational approach. Massigli was confident that an intergovernmental commercial Treaty could tie West Germany into much the same web of economic interdependence as Monnet anticipated, but with the added advantage of keeping Britain in the process and saving France from being locked alone with West Germany into a little Europe. Third, even when Monnet's planners had decided on their preferred route, their disengagement from the formal information network of the Quai meant that they failed to pick up signals that Massigli was relaying that supranationalism could take a form acceptable to the British that would capitalize on their instinct to remain within European processes wherever possible. In particular, Massigli argues that the Plan could have been adjusted to test the implications of a conversation he had with Attlee in which the main problem with the High Authority, as then proposed, was considered not to be its independence from Governments, but the absence of democratic accountability. Fourth, Monnet's two-phase strategy assumed that the benefits of Franco-German reconciliation would not be cancelled out by the wider division of West Europe. It also contained no prediction as to the time that it would take to move on from the first stage to the second, from Franco-German unity to West European unity. In all, Massigli concludes that French policy was a typical piece of Fourth Republic 'chacun pour soi' (Massigli, 1978, p.188).

Confusion within the two Governments was reflected in some turbulent dealings between the Quai D'Orsay and the Foreign Office. On two occasions, compromise formulae that might have allowed British participation in the talks were suggested and then withdrawn. On 30 May, Schuman handed a memorandum to Britain's ambassador in Paris, Sir Oliver Harvey, which outlined the position that even if Britain was being asked to confine the negotiations to the supranational principle, it would be under no obligation to sign up to any Treaty that emerged from the talks.[6] Schuman even went on to invite the British Foreign Office to draw up its own form of words for entering negotiations on such an understanding. However, when London came back with the proposal that it should 'negotiate in a constructive spirit and in full sympathy with the aims of the French proposal', this was eventually rejected by a committee of the French cabinet, Schuman himself finding the British formula to be lacking so long as it included no specific commitment that the talks would be confined to the option of an independent High Authority.[7] Two days later, and as their own deadline approached, the French Government suggested a meeting of foreign ministers to thrash out some basis for negotiating the Plan. However, by the time Harvey obtained instructions to accept the offer, it had been withdrawn.[8]

2.   The charge of conspiracy

An alternative view is that Schuman and, still more Monnet, wanted to exclude Britain all along. The original announcement of the Plan was specifically presented as a proposal for a Franco-German coal and steel authority. The invitation to other countries to join can be seen as being made in full expectation of a British refusal, given the views that the UK Government had developed on supranational approaches to European integration over the previous three years (Bullen in Schwabe, 1988, p.202). According to this interpretation, Britain was thus offered membership of the Schuman Plan in the same way as the Soviet bloc was given the opportunity to join the Marshall Plan: both schemes were deliberately constructed to exclude unwanted guests and their architects could, accordingly, well afford to go through the formalities of offering membership to those who were never going to join anyway.

Only a month before the Schuman Plan, Bidault's proposal for a three-power directoire for the western world, made up of Britain, France and the US, seemed to suggest that Paris still regarded the UK, and not Germany, as its principal European partner. As late as 27 April 1950, Harvey was advising London that

Britain's implicit veto on European institution-building was intact: a 'European system based on France and Germany is unacceptable to France...the essential feature of a European system is the participation of the UK'.[9] Incomprehension at the apparent suddenness with which French policy seemed to break from its immediate past, prioritize the West German relationship and back schemes for European integration which Britain felt unable to join as a full member, tempted some in London to see the Schuman Plan as a deviation from the normal course of things: a hijack carried out by a small clique in Schuman's private office who were prepared to experiment with a policy of reckless hostility to Britain. On 17 May 1950, Hall recorded in his diary that 'ministers all thought that the Schuman Plan was a plot and argued at some length why it was hatched' (Cairncross, 1989, p.112).

The following factors have been cited as evidence of an intention to exclude Britain from the start. First, the Plan was sprung upon the British Government with only two hours warning. By contrast, both the German and American Governments were given some advance notice. Second, this procedure broke an understanding between the US, UK and France that they would not make any proposals towards Germany without first discussing matters between themselves. In addition, the UK was the occupying power with responsibility for the area immediately affected by the Schuman Plan: the Ruhr. Third, the way in which the French Government made and then withdrew two offers to open discussions with the UK during May 1950 roused suspicions that wiser counsels in the French Administration were repeatedly being overruled by a hard core in Schuman's cabinet who did not want Britain in under any circumstances. Fourth, the closed agenda and the rigid deadline to accept that talks should be confined to a supranational authority were interpreted as a kind of blackmail or shotgun diplomacy. To some, Bevin perhaps included, the Schuman Plan was little less than an attempt to 'mug' British foreign policy. If the UK accepted, it would have been defeated in a most public way on the core principle of how European unity was to be institutionalized. A French success in forcing Britain to accept supranationalism could only bring about a dramatic alteration in third party perceptions of the relative strengths of Paris and London.

However, a British refusal also risked a re-ordering of diplomatic hierarchies. Indeed, one version of the conspiracy theory is that a deadly competition for diplomatic influence was being played out within the quadrilateral likely to dominate postwar Europe: France, West Germany, the UK and the US. The closeness of the relationship between the US and the UK had frequently over-ridden French foreign policy goals since 1945. Since the formation of the West German state in 1949, Bonn too had become an influential force in Western counsels, in spite of the de jure limitations on its sovereignty in matters of foreign policy. The formation of a European Community without Britain offered France a once-off opportunity to break out of third place in the western diplomatic hierarchy and escape possible relegation to fourth position behind West Germany. Not only would France enjoy the most intimate and earliest rights of consultation with Bonn, it would also have something of a veto on West German external policy. French hints of disapproval would provoke speculation that the Six were coming under strain, unsettling both neighbouring states and German domestic opinion who expected West Germany to pour its relations with the outside world through reassuringly multilateral frameworks like the new European Community. As the leading member of a continental grouping, Paris would equal or trump London as an access point to Europe and ensure that the UK/US 'special relationship' did not monopolize Atlantic relations.

In addition to the suspicion that France was really engaged in a selfish scheme to re-order diplomatic relationships in its favour, Bevin accused France and the US of plotting against the UK's commercial interests by designing an industrial grouping with a constitution that they knew Britain could not join for political reasons (Massigli, 1978, p.188). Another idea was that Britain was deliberately excluded from the Schuman Plan for reasons of ideology, rather than power politics or economic interest. According to this view, Britain's exclusion was the logical conclusion of the explicitly neofunctionalist idea of European integration with which Monnet and his associates worked. This required that some supranational authority should be present right from the start, if there was to be an identifiable prototype for a fully European government, if publics were to be gradually socialized into the experience of an increasing proportion of public affairs being handled at the European level, if there was to be a force motrice capable of extracting the 'European interest' from the miasma of 'national egotisms' and if there was to be a single, definite point at which pressures for more and more European integration could cumulate.

3.   Monnet and Schuman defended

The defenders of Monnet and Schuman see no conspiracy, only a French Administration that was working to remorseless deadlines to save both its domestic and foreign policies from collapse. If the formation of a Community of Six was to be something of a diplomatic and economic triumph for postwar France, this was a long way in the future. In May 1950, the Schuman Plan was conceived and presented in an atmosphere of some desperation and for motives that were largely defensive. If the Plan had features more likely to lead to Franco-German agreement than the inclusion of the United Kingdom, this was less a matter of intention than of the need for the Plan to meet the immediate exigencies facing the French Government. It was not a matter of choice for France that, in the summer of 1950, sustained economic recovery, alliance building in NATO and domestic political survival all demanded that priority should be given to Franco-German reconciliation. Yet even those, like Monnet, who saw most clearly that the Plan put Franco-German reconciliation before everything else, were not prepared to give up on Britain if its Government could be persuaded to join on terms that would also stabilize the relationship between the main continental countries. In the end, it was the impossibility of achieving these two things at once, and in the hurry that seemed to be demanded by the circumstances of 1950, that sealed Britain's exclusion. It is, indeed, essential to understand the Plan from the French end, if we are to appreciate the depth of the difficulties that were involved in getting Britain on board.

To begin the detailed defence of the Monnet/Schuman position, the Schuman Plan was no more 'bounced' on the British Government than it was kept secret from most of the French Government itself. Only nine people were in on the secret of the Schuman Plan before 9 May and, if the British Government only had two hours warning, the French Council of Ministers only had five (Bosuat, 1992, p.748). The breakneck speed with which the Plan was prepared was dictated by the need to table a French proposal for multilateralizing control of coal and steel before France was forced into retreat on unilateral controls over German industry at the Atlantic Council scheduled for 11-13 May 1950. The surprise of the announcement was a matter of public relations, designed to maximize the dramatic impact of the Plan in French and German politics and to shatter the idea that Franco-German hostility was a fixed feature of the political landscape. There was little if any intention to humiliate or wrong-foot British diplomacy and, in any case, Monnet and Schuman were merely delivering on an agreement, already made with Britain and America in September 1949, that France would make concrete proposals for the future of Germany before the next Atlantic Council.

Nor was there anything conspiratorial in the prior consultations with Acheson and Adenauer to the exclusion of Bevin. Quite apart from the fact that the former only received the advantage of a few hours, the order of consultation merely reflected the reality that Germany and the US were in a stronger position than the UK to veto the Plan. A plan for Franco-German reconciliation could scarcely be pursued in the teeth of German opposition, while experience of meetings of the three occupying powers had frequently taught that any alignment of the US with either Britain or France could usually prevail against the UK or France on its own. It is true that many on the continent continued to believe that European integration could not work without the British, and for some months after June 1950 the adequacy of domestic political support for a Community based mainly on France and Germany was uncertain. However, Britain was critically constrained from mobilizing any continental opposition to a Europe of Six, so long as this was supported by the United States. Monnet's correct identification of Germany and

America as key to his scheme says more about the inherent features of what was being proposed, and a decline that had already begun in Britain's position in continental politics, than it suggests a deliberate coup to wrest for France the diplomatic leadership of West Europe.

As for the behaviour of the French Government between 9 May and 1 June 1950, the most sympathetic explanations were offered by Britain's own ambassador to Paris, who reported that 'the French Government was astonished and pleased at their success in tying up the Germans and were unwilling to do anything that would enable them to escape'.[10] The enthusiasm of Adenauer's personal response on 8 May 1950 and rapid confirmation of acceptance by the German Cabinet by 24 May 1950 would seem to have narrowed the options for the British Cabinet. Monnet and Schuman now knew that they had a good chance of making rapid progress with their main goal of Franco-German rapprochement. There was even talk of sewing everything up in a draft treaty over the summer. By contrast, Monnet's five day visit to London in mid May only served to confirm that the subsidiary goal of including Britain in the negotiations would sow doubt and slow proceedings: 'we would lose the simple principles at the heart of the proposal' (Monnet, 1978).

Again Harvey understood Monnet's motives. He told London that Monnet was determined that 'Anglo-French divergencies' should not be aired in the 'presence of a German delegation'.[11] This 'not in front of the Germans' attitude also accounts for Schuman's apparently strange behaviour in making an offer to hold a conference to resolve Anglo-French differences only to withdraw it. He explained to Harvey that the Germans could not be excluded from such a meeting, which could, in any case, do little more than register an impasse in positions between London and Paris.[12] Although Adenauer was plainly delighted by Schuman's offer, there were important forces in German politics, especially industrial interests themselves, who could welcome British support for any attempt to wriggle out of the full supranational rigours of the proposed scheme. The State Department likewise picked up Monnet's fear that an uncommitted British Government might unstitch the deal with Germany.[13] Although Schuman and Monnet identified coal and steel as an ideal starting point for Franco-German reconciliation and European unification, they were deeply anxious that France would be in an unequal position to Germany in these industries. This imbalance could eventually be neutralized by replacing inter-state bargaining with an impartial supranational authority, but this would only happen after a preliminary round of Franco-German negotiations which could represent a moment of danger for France as the weaker party industrially. Not only was West Germany the stronger producer of coal and steel, the slippage of allied controls meant that its bargaining power was likely to increase with the length of time needed to negotiate the detail of the Schuman Plan. All of this underlined the need for the closed agenda that London could not accept. This would speed negotiations and lock Germany into acceptance of the supranational approach.

Harvey also noted that Monnet and Schuman were coming under acute domestic pressure by the end of May to make an immediate start to the negotiations: 'French press and public opinion' were 'following discussions with considerable anxiety'.[14] The permanent threat of a change of government in France, which might cost Schuman the Foreign Ministry, weaken support for the supranational approach, or lead to some other policy vacillation also made it important that Monnet should lock the negotiations into an agenda that would preserve the integrity of his original conception.

The Foreign Office was, in fact, well informed of the urgency that had inspired Schuman's initiative. Harvey reported that M. Parodi, Secretary-General of the French Ministry for Foreign Affairs, feared 'we are steadily releasing Germany from all her servitudes without doing anything to bind her into the West'.[15] Although the policy of the French Government had been adapting as much as it had been retreating, it was possible for its domestic opponents to present a very different picture in which French postwar diplomacy had been defeated at every turn by the Anglo/American combination: on the internationalization of the Ruhr, the decision to allow the creation of a new German state and the progressive easing of restrictions on the capacity of German industries that had recently been the basis of the Nazi war machine.

Yet all of these changes - and Franco-German reconciliation itself - were essential to the construction of the Atlantic Alliance. Chapter 5 will show how, for all its fears of German rearmament, the French Government cared deeply about the successful formation of a collective defence in NATO. To play its part, France was now expected to make further concessions at the May 1950 meeting of the Atlantic Council and, in particular, to weaken the International Authority of the Ruhr (IAR) without which there would be no further deconcentration of German cartels and no institution to guarantee French producers equal access to the vital outputs of the Ruhr by parcelling these out between export and domestic consumption. To many, this represented the 'last line of retreat in French policy' (Bosuat, 1992, p.738).

The Foreign Office advised that 'all in all, Schuman had good reason to fear that Allied policy in the German coal and steel industries would cause something of a political crisis for him in France.[16] Bidault, who had now been fully converted to the Schuman Plan, felt that 'if we do nothing we are lost. The greatest danger to France is not revolution, or Caesarism, but sleep' (Dalloz, 1992, p.307). Monnet has likewise described the feeling that French policy had reached a dead-end by Spring 1950: 'no one imagined that the present limits on German production could be perpetuated, but no one wanted to subscribe to a decision that would bring them to an end..the course of French politics did not allow it' (Monnet, 1976, pp.336-7). Without a completely new approach, French Governments would continue to be isolated in international conferences, reduced to begging for 'small amounts of coal' or 'brief reprieves' from the full rigours of German reconstruction (Monnet, 1976, p.325).

The completely new approach would have to satisfy America, West Germany and French domestic opinion. Anything less would mean that there would be no overlap between solutions by which the new Atlantic Alliance could be stitched together and a foreign policy that could command a winning coalition in domestic politics. Unless France and Germany could embed their relations in some institution or project in which both had an overwhelming interest, there was a real danger that government commitments to rapprochement would be quite insufficient. Domestic politics would oblige each side to fight its corner in the many unliquidated disputes that remained between the two countries: dismantling, decartelization, the Saar and so on. Old national psychoses could gradually re-emerge and loss of elite control over foreign policy gather momentum. This problem was clearly evident in Franco-German relations. Schuman had, in fact, been committed to reconciliation since 1948 (Poidevin, 1986 (a), p.208) and Adenauer had even proposed a complete political union between France and West Germany. Yet in April 1950 the two countries were if anything moving even further apart, following a unilateral decision to incorporate the Saar into the French economy. Adenauer, who had only a slender majority in the Bundestag, now found himself under savage attack from the Social Democrats who represented him as a stooge of the West incapable of defending German interests.

The answer provided by the Schuman Plan was breathtakingly simple. Administrative restraint of West Germany's economy would be replaced by a new mixture of free exchange and the political regulation of the coal and steel industries of all participating states. Free exchange would internationalize Europe's economic base and make it difficult for any one government to mobilize coal and steel for military purposes. As internationalization would go hand in hand with trade expansion, the decoupling of industrial and military power would no longer depend on the repression of economic opportunity. In so far as institutional restraints remained, they would apply to all ECSC members and would not, therefore, be discriminatory measures, specifically directed at West Germany, like some permanent emblem of war guilt.

The originators of the Plan thus saw themselves as involved in something far more grandiose than a petty conspiracy against British influence in West Europe. For them, the stakes were nothing less than the termination of a failed approach to Franco-German relations that had lasted ever since France had first insisted in the Versailles Treaty of 1919 that, of all West European states, Germany alone should be limited in its sovereignty. From now on all restrictions would apply equally. Monnet even claimed that the Schuman Plan was the peace treaty between France and Germany that had never been signed at the end of the second world war (Monnet, 1976).

The urgency of the French search for radically new approaches to relations with West Germany and America was not confined to problems of European and Atlantic security. The continued economic recovery and reconstruction of France were also at issue. European economies were expected to return to external balance on their trading accounts by 1952. Should individual countries be unable to fund deficits in the absence of American aid under the Marshall Plan, there was a clear danger of a descent into protectionism. Not only would any Malthusian economic competition put an end to all political prospects of Franco-German reconciliation, Monnet also believed that France needed open markets if it was to fulfil its postwar ambition of completing the industrialization of its society and modernizing to a similar level of development as West Germany. A further problem was that France's economic plan - also devised by Monnet - assumed i) access to specific grades of coal and iron ores from Germany and ii) that France would be able to produce around 3 million tons of steel surplus to its own requirements. By proposing that German steel-makers should be allowed to return to full production, the British and Americans threatened to leave the French with excess steel-making capacity. In addition, as Monnet later recalled, 'allied documents showed that on its own, the German steel industry could absorb *all* the coke from the Ruhr'. This would have the effect of limiting industrial production in France and the rest of Europe: a complete and ironic reversal of the original intention to constrain West German output and capacity (Monnet, 1976, p.325).

Against this background, Milward somewhat gnomically remarks that the 'Schuman Plan was needed to save the Monnet Plan' (Milward, 1984). By guaranteeing free exchange, it precluded political interference with French access to the raw materials of the Ruhr. By embedding the next phase of West European market integration - the creation of a Customs Union in coal and steel - in a new Community to which its members had made a massive political commitment, the Schuman Plan created confidence that the future lay with liberalization and expansion, not protectionism and contraction. Indeed, in so far as it perpetuated what Milward calls the virtuous cycle of export-led growth in postwar West Europe, it headed off threats of either excess capacity, or balance of payments difficulties, in any one country.

4.   The indispensability of the supranational principle

In 1950, attitudes within the British and French governing elites to intergovernmental structures could scarcely have been more contrasting. Whereas the former considered the OEEC to have shown that traditional approaches had continued validity in the postwar world, many in the French Government drew the opposite conclusion that the OEEC had demonstrated that the limits of what could be achieved intergovernmentally fell well short of what would be required of any international organization capable of dealing with Europe's problems. Intergovernmental organizations were, according to this view, little more than a cloak of respectability - a facade of unity - behind which individual governments went unconstrained and continued to act much as they would if quite unrelated one to another. They could only deal with trivial, technical matters at the margins of national sovereignty. They soon descended into 'à la carte' relationships in which member states only managed spasmodic acts of co-operation in those rare moments in which their governments all wanted to do the same thing at the same time. Monnet was convinced that 'intergovernmental systems, already enfeebled by the compromises by which they were established, were soon paralyzed by the rule of unanimity' (Monnet, 1976, pp.322-33). Indeed, international organizations constructed on such a basis could even be destabilizing, encouraging everyone to abdicate responsibilities to some abstract totality, when this could never be any more than a sum of the national parts. This had been the bitter lesson of the League of Nations. Powerful support for this analysis came from Adenauer, who failed to see how it was possible to talk of European integration without supranational institutions,[17] presumably on the grounds that any intergovernmental option amounted to no more than the perpetuation of a Europe of separate states.

Although it may seem strange to have it so described, Monnet's case for supranational institutions would have been familiar to the philosophers of the English enlightenment. It resembled John Locke's argument that because individuals are so bad at being judge and jury in their own case, it is rational for them to give up some of the sovereignty they enjoy in a state of nature for the political obligations of a common system of government. Only then can discords be arbitrated and collective action made possible. As with Locke's individual in a state of nature, Monnet believed that nations in a condition of intergovernmentalism were nominally sovereign but actually crippled in their potential by the absence of a disinterested institution. Without this, all proposals for common action contained the cloven hoof of national interest. There were no initiatives that commanded credibility as dispassionate attempts to define a common interest or distribute costs and benefits with impartiality. Willingness to act in common was cancelled out by a time-consuming failure to agree on whose terms action should be taken.

Monnet came to these conclusions through personal experience, rather than abstract reflection. Ever since the First World War, when he had persuaded the allies to expedite the sharing of supplies by applying just the model that he envisaged for the Schuman Plan, Monnet had believed that the effectiveness of international organization could be transformed by shifting the initiative from councils of ministers to multinational executives of civil servants, independent of their separate governments, yet always acting within a mandate conferred by them. Pierre Gerbet writes that:

> Monnet understood..the role that could be played by small teams of independent experts having the confidence of their governments, capable of being able to take a global view of problems..these would form a creative atmosphere, the dynamism of which would drag the governments along (Gerbet in Poidevin, 1986 (b), p.217).

None of these observations should leave the impression that Monnet and his associates were cavaliers seuls, engaged on an ideological frolic of their own. French Governments were expected to press for a postwar settlement that ensured that the European nation state was not reconstructed on the same basis as before. Central to this was the notion that European states and societies would be more and not less prosperous and secure if they all accepted restraints on their sovereignty. All of this was taken as a reversal of an assumption of West European politics that had culminated in the continuous crisis of 1914-50 - that physical security and public welfare were to be achieved through an ever greater intensification of the sovereignty of institutions within the state. The obvious problem was that these efforts could be mutually cancelling and collectively destructive, the classic examples here being the trade war and the arms race. The alternative was that West European states should voluntarily accept restraints on those aspects of their sovereignty that could lead to harmful forms of competition; in other words, that they should run a consensual state system, in which the sovereignty of European states was collegially defined. Harvey reported that although Monnet had probably not yet cemented a consensus for his supranational approach, there was a widespread belief in French governing circles that the British model of voluntarily co-operating nations was 'not integration at all, but merely a modernized form of the old fashioned system of alliances', incapable of solving 'pressing economic and security problems'.[18]

The problem in 1950 was that no progress had been towards operationalizing this aspiration. The policy of European integration was as much stuck in the sand as French policy towards the US and Germany, or the search for external economic balance and industrial modernization. The search for a credible route out of the impasse was as important to the equilibrium of French domestic politics on this as on the other matters. Indeed, it was linked to those other matters, for the supranational principle was the lowest common-denominator of Franco-German reconciliation: anything less would probably not have secured a rapprochement in 1950. The overriding preoccupation of West German policy was that the Federal Republic should be able to participate in the West European states system on a basis of equality. Adenauer thus told Schuman, 'we failed in 1919 because we tried to introduce peace on a basis of discrimination and superiority'; and he went on to call for 'a ceding of sovereignty based on mutuality and not victory or revenge' (Monnet, 1976, pp.336 & 347). What this meant was that if France wanted constraints on German power and assured access to its raw materials, it would have to impose like obligations on itself. Of course this task could have been left to a Council of Ministers, but this would be deeply problematic from the French point of view. Bargaining outcomes on a Council of Ministers would be critically shaped by who would do best in the event of a failure to reach agreements: by who could hold out longest in the event of a stalemate. As France expected, for example, to have more need of German coal, or to be the main loser from any over-production of steel, it was a reasonable surmise that it would be the weaker party: that it would be the demandeur, constantly squealing for the coal and steel authority to help it out of difficulties, while Germany would be able to practise a deadly insouciance and prevarication.

The implication was that the objectives of the Schuman Plan would be insecure under anything less than a supranational authority. There would be no assured access to the German raw materials needed for the modernization of the French economy; and no guarantee that German governments would hold to the intermeshing of trading and production processes that was supposed to act as a substitute for physical controls on the military-industrial capacity of the Ruhr. Indeed, Monnet looked to the new Authority to make some tough decisions that, in his view, were unlikely to be tackled with speed and determination by processes of intergovernmental negotiation: the continued deconcentration of the Ruhr and the sharing of its outputs between exports and home consumption in the event of shortages.

An intergovernmental Coal and Steel Community would be no more than a sham enabling France to cover its retreat on the German question. Indeed, it might not even be that. Jaded by years of false expectations from international processes, it was the supranational character of the new Schuman initiative that caught public and parliamentary imagination in France and convinced many that a consensual international organization really could provide a credible alternative to the forcible constraint of German power.

On the other hand, we do have to consider Massigli's objection that the supranational project was a sleight of hand that rested on a self-fulfilling, but otherwise quite needless, case for new institutions. A supranational constitution, in Massigli's view, was only necessary because it excluded the UK in the first place, for without Britain France needed such a framework to make up for the imbalances in inter-state power that would come from having to work on its own with West Germany in a Europe of the Six.

The flaw in this argument is that the British Government had allowed real doubts to develop about its commitment to West Europe between 1948 and 1950. This meant that if Monnet was to break the logjams described in this chapter he had, in John Young's words, 'to devise a scheme that did *not require* British membership' (Young, 1993, p.29). Hogan's description of French opinion as fearing a British 'desolidarization' (Hogan, 1987, pp.266-7) from the continent is largely confirmed by Harvey's reports just a few days before the announcement of the Schuman Plan: 'they (the French) cannot exorcize the fear Britain's special relationship with the US may become so close and so satisfying that no third parties will be admitted..Britain's Commonwealth relationship is associated with isolationism from Europe'.[19] Subsequent chapters will show that, even while it was most actively engaged in the formation of NATO, Britain's *publicly* stated doctrine was that it would not involve itself in Europe beyond the point of no return.

Meanwhile, its economic policy often appeared unneighbourly to the countries of Western Europe. By setting tight limits on the degree to which it could participate in a continental trade and payments system, rebuffing overtures for an institutionalized Anglo-French partnership and smiling upon the demise of Fritalux -a Customs Union of France, Italy and Benelux - Britain itself undercut the alternatives to a direct and largely exclusive Franco-German relationship (Milward, 1984). Bidault expressed a common feeling that Britain was cramping the political development of West Europe. In his view, France could neither live with Britain nor without it. Monnet's solution - in which a supranational institutional structure substituted for Britain as a means of containing West Germany - can, therefore, be seen to have been based on a keener appreciation of the limited possibilities of Anglo-Continental relations in 1950 than Massigli allows. To the degree that Britain could have acted otherwise towards its neighbours between 1948 and 1950, it brought supranational Europe on itself.

Even if Britain were to become a member of an intergovernmental Coal and Steel Community, there was a real danger that it would be a sleeping partner, turned outwards towards its commercial contacts in the Commonwealth and North America and otherwise only interested in the European group for the defensive reason of ensuring that the Franco-German core did not develop in ways prejudicial to the UK's own coal and steel interests. This would limit Britain's value as a counterweight to Germany and leave France in an unequal position little different to that it feared from a bilateral intergovernmental arrangement with its powerful neighbour. The geography of coal and steel increased the probability that Britain could be a semi-detached member of the Schuman pool, as nothing could change the fact that the industries formed two distinct clusters in West Europe: the UK and a centre that straddled the Franco-German boundary. Even as Community members, the British might be relatively uninterested in decision-making that only concerned the latter. Indeed, in so far as the UK had involved itself since 1945 in the future of German heavy industry, the French had every reason to expect that an Anglo-German bilateral axis was quite as probable as an Anglo-French counterweight. Clearly the former was the worst of all possible worlds from the French point of view.

A further subtlety was that a coal and steel Community with a supranational constitution was more likely to attract the support of the United States. It is too simple to say that France faced a choice between being locked on its own into a supranational Community with West Germany and accepting an intergovernmental alternative in which both Britain and France would be available to balance Germany. Through the Schuman Plan it could, in effect, have a double guarantee against German domination: one presented by supranational institutions and the other grounded no less than the Massigli vision in the distribution of inter-state power in Europe, but this time substituting America for Britain in the role of guarantor. This substitution had important advantages: the greater power of the US; its ability, in sharp contrast to Britain's hemmed in diplomacy, to make sacrifices, or expend accumulated political capital on setting up the ECSC; and the fact that US Administrations were intellectually committed to European integration. They would be external federators and not just external guarantors. By an irony, America's hold on West Germany, and thus its replacement of Britain as France's preferred ally, was made possible by Britain's own assiduity in coupling the US so firmly to the defence of Europe through the formation of NATO.

5.   Conclusion

A popular observation at the time was that the breakdown of May-June 1950 reflected a difference between French cartesianism and English empiricism: the one insistent on agreeing principles up-front, the other concerned to tie down all the details before entering a process. However, there is no need to posit pseudo-cultural comparisons, for the irreconcilability of the British and French Governments is understandable from basic propositions of negotiating theory:

1. Negotiating outcomes are critically shaped by prior decisions on agendas and procedures. Talks about talks thus become the talks themselves.

2. As negotiations proceed, it becomes increasingly difficult for participants to allow them to fail. They may even sign what they regard as a bad agreement, rather than damage their own reputation as reliable negotiators, lose domestic credibility, or dent the solidarity of the states involved in the talks.

3. As a corollary of 1 and 2, many governments will only enter talks, if covered against outcomes that would, in their view, leave them substantially worse off than the status quo ante.

With these points in mind, the British and French Governments can even be praised for taking only three weeks between 9 May and 1 June 1950 to search out the underlying logic of their position. The French had little choice but to entrench the supranational principle at the start of the talks, if they were to avoid what was for them the worst possible outcome of ending restrictions on the German economy without, at the same time, putting coal and steel beyond the reach of any future military mobilization by their neighbour. The British Government, on the other hand, needed an open agenda if it was to row the talks back from Schuman's initial proposals and thus avoid what it considered to be the worst possible outcome - a supranational authority. Harvey aptly summarized the dilemma: Schuman could not agree to anything which did not contain a 'prior commitment' and the British Government 'could not sign a blank cheque'.[20]

A very different conclusion, however, is that Schuman was unable to lure the UK into full talks because association always existed as a 'soft option': something that avoided awkward choices between complete exclusion from a European Community, which many considered dangerous for a mixture of economic and diplomatic reasons, and full membership, which many saw as incompatible with minimum levels of British sovereignty in both domestic and foreign policy. The danger was, of course, that association would be incapable of allowing the British Government to have it both ways, that it was no more than an excuse to postpone fundamental about the UK's position in Europe and that, with time, Britain would face steadily worse trade-offs in making a clear decision to take part or not take part. To this, we will have to return in chapter 6.

Notes

1. Bruce to Acheson, 4 June 1950, *Foreign Relations of the United States*, 1950, Vol.III, p.716.
2. Record of a conversation between Cripps and Monnet, 15 May 1950, PRO [CE 2338/214/181].
3. For a discussion of the logic of alternative coalitions in European integration see Andrew Moravcsik, 'Preferences and Power in the European Community: A Liberal Intergovernmentalist Approach', *Journal of Common Market Studies*, Vol. 31, No 4, December 1993.
4. Record of a conversation between Cripps and Monnet, 15 May 1950, PRO [CE 2338/2141/181] and Minutes of a Meeting of the Economic Policy Committee of the Cabinet, 23 May 1950, PRO [CAB 134/224].
5. Record of a conversation between Strang and the French Ambassador, 1 June 1950, PRO [CE 2726/2141/181].
6. Memorandum handed by Schuman to Harvey, 30 May 1950, PRO [CE 2595/2141/181].

7. Harvey to Younger, 1 June 1950, PRO [CE 2615/2141/181].
8. Harvey to Younger, 3 June 1950, PRO [CE 2668/2141/181].
9. Harvey to Bevin, 27 April 1950, PRO [FO 1041/10/50].
10. Harvey to Younger, 6 June 1950, PRO [CE 2804/2141/181].
11. Ibid.
12. Harvey to Younger, 3 June 1950, PRO [CE 2668/2141/181].
13. *Foreign Relations of the United States*, 1950, Vol.III, p.710.
14. Harvey to Younger, 6 June 1950, PRO [CE 2804/2141/181].
15. Harvey to Younger, 17 June 1950, PRO [CE 3068/2141/181].
16. Note by Wilson, 31 May 1950, PRO [CAB 134/295].
17. Record of a conversation between Henderson and the Federal Chancellor, 29 March 1951, PRO [CE(W) 1543/221].
18. Harvey to Morrison, 4 May 1951, PRO [ZP 18/8].
19. Harvey to Bevin, 27 April 1950, PRO [FO 1041/10/50].
20. Harvey to Younger, 6 June 1950, PRO [CE 2804/2141/181].

3   The Durham Miners Won't Have It: Domestic Sovereignty and the Schuman Plan

It is wrong to assume that either the Labour Government of 1945-51 or the Conservative Government of 1951-5 failed to understand the need for European collaboration in the postwar era. They even accepted that this could involve unprecedented permanency, intimacy and constraint in relations between states. This was clearest in their enthusiasm for the North Atlantic Treaty Organization, which will be discussed later in the book. Both Governments, nonetheless, strove to make the construction of any new West European institutions compatible with settled political forms and identities: with the undisturbed sovereignty of states and, particularly in the case of Labour, with a view of each national society as a legitimately separate endeavour to discover its own approach to economic and social life.

1.   Britain and European Integration: The Sovereignty problem, 1948-50

British Government attitudes on how national sovereignty should be related to the process of European integration had already been thoroughly tested between 1948 and 1950. During these years, the UK was called upon to respond to two initiatives which occasioned arguments of special interest. A Council of Europe had been set up in Strasbourg in 1948 to bring together ministers of fifteen West European Countries. This was fully supported by the British. However, Bevin unsuccessfully opposed a French idea that the Council of Europe should also have an Assembly, made up of parliamentarians of both government and opposition parties in each nation state, and that it should be granted full scope and authority to structure its own debates. It was hoped by some and feared by others that an Assembly would consider itself in some sense a parliament of Europe and give publics some unified and symbolic representation as 'Europeans', to run in parallel with their national democratic institutions: that it would provoke some brainstorming sessions on the ways and means of European unification, perhaps even to the point at which it could become a constituent assembly.

Meanwhile, the Americans attempted to promote European integration on the back of the Marshall Plan. The Organization for European Economic Co-operation was set up in 1948 to administer US aid to West Europe. It was now proposed that when the aid ended in 1952 the OEEC should nonetheless continue as a framework for an ambitious programme in which the West Europeans would i) integrate their markets through a programme of radical economic liberalization and ii) manage their macroeconomic policy in common. If the OEEC was to evolve in such a direction, the Marshall Planners were convinced that its existing institutions - constructed along classic British lines of periodic councils of ministers or civil servants from member states - would be quite inadequate. Although never systematized as such, their proposals for the OEEC were remarkably similar to the structure that would eventually be adopted for the European Community in the Treaty of Rome of 1957. A permanent Secretariat would be formed that would be independent of governments. It would be under the direction of a 'superman' who would be a significant political figure with a public profile of his own. The Secretariat would be responsible for proposing new initiatives, which would then require the consent of a Council of Ministers representing individual West European states. This Council would meet frequently, thus achieving an elite socialization that would facilitate the development of a progressively more ambitious co-operation between the West European states; indeed, the whole process could be considered an embryonic West European government, with the secretariat eventually emerging as an executive, the 'superman' as a President and the Council of Ministers as a Senate of states.

These suggestions compelled the Labour Cabinet to develop what were to remain - at least until 1961 and perhaps beyond - the fixed parameters of any European integration in which UK Governments felt they could participate. The fault line between Britain, the continental movement for European integration, and its American backers is often somewhat glibly described as lying between intergovernmental and supranational approaches to international organization. However, these terms need to be unpacked, for on closer inspection British Governments meant many things when they insisted that they would only accept intergovernmental institutions. Supranationalism, on the other hand, amounted to a complicated political strategy that was not the same as federalism, even though it *might* tend in that direction.

The essential component of the intergovernmentalism preferred by British Governments is usually taken to be the retention of a national veto in all matters of law and policy-making. This was, indeed, important to many, who held that any alternative would be incompatible with the Westminster model of parliamentary sovereignty. There was also a suspicion that Britain might be persistently outvoted under any system of majority voting. The Foreign Office warned that in 'any association operating under federal rules.. the United Kingdom would be confronted by an organized majority with the whips always on'.[1] Majority rule is rarely accepted by those who believe that they will be permanently in the minority and there were three reasons for believing that this could, indeed, be the fate of British Governments in a West European grouping. First, other members would want to use individual policy decisions to catalyze a process of closer integration. Every small matter would thus provoke a federal/anti-federal cleavage with the UK on the losing side. Second, the party politics of West Europe seemed to be some way to the right of those of the United Kingdom with the implication that common policies would reflect an external - and not a domestic - centre of political gravity. Third, Britain was still, in 1950, in a league of its own in matters of economic prosperity. This could tempt the continentals to use a system of majority voting to construct mechanisms that were financially redistributive between member states. The UK would become paymaster for the new Europe. In fact, of all the possible permutations of how individual states might get together in West Europe, that of a union between Britain and the Schuman Six seemed to contain the greatest risk that the UK might find itself in a minority in the three ways described above.

However, British objections to the French and American proposals for European integration between 1948 and 1950 implied that even national vetoes might be insufficient to guarantee the retention of sovereignty. The Cabinet was particularly anxious that there should be no independent centres of authority in European institutions, capable of pushing even veto-holding governments in unwanted directions. A nexus of transnational bureaucracy, European Assembly, private industrial interests and outside powers such as the US could capture the agenda and initiative from national governments. The Treasury warned of 'an open conspiracy of bureaucrats and businessmen which would link the affairs of West Europe..to a point at which so many questions were being settled internationally that one had the substance of West European Government without its form'.[2] In response to a proposal that a supranational executive authority should have the right to make proposals which the Assembly of the Council of Europe could then turn into law subject to the unanimous approval of governments, a UK cabinet memo discussed the danger of government vetoes becoming 'theoretical' on account of the 'pressures to which the Committee of Ministers could be subject'.[3] Hall-Patch felt that the focus of decision-making would move away from national delegations to the Presidency of any supranational secretariat (Hogan, 1987, p.285).

The use by Conservatives of the Council of Europe to launch attacks on the Labour Government, alerted the Attlee Administration to the further possibility that the opposition party might use powerful transnational institutions as a means to embarrass a sitting government and, ultimately, even to infringe its traditional monopoly of domestic policy-making from outside by supporting the transfer of competences to the European level. Bevin warned the Cabinet that a European Assembly could be 'used as a stick with which public opinion could belabour the government of the day'. He went on to explain that he did not like the idea of a transnational public Assembly being able to operate 'even to a limited degree' independently of a private committee of ministers from different countries.[4] All of this amounted to a rejection of the position that independent secretariats or assemblies might be married with intergovernmentalism, so long as governments retained the right to say 'no' to the suggestions of the other bodies. Governments had to be the only significant political actors in international institutions *as well as* the holders of veto rights inter se.

It was sometimes suggested that what constituted an intergovernmental system was not the retention of national vetoes at all, but the principle that even when agreements had been unanimously agreed they should be non-binding. The logic of this position was that even a unit veto system could come to be a significant constraint on British Governments, if at any one time, the latter found themselves bound in by an accumulating corpus of previous agreements, some of growing antiquity, some entered into by UK Governments of another party, all compromising the British doctrine that the Westminster Parliament has unconstrainable rights to repeal all law previously made. Whilst a veto system would protect a British Government from entry into unwanted laws and policies it would obviously complicate any exit from such arrangements and make them hard to amend, as the UK could be held to any commitment by just one state reluctant to change a given policy.

The Labour Government was, indeed, concerned that national vetoes might be insufficient to counter the more entangling aspects of European integration, or to avoid an impression that Britain was solemnly committed to full unification. It was, therefore, eager that its involvement in West Europe should be understood to consist only of self contained and reversible acts of co-operation. These should deal with concrete problems of the moment and not be expected to cumulate over time into a process of institution building. No attempt should be made to intellectualize them as part of a wider process of European integration, or to suggest that Britain and other co-operating states had entered into some implied contract to work towards various 'finalités politiques'. Bevin told Schuman and the Belgian Prime Minister, Paul Henri Spaak, that West European co-operation should develop 'in a traditional British way' and on the model of the British Commonwealth; that is, without any written constitution or programmatic blueprint (Bullock, 1983, pp.616-7).

None of this meant that the Labour Cabinet of 1945-51 looked to a pattern of

European co-operation that would be totally unconstraining: that would miraculously allow the UK and its neighbours to co-ordinate their activities while 'remaining as free as they were before'. With disarming frankness, Bevin and Cripps had informed their colleagues in 1948, 'we shall have to make our plans in association with others. We shall not always be able to do as we wish in our own interests. Changes in our industrial and agricultural structure may become necessary to secure the economic independence of West Europe as a whole'.

It is true that this statement was made in 1948, when the British Government, in the absence of the American security guarantee that was to follow in 1949, felt a greater need to make sacrifices than they would in 1950 to secure coherent European co-operation. However, there was a world of difference between constraint, accepted under an intergovernmental approach, and the operation of any of the European institutional imperatives delineated above. The first would seemingly ensure that the new wine of European co-operation was firmly contained within the old bottles of traditional national institutions: that the formalities of the Westminster model would be preserved: that the British state would remain the only source of institutional authority in British society, no matter how much European co-operation changed the substantive content of government policy: that the British Government and others would remain meaningfully accountable to national parliaments, thus avoiding the forbidding task of constructing a transnational democracy. Any loss of policy discretion would be muffled, ad hoc and probably reversible. European co-operation without the institutional diminution of the nation state would also be in keeping with the principle that, for security reasons, Britain should not integrate itself with the continent of Europe beyond any point of no return. If intergovernmental institutions failed, there would be no problem of transferring functions back to the British state: of UK Governments having to re-develop roles they had divested, while picking up any economic or social debris left by a failed experiment with supranational Europe.

Preference for an intergovernmental approach was a matter of political calculation, as well of political value. It was believed that it would guarantee the UK a *privileged* position in European decision-making. Contemporary UK policy cannot be understood without the claim that Britain had the leadership of West Europe within its grasp. This implied that of all the states in the region Britain, uniquely, had the ability to secure European co-operation on its own terms: to ensure that the compromises needed to secure collective action would fall on others more than the UK. Sir Edmund Hall-Patch would later claim that Britain had 'always secured the greater part of its objectives without due difficulty' in the intergovernmental context of the OEEC, where he was the UK's permanent representative. He would rejoice that:

The Europeans look to us for leadership; they are delighted when we are able to give it; they respond to it in a remarkable manner. During the past four years when we have given a firm lead in the economic field it has invariably been followed.. Our officials were head and shoulders above their foreign colleagues in their knowledge of the issues and in their experience of exposition and negotiation - in this way we achieved the chairmanship of many committees..This meant that a consistent policy, *in line with that of HMG*, could be agreed in advance.[5]

The preservation of British leadership and an intergovernmental approach to European co-operation were inseparably linked in the minds of British decision-makers. Any supranational authority would act as a substitute for British expertise in devising initiatives and brokering deals between states. It would also split Britain's core diplomatic base in West Europe - the small countries that supposedly looked to the UK to deliver them from the dominant or unstable behaviour of France or Germany. The Benelux countries were likely to join a supranational institution, while the Scandinavians remained outside. Worse still, it was unlikely that British leadership could survive any Franco-German reconciliation, which would be one of the principle justifications of the supranational approach. Collective European processes could, finally, erode claims that the UK could serve as the most effective conduit for individual countries seeking access to Washington.

In spite of efforts described in the foregoing pages to clarify a British position on European integration and its implications for national sovereignty, the Schuman Plan did not entirely fit with established categories and definitions, hence the suggestion that any decision about the UK's relationship with the new authority was a little more open than has hitherto been appreciated in the literature. Ernst Haas has rightly described the Plan as a political hybrid (Haas, 1968, p.48) and as late as 1952, the British Foreign Office would, bizarrely, find itself engaged in an internal debate on whether the Schuman Authority was intergovernmental or supranational after all.[6]

It will be seen that this ambiguity was accentuated by the detailed negotiations from which the UK abstained. However, right from the start, other factors had to be weighed against the supranational flavour of a High Authority that would function independently of governments. The Plan was, after all, a self-conscious renunciation of any direct move to a fully developed tier of government at the European level: of any immediate ambition to create a European federation toute entière. Although its authors believed that the same result could be achieved incrementally, sector by sector, the powers of the new authority would for the moment be limited to Coal and Steel and any expansion of competence would require the unanimous consent of member governments. This obviously allowed some to argue that the correct response to concern about national sovereignty was not abstention but participation, for the latter would confer the right to limit and direct the evolution of the new Community from within.

Assuming that the new Community could be stripped of its dynamic potential and limited to Coal and Steel, British membership could have been further facilitated by the observation that there was no question of the new Authority fully displacing the roles of member states even in these two sectors. There would be a system of parallel competence. Although, in the event of conflict, rules set at the European level would obviously override national policies, the former would be limited in their operation to the pre-defined problems of co-ordinating national markets and policies in coal and steel. They could not be ultra vires to the powers conferred by the unanimous consent of governments in the founding Treaty of the Community. Subject to any constraint legitimately developed by the High Authority under the Treaty, national management of coal and steel would be fully operational, and quite probably, diverse in nature. Indeed, for all its de jure independence of governments, the High Authority was likely to be dependent on national civil servants and industrialists for the performance of important functions.

In the event, neither of these two arguments - that the supranational tide could be stemmed from within and that the Coal and Steel Community held to a balanced system of national and transnational institutions - represented a majority view within the British Government. The rest of the chapter and the whole of the next will examine four possible reasons for this. First, the claim that the Westminster model blighted all flexible and creative discussion in British politics about international institution building. Second, evidence that some sectors of the British elite were cowed by the more extravagant claims about the speed and completeness with which Europe was likely to unify in the near future. Third, the argument that the societies of Britain and the Six had recently experienced sharp divergences in the value they placed on national identity and the very factors that made European integration attractive on the continent rendered it unappealing in the United Kingdom. Fourth, the rather different idea that it was ultimately the failure of the Schuman Plan to appear useful to the British Government that shaped the way in which the sovereignty arguments were deployed, sealing Britain's abstention. It was only, to use Claude's language, because British elites failed to see how the Plan could perform a useful 'state supplementing role', capable of meeting their immediate concerns, that the sovereignty issue was not handled in a way that would have allowed the UK to join.

2.   The Westminster model

It is often argued that whilst the Westminster model of rule by a national parliament with an absolute and inalienable sovereignty was well suited to earlier political challenges of national integration and Empire building, it has imposed a straitjacket on both the internal and external development of postwar Britain (Marquand, 1988). Whereas other countries have profitably experimented with devolution at home and new forms of international organization abroad, British political elites have been threatened and bemused by these developments. Because of their intensive political socialization into the assumptions of the Westminster model and the difficulties they accordingly have in conceiving any alternative principle of arrangement to one in which the British Parliament represents the only locus of decision-making with final political authority (Johnson, 1977), they have supposedly found it harder than continental elites to accept that the writ of 'offshore' institutions should run inside their own national territory.

It is suggested that this has had the obvious effect of complicating the adjustment of British domestic politics to the rise of the European Community and the less obvious one of diminishing the influence of the very national institutions that many defenders of sovereignty have sought to protect. British elites have apparently been too preoccupied with the threat of European institutions to exploit the opportunities they present: to understand that they are not simply political competitors but important supports if national institutions are to function as adaptive actors, adjusting successfully to the complexification and partial internationalization of their own economies and societies.

A further problem is that European institution building has proceeded by a process of compromise and consensus, in which intergovernmental and supranational approaches have been mixed and matched. Those inclined to a 'pure' version of one of these approaches have thus tended to be out on a limb in the bargaining - or, to put it more technically, they have taken positions some distance from the median preferences of those negotiating the constitutional features of new European bodies and policies. Without the ideological flexibility to sniff out the centre of political gravity on the intergovernmental/supranational continuum, they have been unable to take the lead, or even to participate in winning coalitions with all the advantages this brings to setting the agenda. Instead, they have oscillated between fears of exclusion and fears of inclusion: fears of going into a process that conflicts with the sometimes idiosyncratic Westminster model of what constitutes a self-governing national community and fears of being left out of a transnational institution with a potential to make decisions important to the UK's immediate political and economic environment (Lord, 1992). This policy paralysis has, in turn, meant that much in Britain's relationship with the European Community since 1950 has been determined by the ability of other countries to form, or just threaten to form, common policy regimes on their own, impose costs of exclusion on the UK and even force it into transnational arrangements mildly prejudicial to its interests, where the alternative would be to incur the still greater risks of complete isolation (Moravcsik, 1993).

Many of these problems lay in the future at the time of the Schuman Plan. But the tendency for the issue of national parliamentary sovereignty to define the limits of flexible reflection was clearly apparent at every level of British political discourse. The Cabinet Committee which considered the Schuman Plan reported that it had taken as 'its *starting point*, the general opposition on both sides of the House of Commons during the debate on the Schuman proposals to both the establishment of a supranational body .. and participation by the United Kingdom in any Federal system'.[7] On close questioning in the House of Commons, it emerged that Churchill would not 'support entry to a supranational authority'[8] and that the government/opposition cleavage on how Britain should respond to the Schuman Plan did not, therefore, extend to any contemplation of a transnational pooling of sovereignty in relation to the coal and steel industries. Amongst the press, even strong supporters of the Plan felt that the government had rightly judged that it had reached the limits of what was negotiable once it had established that Schuman was serious in insisting on a supranational authority. Thus the *Spectator* felt that 'if this really is to be the first step towards a European Federation, then it is plainly out of the question for Britain to join; indeed, even as a first step it would be unacceptable'. *The Times* opined that there was a 'cogent answer' to the question of why Britain could not accept a supranational authority while others could and that this was to be found 'in this country's way of thinking' and that 'any government' would be 'bound to envisage an association' as one of freely co-operating governments.[9] Above all, it was the question of parliamentary sovereignty that defined the somewhat awkward official position that would persist unchanged from the initial recommendation to the Cabinet on 1 June 1950 to Macmillan's eventual decision to apply for full membership of the European Communities on 31 July 1961: join if intergovernmental, associate if supranational. This was awkward to the extent it contained an implicit admission that it could be best to join - if only the issue of parliamentary sovereignty did not get in the way.

3.   The slippery slope argument

In spite of the foregoing, it might have been possible to present the Plan as a limited and technical act of international co-operation: as an agreement that could only be enlarged by subsequent legislation and which would always remain revocable by any future Westminster Parliament. Although this could be an infringement of international law, British constitutional doctrine recognized no constraint on any subsequent repossession of national parliamentary sovereignty. This could even have been used to ease UK entry to the early European Community by suggesting that there was no such thing as loss of British sovereignty: any powers given to an international body would only be 'on loan'. However, the British Government chose instead to accept the Monnet thesis - about which there was nothing hidden or conspiratorial - that a Coal and Steel Community should be but the first step in a continuing process of European integration, incrementally built from specific initiatives. British belief in the dynamic potential of the new Community ensured that it could not be judged on its merits as a proposal limited to the Europeanization of the coal and steel industries, and that juristic observations about the reserve powers of the Westminster Parliament would only provide a 'dignified' veneer for significant and cumulative shifts in 'effective' control to a transnational political process. Those inclined to join would have to accept the risk that membership could lead to any degree of federation and very possibly full European integration.

The Foreign Office described the new Authority as a 'sub-federal machinery..a functional internationalism', designed as a 'step towards federation' and a 'prototype of federal institutions in Europe'.[10] It continuously argued that British acceptance or non-acceptance 'will be interpreted as an expression of our attitude towards a Federal Europe'[11]. Ministers were advised that they should only participate if they were prepared to continue the federal journey; to be 'hustled along the road to full federation through the creation of supranational authorities controlling a widening range of functions or commodities'.[12] Meanwhile, Harvey reported from Paris that Monnet expected the Schuman Plan to be anomalous in a Europe of nation states and that it would, therefore, either 'perish or infect the rest of the community with its supranational form'.[13] Cripps likewise told the House of Commons of the Government's view that 'such a scheme would hardly prove workable in democratic communities without complete federation'.[14] Given the strategic positioning of the coal and steel industries, the new Authority could not long remain unaccountable to democratic institutions. The Permanent Under Secretary's Committee added the observation that West Europe could not indefinitely go on proliferating new authorities without these eventually being brought under a unified system of parliamentary accountability. The sectoral/functional approach would eventually end up in the same place as the federal with a full constitutional structure at the European level.[15]

Indeed, it is a paradox that so long as it remained outside the European Community, the British Government contained some of the strongest believers in the proposition that, once off the starting blocks, European integration would either fail or be rapidly consummated through a remorseless spill-over logic, arising from the impossibility of managing one aspect of public affairs in isolation from the rest. Even the creation of tariff-free markets was considered impossible without i) macroeconomic policy co-ordination and ii) a common currency, conditions that would be impossible without a fully developed European government (Hogan, 1987, pp.110 & 183-4). In the months after May 1950, British assessments even came to see the spill-over from the Schuman initiative as working to an accelerated time-scale. The Plan was rapidly followed by proposals for a supranational authority to manage agriculture and a customs union to cover all aspects of European trade. Above all, France responded to the invasion of Korea and American pressure for rearmament with the Pleven Plan to create a European army, also under a supranational authority. The Foreign Office view was that the pooling of 'defence, coal and steel' would be quite sufficient to create a 'new sovereign, independent state'[16] and that market integration alone

> would inevitably involve an obligation for the economically strong and thrifty to give unlimited credit to the rest, or the establishment of machinery to co-ordinate exchange rates and/or fiscal/monetary policy. This would be impossible without agreement on the objectives of economic policy and would probably require a limited degree of federation.[17]

4.   **European integration and mid-century concepts of nationhood in Britain and the Six compared**

In defending the Westminster model, British Governments may only have been demonstrating the truth that politicians are on the whole domestic creatures soaked in the preconceptions of their own political cultures (Frankel, 1975). The Schuman Plan may have been a fork in the road between Britain and the Six, which if confronted at any other moment than 1950 might have led to less divergent results, for it caught British public opinion when it was at its most satisfied with the nation state and mainstream continental opinion at its most dissatisfied. Unhappily, there is little in the way of hard statistical evidence that would allow us to make a rigorous comparative analysis of popular conceptions of nationhood in 1950. Opinion polling had yet to develop methods of probing real public preparedness to trade national separation against European integration. Some limited polling by Gallup in Britain and France - illustrated overleaf - suggests two public opinions that were remarkably alike, but mainly in their inchoate nature. Publics had yet to be mobilized, troubled or divided on issues of European construction.

For a more satisfying analysis, we are forced to rely on the accuracy of contemporary observation and to imagine how the concepts of nationhood identified in these writings might have affected elite decision-making in the early 1950s. Mid-century Britain was a paradox. Although it was a trading nation whose fragile economic dependence on the outside world pushed it to the brink of financial default three times between 1945 and 1951, the mental maps of publics and elites assumed a self-enclosed polity that was amply able to look after itself and which was only likely to be diminished by contacts in domestic affairs with outsiders.

The Schuman Plan: a comparison of British and French Public Opinion.
British Gallup survey, 1950. Do you think that it is a good idea to pool the coal and steel industries of West Europe, including Britain?[18]

Good	27
Bad	21
Don't know	29

French Gallup survey, 1950. Are you in favour or opposed to the Schuman Plan?[19]

Favour	25
Opposed	13
No Answer	62

Historians, sociologists and other thinkers have captured the intense sense of nationhood - or, as some would prefer to put it, of socio-psychological community - that suffused mid-century Britain and reduced the appeal of any proposal for political integration with Western Europe. Henry Pelling has written of a shared assumption amongst the British that 'somehow or other, things in their own country were arranged better than elsewhere in the world' (Pelling 1984); George Orwell of a feeling that Britain was a 'family with a private language, common memories, and, at the approach of the enemy, it closes its ranks' (Stevenson, 1984); A.H. Halsey of a society which had mysteriously pulled off the trick of combining a high level of class division with an impressive degree of social integration (Halsey, 1986).

The cluster of attitudes that defined British nationhood would for several decades be anchored in the war and the 1940s. The war brought the British public together into an intensely lived struggle for survival that would be perpetuated in the conversation and culture of a whole generation. Indeed, the shared emotions of war happened to coincide with the further integration of the British public into a vivid new media of radio and cinema, providing a heady cocktail of formative experience. The peculiar qualities of Britain's state and society seemed to have been vindicated by its ability to stand alone against Hitler, whilst others fell to the invader with alarming rapidity (Kitzinger, 1973). To many, this cautioned against any move that could weaken the capacity of national institutions to mobilize public loyalties in times of danger, or expose the safety of the UK to the weaknesses and divisions of neighbouring societies.

By contrast, the trauma of 1939-45 - during which almost all European societies were at some stage defeated, occupied, temporarily extinguished as sovereign units, or shamed by the crimes of war - was to much continental opinion the final act in a crisis of confidence in the nation state as a provider of security and economic welfare. The impetus this provided towards integration commanded some sympathy in the UK, but it only seemed to prove that West Europe was a heterogeneous family of states and that there was, therefore, nothing incoherent in the belief that unification might be good for some, bad for Britain and a matter of indifference to others. Everything would vary from country to country, depending upon the health of their nationhood and statehood and their peripherality or centrality to the European continent.

In various reflections that included a request to British embassies in 15 West European countries to reply to a questionnaire on the local politics of European integration,[20] the Foreign Office seemed to incline to the view that there were four very different kinds of European state outside Britain: first, large states, like France, Germany and Italy whose political class inclined towards some degree of integration for its own sake because they were 'disillusioned with the efficacy' of (national) governance and wished to sublimate 'national divisions' or shame in 'some wider association or loyalty';[21] second, small countries like Benelux, where similar doubts about the 'adequacy of the national unit'[22] coexisted with a belief that only European integration could deliver 'stability without absorption and some measure of independence without a corresponding risk of isolation';[23] third, mostly peripheral countries like Sweden, Switzerland, Ireland, Spain and Portugal who had not suffered a crisis of confidence in their 'defensibility' as a result of the war (Bullen and Pelly, 1986, p.292n); and, fourth, states like Denmark and Norway whose record of indefensibility had to be set against high levels of satisfaction with domestic governance, largely successful nation-building, probable peripherality to any European project and the option of an alternative international co-operation confined to Scandinavia.[24] Britain's exceptionalism seemed to be underlined by its difference from all four categories: by its record of defence in war; by its fully developed nationhood and apparently well-adjusted domestic society; and by its peculiar ability to choose peripherality or centrality to European political processes, and to mix them on its own terms, in contrast to other countries, for which these things were much more a question of economic or geographical constraint.

The original six members of the European Community were arguably better prepared than the UK for European integration by a long history of sovereign powers being shifted between new, and sometimes transient, constitutional orders, often with redefinition of the territorial unit of governance thrown-in. Only two -

France and the Netherlands - pre-dated the nineteenth century and even the former could claim to be on its eighth constitution and fourth republic since 1789. In addition the 1939-45 war produced a new political class in these countries, less wedded than British political elites to a given institutional order and more determined to ground their legitimacy on a break with previous approaches to politics. Thus 80 per cent of those returned to the 1945-6 French Assembly lacked pre-war political experience (Rioux in Howarth and Cerny, 1981, pp.85-6). They owed their political socialization and assumptions to the resistance which had developed a strong commitment to the postwar integration of Europe.

In the UK, the war also produced a new and precise social contract, based around the commitment of Governments to full employment and a welfare state. This reinforced contemporary feelings of national integration. It left an impression that the British state for all its constitutional traditionalism, was a highly effective instrument of social transformation and that no-one needed, therefore, look outside the national arena for the delivery of political demands. It also encouraged a notion of 'social patriotism' with the consequence that both the main mobilizers of public opinion - the Conservative and Labour parties - were eager to retain national identity as an element of political appeal and social solidarity in postwar Britain. Far from seeking to abandon any purchase on the idea of national identity, Labour sought to redefine patriotism in terms of its own values and to loosen its connection with the Conservative Party. It was hoped that the new Britain would draw its collective pride from Labour's domestic programme, which would stand as a unique statement of how solidarity, fairness and rationality could be combined in a national community. As Morrison had put it in 1945, 'Planning as it is now taking shape in this country is something new and constructively revolutionary which will be regarded in times to come as a contribution to civilization as vital and distinctively British as parliamentary democracy and the rule of law' (Addison, 1977, p.274). Britain owed it to others, as much as to itself, to ensure that this experiment was allowed to develop without interruption by an excessively close association with the unstable political economies of West Europe.

Indeed, Britain's elite mistrusted the political systems of West Europe and feared that excessively close contact would risk contamination of what they considered to be their own uniquely successful polity. As the US State Department put it, 'The British do not have much respect for the political maturity, resoluteness or discipline of the continental countries...any proposal which would transfer to a European grouping the power to make executive decisions with regard to the British economy would appear to them to be placing their destinies in hands of foreign countries whose abilities they doubt'.[25] In one extraordinary outburst, Bevin told Spofford that it was the connection with the US and the Commonwealth and not any with West Europe that made the British public feel secure in the postwar world, 'People here were frankly doubtful of Europe. Londoners could not rely on Germans..the man in the street was almost instantly struck by the defeatist attitudes of the French'.[26] Mistrust was combined with conceit, as had been shown a year before the Schuman Plan when the British Government had considered a proposal for a Channel Tunnel. A Cabinet Committee advised that:

> An important element in the character of our national life would be altered by the creation of a land connection..the weakening of that unquestioning sense of superiority over the peoples of the continent that forms an essential element of British self-confidence and which has proved of value in recent times.

The report went on to describe the importance to the British people of a sense of separateness and distance that came from 'consciousness of living on an island'; and to question the assumption that 'closeness of peoples' improves relations between them.[27] At the risk of seeming to parody, there was a very British assumption that it is high fences and not a sense of community that makes good neighbours.

5.   The Schuman Plan and state capacity

Cogent though the considerations of the last three sections were, they would not prove insuperable once British Governments decided to apply for full membership of the European Communities. What distinguished 1961 from 1950 was a feeling within the British Government that it *needed* to be on the inside of Community institutions. Once this sense of necessity crystallized, the sovereignty arguments of the 1950s were conveniently turned upside down to allow for the possibility of British membership. Where implied commitments to a federal destination and dire predictions of inherent spill-over dynamics were used as reasons for staying out in the early 1950s, British Governments later claimed that the pace and nature of European integration would always be susceptible to political control, if necessary by just one state that was prepared to use its veto. Likewise, the tension between the Westminster model and the supranational dimensions of the Community suddenly came to be presented as a faux problème - European institutions would be adjusted to British constitutional practice, in large part through UK membership itself. Much of this reflected the plasticity and historical contingency of the very notion of sovereignty. While sovereignty is sometimes used to connote the political body whose decision is final in the making of policy or law, it is, on other occasions, used in an instrumental or utilitarian sense to describe the power of a society to influence its environment (Wallace, 1986; Howe, 1990). Where the first implies that any right of European institutions to a final say must represent a loss of national sovereignty, the second suggests that the sovereignty of states can be pooled or even enlarged in a setting such as the European Community, whose collective frameworks can be used to bring about results that governments cannot achieve individually.

After 1961, the notion of pooling and enlarging sovereignty entered British Government rhetoric. In 1950 this was, by contrast, a minority view. To see why, the remaining sections of this chapter will contrast two assessments of what membership of a European Coal and Steel Community might mean for the capacity of the British state: the opinion of some civil servants that the ECSC could help British Governments achieve important objectives will be compared with a strong belief in the Labour Party that the Schuman Plan would, on balance, be an unacceptable constraint on domestic policy-making and an unnecessary addition to the powers of UK Governments to manage international economic interdependence.

6.   A useful addition to the powers of the British state: a technician's view

A comparison of the economic consequences of various levels of British participation in the Schuman Plan began in May 1950 and continued throughout the remaining two years. Monnet's conversations in May 1950 with Britain's own 'economic planners', a group of senior civil servants who clustered around Sir Edwin Plowden, produced the conclusion that the UK would have to form some kind of intimate relationship European Coal and Steel authority.[28] On 17 May 1950, Hall noted in his Diary that at a meeting between Monnet, Plowden, senior civil servants and the President of the Federation of British Industry, 'opinion became more favourable as discussion proceeded. Everyone agreed that we ought to join if we could do so on suitable terms' (Cairncross, 1989, p.112). Apart from Hall himself, the argument for a close relationship with the Plan was most powerfully developed by David Butt and David Pitblado, respectively the Cabinet Office and Treasury representatives on the inter-departmental working party which was set up to consider the ECSC over the period 1950-2.

The economic assessment that the working party sent to the Cabinet on 31 May 1950 began in a style that did not immediately suggest the conclusion that was reached by Plowden's group. It was observed that the British coal industry was equal in size to those of the Six all put together, while its steel industry was also the largest of the group. The status quo allowed the UK to produce 85 % of its fuel supplies indigenously and to ensure reliable supplies of steel for its engineering industry. In addition to this self-sufficiency in coal and steel, Britain's own pattern of imports and exports suggested that it was not a natural trading partner with the Six in these industries. It imported no coal at all from the rest of the group, exported less than 2 % of its total coal production to the Six, imported only 1.1m tons of steel and exported a mere 100,000 tons. The meaninglessness of a group of seven (Britain and the Six) to Britain's industrial interest seemed to be underlined by the fact that if the UK did have an external dependency in coal and steel manufacture it was not with any of the Six but with Sweden from which it obtained most of its iron ore.

In spite of all this, various members of the working party argued that Britain had one overwhelming interest in some kind of intimate relationship with a European Coal and Steel Authority. The industries in question were subject to *international* crises of over and under-supply. Given the lumpiness, or, to be more technical, the enormous scale and indivisibilities, of capital formation in these sectors, it was easy to miscalculate output and investment. As a result, these industries had historically lurched between over and under supply, thus exaggerating the economic cycle and provoking more general trade wars in West Europe. In 1950, there was reason to believe that Britain and the Six could be on the verge of another crisis of this kind, as the total of steel-making capacity already planned by individual countries exceeded plausible estimates of future demand.

In a clever inversion of the argument that the size of the British coal and steel industries gave the UK a self-sufficiency that made the Schuman Plan irrelevant to its needs, officials in favour of a close relationship with the ECSC argued that a transnational mechanism to secure the stabilization of the two industries was a precondition of a full reconstruction of the West European trading system; that precisely because it was the largest regional producer of coal and steel, none of this would be possible without Britain; and that the parroting of figures that showed low levels of trade between Britain and the Six was beside the point, as no one could expect trade to be significant until such measures as the Schuman Plan were in place. In this vein, Butt argued that 'the potentialities for good of a body which will really take a grip on the coal and steel industries of Continent, and do so more effectively than all the inter-allied machinery of the last five years, are so great that it really would be very short-sighted not to get right in'.[29]

Indeed, the officials in favour of a close, institutionalized relationship with the ECSC argued that currently low levels of trading interdependence with the Six in coal and steel would not save the UK from the consequences of any European over-production. The use of measures to prevent the UK domestic market from becoming a dumping ground for a European surplus would be problematic. First, this might only deflect excess European steel on to UK export markets in the Commonwealth. Second, any decision to close the UK market to a flood of cheap steel would merely transfer a competitive problem from steel to engineering; German engineering would have an advantage over their British competitors in access to cheaper supplies of steel. An up-dated economic assessment in December 1951 drove the point home that the interests of engineering, as a sunrise industry, had to have priority over steel itself in defining Britain's relationship with ECSC.

It is not an ultimate objective that we should be self-sufficient in steel. It is much more important that we should have cheap and assured supplies as the basis of our engineering exports. It would be dangerous to hamper our engineering industries when competitors have access to cheap steel. If the Community's steel were to become cheaper than ours, it is important that we should have access to it.[30]

In addition to these general arguments, the working party considered separate assessments for coal and steel. In spite of opposition to the Schuman Plan from the industry itself, the Whitehall view was that British coal could do well from participation, depending on the success of the UK in pushing the ECSC in some directions and not others and on the response of the industry to the new competitive challenge. It was argued that 'Britain enjoys easy access to ports, good quality coals and coal that is suitable for (European) consumers' plants. Long-term prospects in the coal market are good'. A calculation of the balance between wage costs and productivity suggested that UK coal would face a tough competition with German producers. On the other hand, it would have a clear advantage over the French. An index was compiled that ranked the productivity of British, German and French coal at 1.27, 1.07 and 0.75 respectively. This competitive advantage was partially cancelled out by the higher wages paid to British miners. In the UK, wages accounted for 64.9% of costs, compared with 40.3% in Germany. However, the officials expected continental wage levels to converge on British, rather than the other way round. Although they were deeply sceptical of Monnet's original intention to promote wage 'equalization', they could only admit that any movement in this direction would be to Britain's advantage.

The December 1951 assessment attempted a similar calculation of whether Britain or West Germany would be the lowest cost producer in the event of free trade in steel. It began with the observation that the removal of tariff costs of 20-33% would in itself change the competitive behaviour of management and workforce in ways that made it very hard to predict who would be the winner from liberalization. A further problem was that neither Britain nor Germany had been producing under 'normal circumstances' over the past twenty years. In Germany's case cartelization in the 1930s had been followed by conversion of steel to wartime produce and allied controls since 1945. Nonetheless, the officials took the view that recent restrictions on German production meant that Britain had a temporary lead in the capitalization of its steel industry and that German equipment was therefore 'inferior', that Britain enjoyed lower material and transport costs, and a somewhat better match between its coal and steel industries. Once again, any advantage that West Germany might have in lower wage costs would erode once measures of economic recovery, such as the Schuman Plan, allowed it to attain levels of full employment characteristic of the UK.[31]

Robert Hall drove home the force of official support for a close relationship with the ECSC in a memo to the Prime Minister on 21 June 1950: 'the working party has come to the conclusion that there would be great advantage to Europe and the UK in freer market conditions, co-ordination of investment, regulation of production in a slump and exchange of information'.[32] Not only would the seven as a whole benefit from freer market conditions in coal and steel, but Britain could be expected to do especially well within the group.

The officials went on to anticipate - and then dismiss- two possible objections to their conclusion that Britain needed to form a close relationship with the ECSC. The first of these was that the new Authority might turn out to be incompetent: 'bad planning is worse than market forces'. But such a risk was inherent in all institution building and, in any case, it only sharpened the case for an effective British input to the new authority, as UK industries would be affected by the ECSC in any event. More generally, there was no reason why the Schuman Authority should be a worse judge than national governments of forthcoming slumps and booms; indeed, its economic judgements would probably be a collation of national assessments, but with the added advantage that they could facilitate co-ordination and reduce the danger that Britain and the Six might pursue conflicting policies. The officials were particularly attracted by the prospect of the two main industrial centres in West Europe, Britain and Germany, making their 'investment plans in the critical sectors of coal and steel' with full knowledge of each others' intentions. A transnational authority would force a 'confrontation' between the production and investment plans of West European industries. These could then be adjusted in so far as they implied any mismatch between supply and demand.[33]

The officials also considered the possibility that the general interest of the Seven might not coincide with the particular interests of the UK. For instance, the economic cycle might not synchronize across the group. A policy of expansion or contraction appropriate to the Six might be precisely the opposite to what was required for the British domestic economy. In more contemporary parlance, the Seven might not turn out to be an 'optimum policy making area'. The officials dismissed this second objection for almost identical reasons to the first. In or out of the ECSC, the UK would still be

> exposed to unfavourable external developments. We cannot prevent these taking place by refusing to have anything to do with them. If Britain joined the Authority we would not only have a say in developing its policies, we would be in a strong position to know what the other countries are likely to do and to adjust ourselves accordingly.[34]

The overall conclusion was that it was by no means clear that membership of the Schuman Plan would diminish the ability of British Governments to control the economy. There were sound reasons for believing that some such mechanism would be a necessary complement to national economic management. Butt, for instance, failed to see how it would 'inhibit a general economic policy of a kind that Ministers might be anxious to follow in the next fifty years'.[35] Britain outside the Schuman Plan was unlikely to be more sovereign than inside. Indeed, it risked a long-term competitive challenge to its domestic economy: 'our coal and steel experts view with alarm the consequences of our having to compete with a powerful and integrated group of European industries formed without our participation'.[36]

7.   A useless interference: a Labour Party view

Some of the views expressed above found a resonance within the Labour Party. For instance, in June 1950, Labour's International Department noted recent research which predicted that the total capacity of West Europe's steel industries was likely to exceed demand by 8 million tons by 1953. It went on to suggest that this could be eliminated either by a private cartel, or by cut throat competition or by international planning. The last was clearly to be preferred.[37] However, the majority within the Party was firmly of the view that participation in the Schuman Plan would only circumscribe the ability of Labour Governments to achieve their domestic goals. This perception was fatal to Britain's participation in the Plan, for, as its neofunctionalist originators were the first to admit, proposals for European integration would often be accepted or rejected for their ability to serve the *short-term* goals of dominant national political elites. Without this, an ideological commitment to integration might be insufficient. With this, ideological hostility to integration would not necessarily be decisive.

The perceptions and positioning of different sections of the British elite concerned with the Schuman Plan can be traced by considering the fate of the economic arguments for participation surveyed in the last section. Supporters of these arguments were first weakened by their failure to convince all the economic ministries. Treasury opinion was divided and the Board of Trade was hostile. They then found they could only secure recommendations from the Working Party for a close economic relationship with the Six by making compromises with the Foreign Office. By the time their point of view reached Cabinet it was often too veiled in its analysis and equivocal in its prescriptions to shake the party political preconceptions of Ministers. It was, therefore, assumptions drawn from the elite of the governing party, and not those of leading civil servants, that dominated the handling of the Schuman Plan.

For many in the Labour Party, the Schuman Plan was incompatible with Labour ideas of domestic political economy and, in particular, its guarantee of full employment. After 1947, Government policy had retreated from direct control of the economy. The consensus in the Cabinet was that the nationalization programme would end with plans to bring the steel industry into public ownership. Britain would otherwise remain a market economy. However, this only seemed to make Labour's economic policy more dependent on government influence over the very industries that would be affected by the Schuman Plan. This was made explicit at a strategy meeting held at Dorking in May 1950 with the Cabinet, NEC and TUC leadership in attendance. The meeting concluded that:

> through nationalization we have secured the required power over one sector of the economy, but overall our present full employment situation is precariously held...there is a constant danger that the private sector will jeopardize our full employment programme. There will always be the chance of mass unemployment unless the government had enough control of basic industries like steel.[38]

Meanwhile, the Treasury under Cripps looked to operationalize Keynesian ideas of 'indirect planning'; of stabilizing total demand to ensure full employment and capacity utilization without being drawn into the morass of a fully planned economy in which government would take detailed decisions about the level and distribution of production, investment and exchange. If detailed planning was ruled out, the secret of the Keynesian approach was for the state to locate certain strategic points at which it could inject or withdraw demand from the economy in such a way as to maintain full employment of resources, iron out the economic cycle and prevent the economy getting stuck with high unemployment for years on end, as had been the case in the 1930s. Kenneth Morgan notes that the annual review of the public sector investment programme was to be the chosen channel for government induced expansion and contraction (Morgan, 1984, p.367).

Two images illustrate the grip of the coal and steel industries on contemporary Labour thinking. First, was the idea that these could be managed counter-cyclically to the rest of the economy. Thus one NEC statement explaining Labour's position of non-participation in Schuman argued:

> common ownership is a means of preventing unemployment. When private manufacturers cut down investment in new machinery, they cause nationwide slumps unless counter measures are taken. One counter measure is to expand investment in a publicly owned industry that requires a great deal of new equipment. There would have been no postwar recovery if basic industries had been left in private hands. Shortage of coal and steel would have crippled the economy.[39]

Second, was the metaphor of coal and steel industries as 'commanding heights' that government could occupy in such a way as to ensure that decisions about investment, production and demand for raw materials in these industries would send powerful multipliers throughout the rest of the economy. For example, the car industry, which was the single largest contributor at the time to the annual rate of economic growth, was obliged to shift between 50 and 75% of its production into exports, or face a reduction in the flow of steel (Milward, 1993). The Government saw this as a means of easing the balance of payments constraint on the achievement of full employment in the rest of the economy.

Just as the state seemed to be close to discovering the elixir of economic management, the Schuman Plan appeared to threaten to constrain the degree to which a British Government could use two of the most important taps to raise or lower demand in its own economy. The National Coal Board's submission to the Official Committee established to consider the Schuman Plan began with the question, 'can any Government discharge its generalized responsibilities for employment, price levels and the balance of payments, when an important sector of its own economy is put outside its jurisdiction?'[40] Cripps likewise told the House of Commons, 'Whatever is done to these industries will have an effect on our whole industrial life..Parliament has always proved cautious as the removal of any important element of our economic power or policy'.[41] Also in June 1950, Labour's long awaited statement, *European Unity*, began by asserting that 'unless Governments intervene to correct the harmful effects of the market economy and to stimulate the beneficial', social justice and democracy would be impossible and economic stability unlikely. It went on to claim that the 'coal and steel industries held the key to full employment and stability in each country', as these were strategically placed to pump-prime the overall economy in any recession. Investment in coal and steel would quickly create new orders for other industries, while increased output would provide key raw materials for the rest of the economy, thus ensuring that investment could resume with confidence that recovery could proceed without running into supply bottlenecks.

Although written by Denis Healey, then only an official in the Labour research department, *European Unity* had been commissioned by Bevin and approved for publication by a meeting of the Labour's National Executive that included Attlee and Morrison. In Strang's view, 'The Labour Party statement, though ill-timed and in places ill-expressed, was, in its main thesis, along the true lines of British policy' (Bullen and Pelly, 1986, p.181). An important aspect of the pamphlet is that it went beyond the economic arguments of the last two pages to present three political reasons why Labour should prefer Keynesianism in one country to participation in the institutions of the Schuman Plan.

1. Incompatibilities of Ownership Structures. The pamphlet argued that 'the unwillingness of other European Governments to control their coal and steel industries' was the 'greatest gap in European co-operation'. Britain's nationalized industries would have to co-exist in the Schuman Authority with the privately owned coal and steel companies of the Six. As these were precisely the industries where the free market was most prone to the welfare losses and instabilities of oligopoly capitalism, those who had not nationalized their coal and steel would make the economic cycle more unstable for those who had. It would be better to keep the British and continental markets apart, or for Britain to have reserve powers of national protection. This might be possible under an association agreement, but not as a full member of the Schuman Plan.

2. Retreat from Economic Democracy. The Schuman Authority would only enjoy weak legitimacy in member societies. In other words, there would be a low level of automatic consent for its decisions and little public understanding of its operations. This, in combination with the considerable role that was anticipated for an independent technocracy, would make it over dependent on the very monopoly interests it was supposed to regulate, while freeing it from any countervailing need to satisfy the public interest. This argument can only be fully understood in view of an assumption shared by many in the Labour movement that a public interest in full employment always had to be protected against strong private interests in running the economy at less than full capacity. Left to themselves, strategically placed industrial interests would form cartels, restrict supply and make monopoly profits at the expense of some unemployment of resources.

If only those who represented society as a whole had an interest in full employment, it followed that parliamentary democracy and full employment went together. Not only did this justify the nationalization of certain sectors, such as coal and steel, in which cartelization was endemic, it also made it important that all public agencies with an influence on the macroeconomy should be fully accountable to parliament. Left to themselves, those who ran such agencies might be induced into overly restrictive policies through their position in a network of interlocking elites and technocracies, or as some in the Labour movement would have it, their class interests.

In suggesting that coal and steel should be subject to a transnational authority, only weakly accountable to a representative body, the Schuman Plan was more than a challenge to the recent nationalization of those industries. It also seemed to be a set-back to a wider project to secure a democratic monopoly over economic management, in the name of which the Bank of England had been nationalized as one of the first acts of the Labour Government in 1945. All of this explains the initial reaction of Attlee and Cripps to the Plan, which was to explain to the French Government that the problem was not only one of national sovereignty, but the failure of Schuman's scheme to allow for adequate accountability to any democratic process. It also explains why the National Executive of the Labour Party supported international planning of the coal and steel industries but rejected the Schuman Plan as an appropriate institutional mechanism. Labour representatives at the International Socialist Conference on the Control of European Basic Industries in June 1950 were instructed to secure a declaration that the

> Socialist Parties of Europe have always urged that Europe's basic industries should be planned as a whole. In any given form of international organization, the essential principle of democratic control and democratic procedure must be preserved - this control would involve representatives of trade unions and consumers.[42]

3. Domination by a non-Socialist majority. Even if the Authority were to develop democratic institutions, the Six was not considered an appropriate grouping for Labour Britain, as it was likely to be dominated by an anti Socialist majority. *European Unity* pointed out that in the Consultative Assembly of the Council of Europe only one in four of the delegates were Socialists: 'we could not guarantee that full employment, fair shares and social consensus would be the basis of a European Union. In its social and economic policy, any united Europe would stand to the right of the USA'. The pamphlet went on to imply that Labour would be better off taking its chances with an alternation of power with the Conservative Party in the 'winner-takes all' system of the British state than entering common policies with continental political parties: 'even the Conservative Party recognizes that social consensus in Britain depends on using economic methods closer to the Labour Party than those of the German, French or Italian Governments'. Continental socialists did little to allay these suspicions within the Labour Party. Dr Schumacher, the leader of the German Social Democrats, would later tell Morrison that the Six states suffered from the 'four c's'. They were conservative, clerical, cartelist and capitalist.[43]

The overall drift of arguments such as those presented in *European Unity* was that Britain should only merge its economic fate with continental Europe after some convergence by other countries on Labour's own preferred model of political economy. There would seem to be a pattern in the history of European integration that political parties with very precise preferences for state-market relations find it hard to accept common institutions and policies, as they know that these can only be constructed through compromise with the economic assumptions of other political families. It is highly improbable that - at any one time - politicians of their own persuasion will occupy dominant positions in the governments of all other member states. The problem of how to make Labour's domestic settlement compatible with what was in many ways the other great experiment in political economy at the time, the formation of a supranational European Community, was no better flagged than in a Labour Policy statement two years earlier, in 1948. This observed that:

> a nation's economic activities are so complex and interwoven, and the part played by them in government so increased, that any attempt to disentangle separate spheres of competence would involve serious dislocations in the economic and social life of the states concerned; and that under a uniform trading policy, governments would lose control over their financial and fiscal policies. *It would only work if the whole area were either a free enterprise Union or a fully planned socialist society'.*[44]

This belief in the indivisibility of economic control was similar to the 'spill-over' logic of the neofunctionalists. However, in Labour's case, it was used to draw exactly the opposite conclusion: the problem of attaining a critical mass of economic control should be met by deepening the relationship of the state within its own national society, not by widening the political reach of the state through mergers with others in international institutions. To return to our earlier theme, preference for the first over the second course reflected an underlying Labour confidence in the possibility of national self-sufficiency. However, it was also the product of mistrust of continental political systems. In 1950, these had yet to establish a reliable track-record of democratization. Anti-democratic forces of the far left or right remained strong and continental authoritarianism, aided and abetted by Catholic traditionalism, was a special bugbear of many in the Labour Party. The Six might well follow Britain and Scandinavia towards a higher level of economic development, welfarism and consensual Social Democratic politics, but, in the meantime, it was wise to keep the management of British and West European societies in separate compartments.

The *New Statesman*, picking up the point about the incompatibility of economic models, argued that the obstacles to UK participation in the Schuman initiative of 1950 had, in this one respect, grown since the similar Briand Plan of 1929. Over the intervening years, there had been a 'divergence' between the welfare states of Britain and Scandinavia and the 'free enterprise governments' of the Six. The result was that:

> the countries of reformist achievement - Britain and Scandinavia- were complacent about the advantages of pooled sovereignty as they see it as a threat to their own welfare economies. It is where Social Democracy is weak - in France and Germany - that a demand for a frontal assault on national sovereignty is at its strongest.

Nevertheless, the editors concluded that Labour was drawing precisely the wrong conclusion from all of this. If the Six really were looking to European integration to facilitate the introduction of welfarism at home - and if the two opposing attitudes towards national sovereignty in the different countries merely reflected the different stages they reached in the process of social democratization - was it really wise to leave the 'European Union' unduly exposed to an 'unholy alliance of the Vatican and the industrialists of the Ruhr and Comité des Forges?'[45]

However, where Labour opinion did share the *New Statesman's* doubts about the undivided sovereignty of European states, attempts were more normally made to wrestle with this problem without embracing federal or supranational approaches. One line was that international capacity management of basic industries would be more, and not less, effective in a loose intergovernmental framework. Any alternative would split control of the microeconomy of key industries from the macroeconomy of overall demand for goods and services. Supranational institutions would manage the first and governments the second. There would be no guarantee that supply and demand would come into balance in such a way as to ensure full employment of resources.[46]

Another line was that Federalism was a political archaism that made no allowance for the expanded potential of intergovernmental approaches in a context of modern communication and co-operation: 'the Federal idea comes to us from an age when the only alternative to the federation was a pattern of treaties in which states promised to act together if certain circumstances arose. There are now other ways to produce a dependable bond'. It was suggested that economic union could, of itself, change the behaviour of states from competition to co-operation without any need for formal political union; that common policy frameworks could be developed flexibly and with reserved rights for states to act independently in pursuit of distinctive social models; and that the state should be preserved as the sovereign intermediator between publics and international processes, as it possessed a capacity to react quickly in crises that could not easily be transferred from national to supranational level. However one curiosity in contemporary Labour thinking is provided by the 1948 party statement on European Unity. This acknowledged that defenders of national institutions might not have a monopoly of the democratization argument. A case could also be made for federal institutions with formal democratic structures, for the transfer of policy-making to hugger-mugger intergovernmental discussions might only de-democratize the nation state.

> Federation can, however, produce one advantage which the functional approach may easily forfeit. It allows issues to be debated in democratic institutions under the guiding influence of public opinion. There is a danger that if West Europe is organized exclusively in expert committees, far removed from the public gaze, vested interests

and bureaucratic inertia may slow down progress.[47]

To return to the hypothesis that proposals for European integration are only likely to be well received if they are useful to the short-term goals of dominant national elites, this obviously applies to the politics of winning elections and sustaining internal party cohesion as much as to substantive goals of domestic policy. The Government had won the February 1950 election with a precarious majority of only six. It was clear that a second election would have to be held in the near future which would be a challenge to the Government's survival. Contrary to some claims that Labour was confident that long-run electoral trends were working in its favour and that it could expect to be the natural party of government after 1945, the party leadership concluded:

> it is vital that Labour wins the next election. Five years of Conservative rule will not necessarily create the conditions for Labour victory. A Conservative Government could benefit from our past achievements..if it became identified with the improved situation, it would be even more difficult for us to regain power.[48]

Two electoral problems were identified: the 'working class Tory' and the erosion of Labour's demographic base through the increased suburbanization of the British population. Labour leaders concluded that they would have to move in the direction of what political scientists call a catch-all party (Kircheimer, 1966, pp.177-200), substituting a 'broad-based appeal' for a 'class appeal'.

All of this was thought to have three implications for how Labour should respond to the Schuman Plan. First, any erosion in the credibility of Labour's absolute commitment to full employment would cost the party its main comparative advantage over the Conservatives and the basis for its broad-based appeal. Second, demographic shifts to new towns and suburbs made it all the more important that Labour should do what it could to maintain the old heartlands of its electoral base. The 1945-51 Government had developed an extensive regional policy of aids to areas such as those where coal and steel were located. The Schuman Plan could call some of these supports into question. Third, the switch to a catch-all strategy had to be effected without any divisions in the party or loss of the more traditional elements of Labour support. The problem here was that the nationalization of coal had a peculiar place in Labour emotions. Morgan explains that on 'vesting day, 1 January 1947, there were mass demonstrations of rejoicing in mining communities from South Wales, to Nottinghamshire, Durham and Fife' (Morgan, 1984, p.106). The Government placed a heavy emphasis on obtaining trade union consent to their position on the Schuman Plan. When the Cabinet came to consider making counter proposals its first concern was that it had not yet 'been at liberty' to 'discuss things' with trade union colleagues.[49] The attitude of many was that the miners and Labour had not worked for half a century to nationalize coal just to transfer it to some foreign body whose socialist credentials were highly suspect. On the other hand, the nationalization of steel, which was still in progress at the time of the Schuman Plan, was critical to inner party unity. The left was prepared to accept that a limit should be set to public ownership, but only so long as this included steel. The Dorking meeting concluded that 'to drop proposals (for steel nationalization) now would cause bitter controversy in the party and leave us with a disunited party on the eve of the election..it would be fatal it we were to enter the next campaign on the retreat'.[50]

A further reason for reluctance to lose control of key industries was provided by memories of the winter of 1947. Right up until 1951, the Labour movement was haunted by the possibility that the UK economy might once again be brought to a halt by shortages of key supplies, that this would be taken as conclusive proof of the unworkability of socialism and that disastrous electoral consequences would follow. In November 1950, it looked as though stocks of coal would fall below the level of 6.7m tons that had preceded the crisis in January 1947. The Cabinet was warned that this would be 'fatal to the Labour and national interest'.[51]

8.   Domestic society and the international economy

Many of the notions of sovereignty that percolated through British politics were rooted in an age in which government had a limited agenda. Britain prior to 1914 has, after all, been described by A.J.P. Taylor as a society in which most people only encountered the state through the local post office or policeman on his beat (Taylor, 1965, p.1). Likewise, it was not until the 1906-10 Parliament that more time was given to the discussion of economic than religious questions. To insist on the undivided control of domestic society by national institutions may have made sense in a night watchman state, or in a polity concerned with confessional matters of religion and education. It is less clear that such a principle is appropriate to a state that assumes precise responsibilities for economic growth, welfare, employment, inflation and so on. The problem being that all these objectives may have to be achieved in an economy open to influences from the outside world.

In spite of this, the Labour Government of 1945-51 thought that the western world could combine sovereign domestic polities with open economies. The key to this was to persuade other countries that all should aim at internal equilibrium - full employment of domestic resources. External disequilibria - balance of payments deficits and surpluses - would then only be temporary, as one country would not get stuck with a deficit just because another was trying to depress demand beneath that necessary for full employment. Countries would be able to make sovereign choices about the level of domestic welfare spending on the assumption that over the long-run there would be no balance of payments constraint. However, it had to be recognized that the western world was starting from a position of a near-barter economy with massive distortion of markets by trade and payments restrictions (Milward, 1984, pp.217-22). Private trade was almost non-existent, most commerce being conducted via intergovernmental contract with each country aiming at bilateral balances with all others.

The key issue of international political economy at the time was how to get out of this mess. Britain was officially signed up to the American goal of a multilateral international economy. That is to say, a condition in which currencies would be fully convertible and tariffs and quotas would eventually be removed. However, opinion in Whitehall was that this would be the work of a generation and that progress would necessarily be incremental. Short of being able to move by one stride to a fully self-adjusting international economy, there would be many instances in which to remove particular tariffs or restrictions on currency convertibility would create balance of payments problems for individual countries, which would then be restricted in their ability to run their economies at full employment or construct the welfare policies of their choice. The UK Government favoured a solution in which western countries eased up on trade and payments liberalization - indeed, in which they accepted that it might even be wise to make tactical retreats from this goal. The British view was that failure to run economies at full employment would be far more costly in lost economic growth than any distortions caused by low levels of international economic integration. Priority should, therefore, be given to the former aim and countries should even be entitled to raise or reimpose restrictions where they could prove that the domestic policy of their choice would generate more trade growth than would be lost, for instance, through an increase in a tariff. Otto Clarke from the Board of Trade thus prepared a proposal to put to the US for 'an expanding world based on planned foreign trade' (Cairncross, 1989, p.123). Meanwhile, his political boss, Harold Wilson, was of the opinion that 'controls on the location of industry, foreign exchange, import licensing and capital issues would be essential to our success' (Pimlott, 1992, p.130).

British officials further claimed that a circumlocuitous route of this kind might eventually be the only feasible way to reach the long-term goal of multilateralism. By proceeding piecemeal and waiting for moments when liberalization could be achieved without adjustment costs that would necessitate periods of unemployment in particular countries, political pressures for the reimposition of restrictions would be avoided, as would 'hysteresis': a condition in which capital and labour becomes unemployable precisely because of the experience of unemployment. Premature moves towards liberalization would only provoke crises such as the convertibility crisis of 1947 which explains the hyper-sensitivity of British policy-makers to so many proposals of European market integration that could involve even a short-term loss of foreign exchange.

Before 1950, the British Government had already signalled that its support for schemes of European integration and reconstruction would be strictly bounded by domestic commitments to the welfare state. Describing a like political hang-up across the rest of Western Europe, Milward argues that 'aspirations to a better world served to strengthen the inflexible approach to trade and payments' (Milward, 1984, p.220). In Britain's case, this often amounted to a flat refusal to accept even the tiniest balance of payments risk. A French proposal at the beginning of 1950 to remove quotas on 60% of imports was opposed on the grounds that the UK could not afford to lose further gold and dollar reserves to two of the smallest states in Europe - Belgium and Switzerland (Hogan, 1987, p. 300). Conversely, in its efforts to head off Fritalux, Britain was prepared to perpetuate the sclerosis of the European trade and payments system for what was little more than a scam to ease its own currency problems. Germany at the time was in deficit to the UK but in surplus to much of the rest of West Europe. This was an artificial imbalance created by Britain's own decision not to extend the lowering of its import quotas to West Germany. The obvious solution was to rectify this inequality of access to UK markets. Instead, the UK proposed that other countries should settle their debts to Germany in sterling, which Germany would then use to cover its deficit with Britain. Apart from this betraying a determination to hang on to what was probably the largest single distortion in West European trade, it would, as Hogan points out, have wrecked attempts to form a multilateral payments system. Germany alone of the continental countries would become a quasi member of the sterling area. It would be syringed out of West Europe into a bilateral - but discriminatory - relationship with the UK: an arrangement that would only make it harder for it to form a non-discriminatory trade and payments agreement with its other neighbours (Hogan, 1987, p.307). Yet, efforts to make a cost-benefit analysis of the Schuman Plan on Britain's balance of payments constraint - and thus its domestic economic discretion - were probably doomed to failure. This was because it was never quite clear what was at issue: whether the Plan was dirigiste or liberalizing in intention and, if the second, whether its introduction of a Customs Union to Coal and Steel was but the first step towards a more general application of that method to the integration of European markets.

These ambiguities meant that more inchoate fears often dominated over the relative optimism of those efforts that were made by the official working party to reach definite assessments of the likely impact of the Plan on Britain's competitive position. Since 1947, the Board of Trade had opposed a West European Customs Union on the grounds that 'it would lead to a decline in industries here in favour of competitors elsewhere' (Milward, 1984, p.237). According to Milward, the BOT was worried that 'important sections of Britain's capital goods production, particularly steel and chemicals, would need permanent protection once the restrictions on German volume production were removed'.

The Korean rearmament programme forced the British Government to abandon the assumption that the domestic welfare state could develop in complete isolation to the external economy. But this was not seen as changing the politics of sovereignty. It was still for the UK alone to decide how it was going to trade domestic priorities off against international commitments; and it was felt that in weighing the internal against the external, British Governments still had sufficient degrees of freedom for it to be a nonsense to consider the UK as anything less than a fully capable self-governing nation. Even when 10% of national income was being put into the rearmament effort after 1950, the Government doggedly resisted outside pressures to prune its domestic programme. In 1952 Churchill told Congress, 'Our standards of life are our own business and we can only keep our respect and independence by looking after them ourselves. To Truman, he remarked, 'This is the UK's form of a declaration of independence' (Gilbert, 1988, pp.677 & 688). Neither change of circumstance nor change of government provoked the thought that participation in the Schuman Plan was being rejected in the name of an autonomy of domestic management that was already eroding.

9.   Conclusion

A neofunctionalist explanation of why some countries sign up to a scheme of European integration like the Schuman Plan, while others remain aloof, would probably highlight two factors:

1.   The choice of a *starting point* likely to yield sizeable benefits in the near term. Material temptation should be substantial enough to dissolve any reticence about loss of sovereignty or domestic control: for the 'low politics' of transnational technocratic management to appear more appealing than the 'high politics' of sovereign statehood. The anticipated gains from integration should also serve the immediate goals of dominant elites and get them out of some of their fixes. This will incline them to take the lead in meshing their political energies in the new European framework, where they might otherwise consider this a threat to their dominance in the domestic arena.

2.   The goal of an *end point* in full European integration, although vague and aspirational, should help to consolidate a consensus around any particular proposal in the necessarily incremental process of unification.

On both counts, the Schuman Plan proved unattractive to Britain's governing elites.

Collaboration with continental Coal and Steel seemed insufficiently 'useful' to offer a tempting starting-point for collaboration. On the hand, full unification was not an end-point that many wanted to reach.

Notes

1. 'Should Western Europe federate without the United Kingdom?', Memorandum by the Permanent Under-Secretary's Committee, 13 February 1951, PRO [ZP 18/19].
2. 'Western and other Unions', Clarke to Bridges, 27 September 1948,
3. 'The Council of Europe', 20 March 1950, PRO [CP (50) 40].
4. 'European Unity', Memo by the Secretary of State for Foreign Affairs, PRO [CP (49) 3].
5. Hall-Patch to Eden, 8 July 1952, PRO [M 551/88].
6. Memorandum by Dixon on relations between the restricted Communities and the Council of Europe, 8 September 1952, PRO [WU 10733/191].
7. 'Integration of Western European Coal and Steel Industries', Report by a Committee of Ministers, 1 July 1950, PRO [CAB 129/40].
8. *The Times*, 28 June 1950.
9. *The Spectator*, 9 June 1950; *The Times*, 4 June 1950.
10. 'Constitutional problems involved in a supranational authority as envisaged by M. Schuman', 16 June 1950, PRO [CAB 134/295].
11. Note by the Foreign Office, 16 June 1950, PRO [CAB 134/295].
12. Wilson to Butt, 5 May 1951, PRO [CE(W) 1543/198] and memo by Permanent Under Secretary's Committee of the Foreign Office, 9 June 1951, PRO [ZP 18/20].
13. Harvey to Bevin, 1 March 1951, PRO [CE(W) 1543/48].
14. *House of Commons Debates*, 26 June 1950, Vol 746, Col 1949.
15. Memorandum of the Permanent Under Secretary's Committee, 9 June 1951, PRO [ZP 18/8].
16. Gallagher to Hood, 26 September 1952, PRO [WU 10733/242].
17. 'Boothby's Strasbourg proposal', December 1951, PRO [MH 581/98]17..
18. George H. Gallup, *The Gallup International Public Opinion Polls*, Great Britain 1937-75, Volume I, Random House, New York, p.223.
19. George H. Gallup, *The Gallup International Public Opinion Polls, France 1944-75*, Random House, New York, 1976, p.144.
20. Analysis of Replies to Foreign Office Circular Dispatch of 16 April 1951, 20 July 1951, PRO [ZP 18/21].

21. 'Memorandum on the consequences of contemporary movements in Western Europe towards forms of economic integration having federal consequences', 19 July 1950, PRO [WU 10711/22].

22. This term is used in Harvey to Morrison, 4 May 1951, PRO [ZP 18/8].

23. Analysis of Replies.., 20 July 1951, *cit.*

24. Ibid.

25. 'Essential elements of US-UK relations', 19 April 1950, *Foreign Relations of the United States*, Vol III, 1950, p.874.

26. Memorandum by Pierson Dixon, 23 August 1950, PRO [FO 800/17].

27. 'The Channel Tunnel', 15 July 1949, PRO [CP (49) 153].

28. 'Political problems involved in the Schuman proposals', The Foreign Office, 31 May 1950, PRO [CE 2820/2141/181].

29. Butt to Hall, 4 July 1951, PRO [T 230/182].

30. Report by a working party of officials on the Treaty constituting the European Coal and Steel Community, 31 December 1951, PRO [F.G.(W.P)(51)43].

31. Ibid.

32. Hall to Attlee, 21 June 1950, PRO [PREM 8/1428].

33. Opinion of the Coal Board, 18 May 1950, PRO [CP 378/C4/A]; also Report of the working party on the proposed Franco-German Coal and Steel Authority, 31 May 1950, PRO [CE 3170/2141/181].

34. Hall to Attlee, *Cit.*

35. Memoranda from Butt to Pitblado, 9 & 19 June 1951, PRO [CP 378/01/8].

36. Younger to Strang, 2 June 1950, PRO [CE 2773/2141/181].

37. Background notes for the International Socialist Conference on control of Europe's Basic Industries, 16-18 June 1950, *Labour Party Archives*, Harvester Press, Microfiche 391.

38. Summary of discussions at Dorking, 19-21 May 1950, *Labour Party Archives*, Harvester Press, Microfiche 389.

39. Draft Policy Statement for discussion at NEC, 12 July 1950, *Labour Party Archives*, Harvester Press, Microfiche 393.

40. Opinion of the Coal Board, 18 May 1950, PRO [CP 378/C4/A].

41. *House of Commons Debates*, 26 June 1950, Cols 1941 & 1949.

42. 'Report on the International Conference on Control of European Basic Industries, 16-18 June 1950, London', *Archives of the British Labour Party*, Harvester Press, Microfiche 392.

43. Record of a conversation between the Secretary of State and Dr Schumacher, 21 May 1951, PRO [C 10110/180].

44. 'Feet on the Ground: a study of European Union, The Labour Party, 1948, *Britain and Europe since 1945*, Harvester Press, Microfiche 259.

45. *The New Statesman*, editorials of 3 June 1950 and 10 June 1950.

46. Background notes for International Conference on Control of European Basic Industries, 16-18 June 1950, *Labour Party Archives*, Harvester Press, Microfiche 391.

47. 'Feet on the Ground', *cit.*

48. Summary of discussion at Dorking, *cit.*

49. Conclusions of a Cabinet Meeting on 22 June 1950, PRO [CAB 128/17].

50. Summary of discussions at Dorking, *cit.*

51. Coal Emergency Powers, 14 November 1950, PRO [CP(50) 271], Man-power in the Mines, 1 December 1950, PRO [CP(50) 297].

4 At the Intersection of Three Circles: External Sovereignty and the Schuman Plan

Churchill made a speech in summer 1950 that crystallized into a simple image the world outlook of most political and opinion in Britain. Britain's position in the world was defined by its unique location at the intersection of the three circles of free nations: the British Commonwealth, United States and 'United Europe'. Churchill's doctrine was to provide the conceptual framework by which Britain's full participation in the Schuman Plan was rejected as incompatible with the overall pattern of Britain's foreign policy.

First, the three circles had a clear order of priority in their claims on British foreign policy. Churchill made it clear that the 'first circle for us is naturally the British Commonwealth and Empire...then there is the English speaking world...and *finally* there is United Europe'. It is hard to avoid the impression that this order of priority was automatically assumed and insufficiently questioned by those who considered how Britain should react to the Schuman Plan. This led to a style of decision-making in which consideration would only be given to participation in European integration if *no objections* could be found in terms of the Commonwealth and US/UK relationships. The Commonwealth and Europe were not to be traded off against each other as priorities with equal validity. In autumn 1949, Bevin had made it clear that 'we cannot accept obligations in relation to Europe which would restrict the implementation of our responsibilities elsewhere'.[1] In an exchange of Cabinet papers on the Schuman Plan in July 1950, the Ministry of Defence was determined that the United Kingdom should not commit itself to any arrangement that should limit its ability to co-operate fully with the Commonwealth'.[2] Two days later, the Commonwealth Relations Office repeated a statement that had been made the previous November to all 15 European members of the OEEC and then relayed to all Commonwealth countries: 'we could not integrate our economy to that of Europe in any manner that would prejudice the full discharge of our responsibilities as leading members of the Commonwealth'.[3]

Second, the three circles doctrine required British Governments to insist on being scaled as a world and not as a regional and European power without rights and responsibilities in relation to the entire international system. If it was impossible for Britain, or any other country, to look forward in the foreign policy field to a definition of external sovereignty that matched ideas of domestic sovereignty as undivided control, it was at least possible for its Governments to claim that they were no less sovereign than any other single state in the global system in rights of access to all levels of negotiation and decision in the international arena. Postwar British Governments thus set themselves the ambition of having rights of participation in all fora right up to what they called the 'top table'. It was considered of the greatest importance that future conferences to decide on the structures and rules of world politics, or just to mediate crises, should be held in the style of Potsdam or Yalta. That is to say, they should consist of the three powers victorious at the end of the second world war: the US, USSR and UK. Sensing the precariousness of this claim when the other two were superpowers, which the UK manifestly was not, British Governments put forward a distinctive view of the hierarchy of states that would ensure the UK a unique position in the postwar order. If not a superpower, Britain was to be considered as quite different from the all the other states in the international system by virtue of the global nature of its contacts and involvements, its massive over-representation in the processes of international trade and finance, the dependability and sophistication of both its domestic political system and diplomacy, its status as founder member of the wartime coalition, its permanent seat on the security council and its membership of the nuclear club.

However, Britain's foreign policy-makers felt it essential that no opportunity should be missed to assert or defend this view that the UK, and the UK alone, was quite distinctive as an international actor: that it was a third power in the world order, somewhere between the superpowers and smaller states that could only expect minor foreign policy roles after 1945. For, Britain's postwar diplomats strongly believed in the subjective dimension of international power; in the self-fulfilling nature of conventions as to which countries should enjoy certain roles in the world system, regardless of their physical power. They would have recognized Edward Kolodziej's later assessment of Gaullist diplomatic thinking: 'each specific transaction' had to be considered as 'contributing to a grammar of relationships, norms and expectations' (Kolodziej, 1974, p.13).

Third, the three circles and commitment to an integrating Europe represented two contradictory philosophies of foreign policy. The three circles idea was that international influence would be maximized at the intersection of the existing, somewhat loose, sub-systems of the international order, whilst the European idea looked to the creation of a new sub-system and the progressive intensification of its internal relationships. The first was a diplomacy of manoeuvre between several international centres where the second was a diplomacy of prior commitment to just one. All of this greatly simplifies ideas that were much more complex and varied across individual countries and politicians. However, it was in terms of a simple contrast between the two approaches that British Governments came to believe that even an apparently modest project for a European Coal and Steel Community would not only pose problems of domestic autonomy, such as those surveyed in the last chapter. It could also infringe Britain's external sovereignty: its freedom to pursue a foreign policy of its choice. Joseph Frankel puts the point well when he argues that, under the assumptions of their own doctrine, British Governments had to avoid absorption into any one of the three circles (Frankel, 1975). The Foreign Office drew a like conclusion at the time: 'We are determined to play a role in all three circles and none can command our exclusive allegiance'.[4]

In retrospect we can see the Three Circles idea as at once prescriptive, egocentric, ambitious and conservative:

Prescriptive because it depended on many other states in the international system behaving exactly as expected of them by the British. The US was supposed to accept the UK as trusted consultant and senior ally and accord it a 'special' access to Washington decision-making that would not be available to others. West Europeans were expected to follow a British lead, looking to the UK to organize their collective responses to common challenges. And the Commonwealth countries were meant to continue to welcome London's guidance in external affairs, even if this meant limiting their ambitions to a foreign policy of their own.

Egocentric because the notion that Britain alone connected three key international sub-systems was like drawing a map of the world and placing the UK at its centre (Frankel, 1975). There was more than a hint of a status obsessed approach to foreign policy, in which it was important to British elites that they should feel that they were always seated at the 'top table' of world powers, giving a lead to the diplomatically backward, advising the great and retaining a presence in every corner of the world, whilst lesser neighbours were increasingly holed up in their own region. Wrapped up in this, of course, was a fatal nostalgia for a world that was fast disappearing (Hill in Smith, Smith, White, 1987).

Ambitious because it was hoped that at the same time as penetrating to the core of each circle, Britain would function as a pivot between them all. By using its special relationship with the US to communicate the concerns of others, Britain would retain the leadership of West Europe and the Commonwealth. It would, conversely, become invaluable to Washington, rebalance the inherent inequalities in the US/UK relationship and approach its ally as an equal rather than a supplicant by showing that it could co-ordinate Europe and the Commonwealth in line with US goals and priorities. Through the deft structuring of relationships, Britain would ensure influence even in the face of a relative decline in the substance of its power. As the only power with privileged access to the innermost counsels of the United States, Commonwealth and West Europe, others would supposedly always be better off using the United Kingdom as an intermediator, rather than dealing direct with other power centres. This would allow British Governments to ensure that the mutual adjustments of various parts of the international system could always occur on terms acceptable to themselves. Amongst the middling powers of West Europe, it alone would remain a 'structure-maker', rather than a 'structure-taker' in the international system.

Conservative because the unlikely combination just described depended on freezing a rare conjuncture of relationships that probably only briefly existed immediately after 1945, if at all. The three circles idea depended on there being limits to the creative diplomacy of others. Yet the lesson of the Schuman Plan was that Britain could only avoid its own absorption into European integration. It could not stop others in Europe from integrating.

To carry these points further, it is important to see how British foreign policy-makers analysed the Schuman Plan in terms of each of the three circles. Only in the concluding chapter will we return to some more general remarks about the three circles idea and European integration as contending routes to international influence in the postwar world.

1.   **Dwelling amongst our own: Britain, the Commonwealth and the Schuman Plan**

In his study, *The Commonwealth and Britain*, Dennis Austin remarks that by '1945, Britain, Canada, New Zealand and South Africa had come close to being a civil society of shared beliefs and agreed ends' (Austin, 1988, p.7). If not an extension of national identity, the Commonwealth was perceived as a family relationship. Churchill told the June 1950 debate on the Schuman Plan, 'we have our dream and our own task. We dwell amongst our own.'[5] Anthony Eden is recorded as believing that the bar to a full relationship with West Europe was predominantly a matter of emotion and identity: 'open the personal mail arriving in any post office in England and you would find that 90% of it came from beyond

Europe' (Shuckburgh, 1986). From the Labour side, *European Unity* claimed that in 'every respect, except distance, we in Britain, are closer to our kinsmen in Australia and New Zealand than we are to Europe' and a policy statement a month later went on to assert 'there is between Britain and the Commonwealth a fine-spun mesh of inter-relationships. There are family and cultural ties, a common democratic and legal heritage. We are peoples with the same principles and the same ideas of how to go about things'.[6]

Where British and continental politics were divided by dissimilarities of political culture, reinforced by the different ways they had experienced the events of the 1940's, Britain and the dominions had recently fought the war together. At least at the level of their political leaderships, this gave them that sense of mutual obligation and outlook that has so often made wars creative of new political communities. Indeed, nothing could have seemed more natural given shared language and the fact that the Dominions were largely peopled by first and second generation emigrants from Britain. Although France, amongst Britain's allies of May 1940, had the greater interest in repelling Hitler, it was the Dominions which had chosen to fight on alone with the UK, in spite of the geographical distance that gave them the option of seeking their security in non-involvement in Europe. Right up to the 1970's, Britain would find it hard to approach questions of European integration with a certain guilt complex at betraying old friends for an association that included the very enemies that the Dominions had helped Britain to resist. In the 1950's, the Commonwealth also seemed a part of Britain's defences of last resort. It still seemed unwise for the UK to put all its faith in a continental glacis or to risk one day being left alone again in the European security system without being able to call on the 'kith and kin' from the Commonwealth.[7]

Persistence of an organic notion of the Empire/Commonwealth as an extension of the demography and territoriality of the United Kingdom itself was evident just two years before the Schuman Plan when senior ministers considered a scheme to resettle between 3 and 15 million of Britain's own population in the Empire/Commonwealth over the next 25 years. In a piece of economic prescience that should have been applied to other aspects of British postwar policy, it was noted that the UK was only 'precariously prosperous'; that if it did ever reach an economic equilibrium in which it could pay for its imports, it would be an 'unstable state, always liable to be upset by events from outside'. On the other hand, the Dominions and Colonies were in need of 'a greater population to develop their secondary industries'. Why not spread out Britain's great 'skills in manufacture' which represented a 'dwindling asset' when confined to an over-crowded island with a depreciated capital stock? From a strategic point of view 'we should be able to stand a great deal of knocking about' if 'industries were more scattered than now'; indeed, a strategic system based on wide spaces, rather than confined populations, was more defensible in an atomic age.[8] What was significant about this was that Britain and the Commonwealth were seen as constituting a 'we' to a degree that, arguably, Britain and West Europe would never be seen as being even after many years of EC membership.

In justifying Britain's abstention from the Schuman Plan, *European Unity* argued that 'Britain has to remember that it is the nerve centre of a Commonwealth that extends over every continent..not just an island off Western Europe'. It went on to claim that the example set by the British Commonwealth was a 'nucleus of a world society. Citing the successful transition of the Indian subcontinent to full independence within the Commonwealth, it argued that '400 million Asians' had been made into 'friends and equal partners', establishing a 'bridge between East and West, between white and coloured'. It went on to claim that 'Britain's economic ties with the Commonwealth at the centre of the sterling area are big factors in world unity. We will never weaken these links'.[9]

Here was the beginning of an argument that would become familiar in future opposition to British participation in European integration. The European Community and the Commonwealth were presented as competing models and ideals of international organization: the first was supposedly selfish, introverted and regional, where the second linked Britain to a representative cross-section of every kind of society in the free world, sustained its awareness of all sorts of global problems and institutionalized its responsibility for poorer countries. To several on both the left and right of British politics, the Commonwealth was an innovation in international relations to match Britain's new domestic settlement, both of them unique models for a better world, too important to be swallowed up in the process of European integration. Eden thus argued that Britain 'had an unusual understanding of North-South relations and an unusual instrument, the Commonwealth, for handling them' (Shuckburgh, 1986, p.18). That the Commonwealth was informal, where European structures would be bureaucratic, unaccountable and prescriptive, was just another sign that British institutional ingenuity could not be mixed with the cumbersome devices demanded by the weak political cultures - and long history of international mistrust - to be found on the continent.

In fact, British policy in 1950 sought to *intensify* the Commonwealth relationship. There was no question of liquidating the system, in order to concentrate on West Europe. Churchill was quick to make this point in a memo to the new Cabinet in November 1951: 'I never contemplated Britain joining the Coal and Steel Community on the same terms as continental partners..our first objective is the unity and *consolidation* of the British Commonwealth and what is left of its Empire'.[10] The Commonwealth was to be Britain's new power base in its dealings with the US. It would supposedly ensure that the UK's subordinate status to the US in the defence of Europe would be balanced by its great power independence outside Europe. As Peter Hennessy explains, it was very easy at a time of world shortages, to equate political power with access to raw materials. The 'Commonwealth was seen as a source of geological jackpots'. Its intelligent development would 'have the US eating out of Britain's hands in a few years' (Hennessy, 1992, p.217). The British Government thus took the 'simultaneous decision to quit India and penetrate deeper into the Middle East and Africa' (Gallagher, 1982, pp.144-6).

Even as the Empire/Commonwealth became more ramshackle with an ever greater number of internal distinctions between the metropolitan power, the old Dominions, the newly independent countries of the Indian sub-continent and the remaining colonies in Africa, Britain's ever optimistic policy-makers saw differences as complementarities that would bind the whole together into a system more intimate and self-sustaining than before. Uniquely amongst the European countries, Britain would succeed in turning the retreat from Empire into a constructive act of statesmanship in which former colonies would be reorganized into a voluntary association of states; and, most remarkably of all, an association in which freshly independent Commonwealth states would willingly function as the international power base of the ex-imperial power. The Commonwealth would be turned into a useful conduit of development finance for these countries. States without a long track record in Foreign Policy or security systems of their own, would apparently find it useful to tap into the established diplomatic infrastructure provided by Britain and the rest of the Commonwealth, or to draw on any security guarantees that seemed to be implicit in being a valued member of the club.

2.   Imperial Preference and the Sterling Area

The Empire/Commonwealth of 1950 possessed both structure and fragility. In the absence of either, British Governments may have been able to take a more relaxed attitude towards European integration in general and the Schuman Plan in particular. Consideration of this point best begins with the distinctive system of trade and payments which formed the substance of the Empire/Commonwealth relationship. Imperial preference gave the Empire/Commonwealth access to British markets on better terms than any other country. A series of special understandings about the supply of key commodities was also valuable in a world recovering from the dislocations of war. In addition, the Sterling Area, which was largely co-extensive with the Commonwealth, meant that members could be sure that the pound would be accepted as a means of exchange. This was important so long as international liquidity was short and the alternative to trading in sterling was the expenditure of precious dollars.

Participation in the Schuman Plan would mean establishing a Customs Union in Coal and Steel with the Six. These two commodities would circulate freely within

West Europe. However, they would be subject to a common tariff against outsiders. This was not in itself of great concern, as Britain was on the whole an exporter and not an importer of coal and steel from its imperial system. What was more worrying was that many expected the ECSC, under the self-proclaimed expansive logic of the Schuman Plan, to be just the first stage in the formation of a comprehensive West European Customs Union. As early as September 1950 French minister, Michel Petsche, came up with just such a proposal and, at the end of 1951, the Whitehall working party on the Schuman Plan concluded that 'the necessary consultations in the coal and steel context will tend to draw the countries together in their overall trade policies'.[11] A West European Customs Union would either displace the Commonwealth countries from preferential access to British markets, or attempt to combine the two principles of Imperial preference and European economic integration, probably at the price of substantial dilution of both. In a communication to the Commonwealth Governments, Patrick Gordon Walker summed up the position of the Labour Cabinet as follows:

> Our participation in a single market for coal and steel with consequent lowering or removal of tariff barriers, would establish a special trading relationship with the Community, and this would make it difficult to preserve a special relationship with the Commonwealth which is the cardinal point in our commercial policy.[12]

The objections that the Board of Trade had made since 1948 to a full West European Customs Union are, therefore, directly relevant to British rejection of the Schuman Plan. These were that Britain traded more with the Commonwealth than with any other part of the world; and that it was this commerce - not any putative West European trading area - that corresponded to the natural order of things in the international system. By linking primary producers with manufacturers in more developed countries, the Commonwealth supposedly constituted a rational division of labour. Its development of elaborate trade and payments mechanisms could not, therefore, be dismissed as the product of a temporary disruption of Britain's local markets in West Europe since the 1930s. On the contrary, of all possible trading relationships, the Empire/Commonwealth offered Britain the best opportunities for the future, for the West Europeans were apparently too alike, too complementary in their production, to become significant trading partners. Indeed, much of the remarkable improvement in Britain's balance of payments since 1945 had been with the Empire/Commonwealth, indicating that these were dynamic markets at the *margin* and not just in terms of acquired levels of trade.

By 1950, Britain had also made the Commonwealth the basis of an elaborate complex of deals by which member states could - as far as possible - expect assured supplies of the key commodities they needed. This was important in a world of shortages and, indeed, for the domestic policy of full employment, as a complex modern economy could clearly shudder to a halt if bottlenecks developed at any point in the production process. Britain's position at the centre of this web, and its occasional ability even to find some surplus supplies for non-Commonwealth states, was also considered a key Foreign Policy asset. The 1948 Labour Party statement on European policy considered that 'Britain's strength as a world power and consequently her value to a European Union, depend above all on the close association between herself and the Commonwealth. The Commonwealth can supply Britain's food and raw materials to a degree to which West Europe could never equal'.[13] The problem was that Britain's position as a supplier of last resort of coal and steel was considered to be its essential contribution to the Commonwealth bargain. Under the Schuman Plan, priority would have to be given to West Europeans in the event of any shortage.

The extensive use of sterling - mainly but not exclusively by Commonwealth countries - was seen as contributing a further decisive advantage to Britain's commercial interest, inclining several countries to buy UK exports, where they might not otherwise have done so.[14] It is hard to believe that there was ever a point at which around 50% of all international trade was conducted in sterling, or when Britain alone imported as much as the United States (Milward, 1984, p.238). Yet, both of these were the case just before the Schuman Plan. Susan Strange explains that collectively the sterling area had a substantial dollar earning capacity; that it could, therefore, function on slender reserves and cushion individual members from the need to deflate their economies in response to temporary deficits. However, she also distinguishes a Labour view of the sterling area as a 'defensive monetary bloc' from a Conservative belief that it was essential to the revival of the City of London as an international financial centre (Strange, 1971, pp.65-9). Other authors have argued that the unrivalled access of financial elites to government, afforded by social contact and geographical proximity, underpinned official preference for intensifying the sterling area, rather than diversifying economic contacts towards West Europe. They also claim that the postwar policy of consolidating the Empire/ Commonwealth only lasted as long as this was considered the best means of promoting the international use of sterling (Cain and Hopkins, 1993, pp.265-97).

The problem was that the war had left Britain heavily indebted to its own imperial system. Given that the size of sterling liabilities was publicly known and that the UK would have great difficulty satisfying all its creditors at once, there was a permanent risk of a 'run against the bank' by those afraid that their sterling holdings would fall in value if they did not encash them before others did so. Anything such as the Schuman Plan that could be taken as a signal that the UK was beginning a retreat from Imperial Preference would weaken the one factor that made it worthwhile to hang on to sterling: the probability that Commonwealth countries would need pounds for the indefinite future to settle their trading bills. Given the Board of Trade's general pessimism about the ability of Britain to compete with Germany in sophisticated manufacture, there was also a possibility that membership of the Schuman Plan would lead to a net trade loss, particularly during a transitional period during which British industry recapitalized and reorganized itself to attain a higher level of productivity than it was used to in its dealings with the 'softer' Commonwealth markets.

John Darwin has quoted a US diplomatic report of January 1950 to illustrate how the Empire/Commonwealth had become a system that functioned without any margin: 'even trivial things..a million pounds gained or lost in overseas trade become problems of major dimensions that require cabinet attention' (Darwin, p. 164). Together with memories of the convertibility crisis of 1947 and an absolute domestic commitment to full employment, the wish to perpetuate the Commonwealth thus completes our picture of British hyper-sensitivity to any proposal for European integration that might cost it foreign exchange. During the European Payments Union negotiations, the British Government came up with an evocative phrase that said everything about the limits to the West Europe/Commonwealth relationship that it was prepared to contemplate. The UK was prepared to go into a multilateral currency clearing system with the West Europeans in which it would have to settle a certain proportion of its trading liabilities in gold and dollars, but only so far as it was able to erect a *sluice gate* to control the level of transactions between West European and sterling markets.

3.   Preserving the credibility of the Commonwealth commitment

In 1950, the British Government was, in effect, proposing for the indefinite future to run a two-tier imperial system, as summed up in the very term Empire/Commonwealth. The movement to self-government and Commonwealth status was expected to reach a plateau with the grant of independence to the Indian sub-continent in 1947. Most other territories were expected to remain as colonies for which Britain would be directly responsible for a good fifty years or so (Morgan, 1984). Yet the Indian army would no longer be available to put down any colonial émeute and many of Britain's troops were tied up in the Middle East, rather than the Empire proper.

The Commonwealth/Empire increasingly rested on consent and the avoidance of trouble. British Governments lived under the threat of a colonial crisis ramifying disastrously through an already overstretched series of policy commitments at home and abroad. The two tier system already risked 'demonstration effects' with those who had not yet received independence looking to enjoy the same self-government as those who had, or to dispute Britain's timetable for change. A military defeat, or even a display of diplomatic weakness, could betray the hollowness of British power and encourage rebellion to spread like a forest fire through the geographically dispersed system. Denis Healey, who as Labour International Secretary was close to the foreign policy-makers of the time, would later write that 'the British Empire was seething with revolt, encouraged by our wartime ally, the United States' (Healey, 1990, p.98). Although it had abated somewhat by 1950, the known hostility of the leader of the western world to colonial Empires, did nothing to shore up Britain's imperial position. On top of this, there was always the danger that Britain might have to fight its way out of Empire, get bogged down in one remote conflict, or suffer economic shocks to its own productive base brought about by change too sudden for private actors to adjust. It was also assumed in 1950 that 'scuttling from Empire' would be disastrous domestic politics. All in all, the right course seemed to be to make the best of an imperial commitment that would continue for the indefinite future.

The economic fragilities mentioned in the last section, and the political ones in this, came together to make it an axiom of British Foreign Policy that nothing should be done to cast the slightest doubt on the long-term commitment of Britain to Empire. British policy would be repeatedly inhibited by concern that anything beyond loose Association with a European Community could be interpreted as the beginning of the end of the Commonwealth. Governments and other elites in the Empire/Commonwealth would immediately start to adjust to the expectation that the post-imperial system would eventually be liquidated. The nightmare of disintegration and scuttle would quickly be substituted for hopes of a managed transformation of the Empire-Commonwealth into a system that would be self-sustaining even in the postwar world. Whilst by no means ruling out all options for more European co-operation, the Commonwealth Office pointed to the danger that even before it had defined its relationship with the Schuman Plan, Britain was reaching the limits of the involvement that it could afford with the continent: 'the whole nexus of our relations with European countries in recent years - in the Brussels Treaty, OEEC, the Council of Europe and, to some extent, the Atlantic Treaty Organization - has inevitably brought into question the United Kingdom's relation to the rest of the Commonwealth'.[15]

Apart from it being necessary to avoid anything that would prejudice any of the vital economic relations set out above, there were two further dividing lines between safe and unsafe involvement with Europe. First, the Empire/Commonwealth reinforced the British Government's aversion to supranational institutions, for these would mean that matters touching its affairs could be decided without Britain's consent; that an uncomprehending European authority could blunder into measures capable of upsetting one of the many precarious balances in Empire/ Commonwealth relations; and that the UK might steadily lose control of what it considered to be its own sphere. Referring to the Commonwealth and the sterling area, Bevin argued that 'we must decline to accept limitations in a purely European association on our ability to make decisions (on matters that are) our own responsibility, and we cannot agree that any organs to which we belong should acquire authority of a supranational character'.[16]

Second, the Empire/Commonwealth provided a further reason why collaboration between European states should not be presented as a stage towards their integration.[17] In answer to the charge that it was a betrayal of British pragmatism not to stay with European integration until such moment as it involved an irrevocable choice between Europe and Commonwealth, UK Governments argued that they could foul up both political sub-systems by not clarifying their refusal of implied commitments to work for the progressive unification of West Europe. Once Britain was inside a European Community, the plans and expectations of both private actors and other governments would start to adjust to the fact of its membership. Commonwealth countries would doubtless start to diversify their relations towards the United States or other members of their own regions. The point of no return - at which the Commonwealth could no longer be saved, or Britain could only be extricated from Europe at great dislocation to itself and its neighbours - could come all too quickly. The Permanent Under Secretary's Committee of the Foreign Office concluded that the Six could afford an experimental attitude to the construction of new European institutions in a way that Britain could not: if these structures proved unworkable, 'the individual European countries could go their separate ways and return to the same situation as before'. Britain, by contrast, 'would have had to break its Commonwealth and sterling area'[18] in the meantime.

It was suggested at various points between 1948 and 1952 that the two projects of integrating West Europe and modernizing the British Empire/Commonwealth could be purposefully co-ordinated in such a way as to avoid the difficulties set out in the last few pages. This might have been consonant with three circles philosophy, positioning Britain as the fly-wheel of two of the spheres, simplifying the UK's relations with both and ironing out possible contradictions that could have forced Britain into a choice of one or the other relationship.

It is instructive to analyze the reasons for rejecting this option. First, the ambition of consolidating the Commonwealth as Britain's power base in the postwar world was seen to depend on the privacy of its relationship with the UK. Eden argued that 'any formal association between the Commonwealth and West Europe would weaken the special relationship between the United Kingdom and the Commonwealth countries'[19] and the Foreign Office felt that 'our position as a major power depends on the cohesion of the Commonwealth and sterling area. We could not hope to maintain their cohesion within an economic union' of the Commonwealth and OEEC.[20] Second, there were thought to be limits to which a merger between West Europe and the Commonwealth was possible without splitting the latter. The Canadians would probably prefer to enter a dollar area with the United States.

Moreover, a Commonwealth that had been unwilling to accept 'a greater degree of unity' even within itself was likely to come under political strain if exposed to European enthusiasm for institution-building and Treaty signing. Thus Bevin told Schuman that Britain had 'already had enough constitutional difficulties within the Commonwealth' without putting it under the strain of formalizing a relationship with Europe.[21] It was precisely on the avoidance of such formalities that the survival of the Commonwealth depended. Third, joint projects between West Europe and the Commonwealth were thought likely to entangle Britain in an even more remorseless spill-over logic than any that would operate in a European Community alone. Eden warned that 'a unified control over the economies of the sterling area and Western Europe could hardly be established without agreement on the detailed objectives of economic policy and it is doubtful whether this could be achieved without a measure of political federation'.[22] The Foreign Office added the twist that a 'single market' between the Commonwealth and West Europe would require the co-ordination of many other policies besides, especially those concerned with the management of currencies.[23] Fourth, the United States was prepared to accept some discrimination against its commercial interest in order to promote the integration of West European markets, but it could not accept joint ventures between the Commonwealth and West Europe: to have done so would have been to collude in its own economic isolation.

In spite of all the above, there was much evidence at the time that the Commonwealth would provide but a precarious substitute for Britain's full involvement in West Europe. Signs of fragmentation were already apparent. The Cabinet was warned that the South African nationalists, who would come to power in the same year as the Schuman Plan, were 'aiming at a secessionist Republic outside the Commonwealth'.[24] India's refusal in 1948 to remain in the Commonwealth on the basis of loyalty to the crown and its insistence on substituting some notion of Commonwealth citizenship was pregnant with implication. It demonstrated that as countries became independent, London could not dictate the terms of the Commonwealth relationship; it had to be negotiated between equals. Indeed, the objection of the other eight Dominions to India's position illustrated that the Commonwealth was increasingly a relationship held together by agreements to differ, by allowing members to go their separate ways behind a facade of unity.[25] Canada was lukewarm about proposals for Commonwealth defence co-operation, seeing its security interests as being best served by its own direct contacts with Washington. Australia and New Zealand increasingly looked to the US to provide its security. Canada was also the most obvious loser from any perpetuation of the Commonwealth as a trading and financial unit. A large part of the sterling area deficit arose from Canadian trade with the US and a good proportion of Britain's own balance of payments problem arose from its dealings with Canada. This meant that the health of the whole system depended upon Canada maintaining tariffs against the US and accepting payment from the UK in sterling rather than dollars. Both of these meant foregoing the enormous potential of increased trade with its southern neighbour and by 1949 there were clear signs that Canada was going restive with this pattern of economic relations.

When they were not rejecting European integration in the name of Commonwealth unity, British policy-makers could, in fact, be remarkably hard headed, even dismissive, about the prospects of the latter. In October 1949, Bevin wrote that

> there are no political tendencies in the Commonwealth today which suggest that it could be consolidated as a single unit. It has no central authority and is unlikely to create one. Its members are increasingly framing their policies on the basis of regional and local interests. Only Britain is in a position to offer leadership, but it seems unlikely that proposals originating in London are likely to be welcome.[26]

The new states had not acquired their independence just to accept the self-abnegation that would have been involved in giving up all claims to a foreign policy of their own in order to follow the lead of the UK. On the contrary, the advantages of demonstrating sovereign statehood by differing from the UK always had to be weighed against any benefits of Commonwealth co-operation.

Nor was the Commonwealth a system in the sense of either homogeneity of interests or regional proximity within the international system. Indeed, one of the main centrifugal forces was that most of its members had only a short-term interest in concentrating all their relationships on just one metropolitan power, the UK. As Bevin correctly predicted, the implicit security guarantee afforded by friendship with a nuclear superpower like the US would ultimately prove far more attractive than Britain's overstretched conventional capabilities. Moreover, the need of the Commonwealth for investment capital could not be satisfied on any significant scale by the UK. The aim of rebalancing Britain's economy by placing it at the centre of a complex system of raw material trade between the Commonwealth and the rest of the world suffered from the fatal flaw that a substantial investment in industrial capacity for Asia and Africa would have to be made up front and this would compete with domestic British priorities. For example, the hope of selling Rhodesian coal to Argentina in order to bridge the deficit on British food imports came up against the obvious problem that a whole new railway system would first have to be constructed in southern Africa. Only the US could provide finance of this kind and it had no interest in channelling dollar aid through London in a way that would have been compatible with maintaining the exclusive political relationships that sustained the Empire/Commonwealth as a British-led sub-system of world politics: 'the attraction exerted by the pound sterling and the Royal Navy is less than that of the dollar and the atomic bomb' (Bevin).[27]

The Commonwealth seems to have shown less concern about the prospects of the UK becoming more closely involved in West Europe than the British Government showed on its behalf. The summary of High Commissioners reports on reactions to the Schuman proposals showed that the Canadians seem to have supported the US view that Britain was, if anything, over-cautious about European integration; the Australians to have given no detailed consideration to the problem at all; and India, Pakistan and Ceylon to have been without any opinion. Only New Zealand seemed fully to support the British Government's position.[28] This would also correspond with a US assessment that the UK was investing hopes in the Commonwealth that were shared by none of its other members, 'except possibly New Zealand'.[29]

4.   Britain, the United States and the Schuman Plan: exceptionalism granted?

The intersecting histories of European integration and Britain's claims to a special relationship with the United States came into clear conjunction with the proposal of the Schuman Plan. Just two days after Schuman's announcement on 9 May 1950, Bevin presented Acheson with a paper intended to pin the US Administration down to procedures that implied the UK/US relationship was special and thus prior to others. Bullock recounts how Acheson insisted that all copies of the paper should be collected and burned: ' with the first initiative to come from the French fresh in his mind, he also had to mind the undesirability of allowing the USA's special relationship towards Europe to be pre-empted by the UK's claim to a special relationship' (Bullock, 1984, p.772). It is, indeed, tempting to see this as the cremation of Britain's claims to a privileged status in its dealings with the US and to conclude that such pretensions reached a clean cut-off point in May 1950, as they could not possibly survive a credible scheme of Europe integration. However, it is important to understand that history was not as tidy as this if we are to make sense of two further issues: first, the absence of any attempt by the US to push Britain into the Schuman Plan; second, the comparative insouciance with which London concluded that aloofness from a European Community need not have serious implications for its relations with Washington.

The full force of enthusiasm for European integration in Washington was reported to London by Britain's ambassador, Oliver Franks, who put it all down to:[30]

1. A wish to end Franco-German rivalry which since 1914 had twice contributed to world wars from which the US had been unable to remain aloof.

2. A belief that Europe could only recover its economic viability and be taken off the backs of the American taxpayer, if it developed continental-wide markets and common political structures to manage them.

3. A fear of assuming responsibility for a politically unstable West Europe. European integration was expected to stabilize the internal political development of European states and societies, as well as resolve conflicts between them.

4. An 'emotional feeling' that because the US had itself evolved from 13 states into an integrated nation, 'integration was a good thing and that criticism of it comes close to being criticism of the US Constitution itself'.

These points will be expanded in chapter 5. For the moment it is sufficient to note that, until the Schuman Plan, unification scarcely seemed possible without Britain and its refusal to participate thus appeared to be a form of obstruction. It is hard to over-state the degree to which British attitudes to European integration were regarded as a critical obstacle to the construction of a stable postwar order, for they seemed to render insoluble the dilemma at the core of American foreign policy. This dilemma was one of striking simultaneous equilibria in superpower relations and in the politics of West Europe, knowing that whatever was decided in relation to the one would affect the other. If the containment of the Soviet Union was impossible without incorporating the Federal Republic into the West, it was unlikely that there would be inter-allied agreement on the mechanisms of containment without some rebalancing of the politics of West Europe to make up for the return of West Germany to full statehood, let alone any German rearmament (Hogan, 1987, p.22). Britain seemed to be essential to this rebalancing. Only it could match the clout of West Germany in any integrated political unit. The Americans were also eager to use economic integration to tie in the Germans and Britain was by far the largest economy and trading nation in the area. Its capacity to disrupt remained substantial, even if its ability to take the initiative appeared increasingly disappointing. American thinking also emphasized the need for one state to act as a leader in any process of integration. Germany was excluded from this role, France seemingly lacked the domestic stability and only Britain had the confidence of the smaller countries of West Europe.

Nonetheless, in the months leading up to the Schuman Plan there had been a growth in US support for at least beginning the process of European integration without Britain. The decision in September 1949 to give France responsibility for coming up with some proposal to integrate West Germany more closely with its neighbours seemed to be a self-conscious attempt to build up French leadership. A month later, Acheson seemed to 'recognize British exceptionalism' by conceding that Britain should be exempted from any process of European integration (Hogan, 1987, p.271). Within the State Department, a group associated with George Kennan began to argue that American attempts to involve Britain had been the main reason why European integration had made little progress since 1945 and that it would soon gather pace if the UK was left out of the process. Britain's delicate balance of payments, and its insistence on putting the Commonwealth and domestic policy first, meant that it had little room for manoeuvre in relation to West Europe. Far from being able to give the expected lead, its European policy inclined towards immobilism, even outright unneighbourliness.

Monnet-like, Kennan also concluded that an organization based on traditional inter-state relationships would just become the site of a German hegemony. The German problem could, therefore, only be solved by some element of European Federation. Better, in his view, a small Europe that could move faster towards Federation without Britain than a large Europe that would always be constrained by the UK's preference for intergovernmentalism. Indeed, the rationale for diluting the European project in order to accommodate the UK disappeared as progress was made with the construction of NATO after 1949. As seen at the end of Chapter 2, there was little need to get Britain involved as some external counterbalance to Germany, if this role was passing on to the US. Not only would the US play the role of guarantor more convincingly than Britain, physically coupling the power of the greatest military machine in the world to the de facto containment of Germany through the permanent positioning of its troops in the Federal Republic. US publics and elites were also more enthusiastic than the British for any project of European integration. An American force motrice would be substituted for a British drag anchor. Just as the successful formation of NATO made it possible for the British to back-peddle on the assumption of the Bevin Plan that the UK might have to accept a more integrated Europe if the latter was to be defensible, the US Administration began to see that the new Alliance could render feasible a Europe without Britain. In a curious sense, NATO cost Britain its perceived indispensability to European integration and thus its veto over the process.

However, on the eve of the Schuman Plan, US foreign policy-makers were by no means settled in the view that Europe could integrate without the UK. Kennan had an influential opponent in Charles Bohlen who continued to argue that there was no alternative to a Europe in which Germany was integrated and Britain included; that the US had little choice but to hold out for a Europe that was both supranational and British-led; that the weight of the UK in the political economy and security of West Europe left no alternative to its inclusion in the management structures of the continent; and that US should not lift the pressure on Britain to get fully involved in West Europe - it should intensify it by taking over the UK's world roles and providing financial support for a graceful redirection of British interests towards West Europe. The US could, for instance, ease any balance of payments risks associated with British involvement in European economic integration by offering to underwrite the liabilities of the sterling area.[31] In March 1950, a meeting of all the US ambassadors to West Europe inclined more to the Bohlen than the Kennan view, suggesting that just two months before the Schuman Plan they doubted that the governments to which they were accredited were yet ready to accept a European entity built around a Franco-German core without Britain.

The inertia of settled assumptions and the tendency of bureaucracies to suspend rather than resolve their differences meant that the Kennan and Bohlen views existed for some time side by side, sometimes even in the mind of the same person. It was in many ways the Plan itself that consolidated change. The manner of its announcement and the imaginativeness of its conception created a more uniform confidence in Washington that, in some matters, leadership of a new West Europe could pass from Britain to France (Schwabe in Schwabe, 1988). It is impossible to understand the impetus that would carry the Plan to its fulfilment without some idea of how it provoked a new transnational coalition between influential elements of the French and American government machines: both had been thrashing around for two years trying to find some means to solve the German problem in an integrated European unit, both were frustrated by UK policy and both came to see the Schuman Plan as a last chance if postwar West Europe was not to slip back into the same patterns as the interwar continent.

However even ambiguous signs from autumn 1949 that the US was changing its mind on the necessity of British involvement in European unification were seen in London as little less than a triumphant vindication of British foreign policy. It was especially welcome that US official opinion seemed to recognize that the Empire/Commonwealth was of general benefit to the West; that the ties of individual Commonwealth countries with the UK were not transferable to other members of the western coalition; that Commonwealth cohesion could be damaged by Britain's involvement in certain kinds of European integration and that the UK could not abandon its responsibilities without causing economic dislocation and a security vacuum, particularly in Southern Asia. Kennan argued that 'dissolution of the empire was not in our interest as there were many things the Commonwealth could do which we could not do and we wished them to continue doing'.[32]

More broadly, the US Administration seemed now to accept that the limits that Britain laid down for its participation in European integration had to be respected: the US could not afford to alienate the only ally that had a robust domestic polity, a governing elite that could be relied upon to share the objectives of the US and a set of global capabilities and connections that were likely to be a net asset, rather than an overall liability, in the task of worldwide containment. In April 1950, the

State Department concluded that were the US-UK relationship to break, the 'eclipse of the whole Eastern Hemisphere would follow' and North America would be isolated within the world system. Britain had to be seen as:

> the cement which holds the Commonwealth together, our principal partner in strategic planning, a major force in ensuring political and economic stability in the Near and Middle East, a collaborator in resisting communism in the Far East, a collaborator in developing multilateral trade, a leader in furthering the development of dependent areas and a principal supporter of the UN.[33]

Any contribution that the British Commonwealth could make to global security and political stability assumed a new importance with the fall of China, the adoption of the containment doctrine, the explosion of the first Soviet atom-bomb and the invasion of South Korea. The new 'Sino-Soviet bloc' was seen as having a significant strength in its possession of the internal lines of communication of the Eurasian landmass whilst the non-communist world was precariously strung out along an arc of crisis running from East Asia through South Asia to West Europe. It was considered essential to the overall credibility of US foreign policy that it should now draw the line at the expansion of the communist world and, as there were few points along the southern section of that 'arc of crisis' that were not in some way covered by the Commonwealth or other British post-imperial roles, the infrastructure that the latter provided in terms of diplomatic contacts, military bases, commodity exchanges, a payments system and development aid suddenly seemed to be a valuable contribution to stability. Indeed, containment, implying as it did that the west would meet communist aggression no matter what form it took, or where it occurred, was necessarily a doctrine that required enormous resources and constant watchfulness. The idea that Britain might perpetuate the Commonwealth into the postwar era by making it relevant to containment - by making it the principal dowry that the UK would bring to a privileged alliance with the US - had some appeal on the American side in 1950-2. The April 1950 State Department Paper on US/UK relations mentioned above had been almost euphoric about the Commonwealth, describing it as 'more important than any other existing grouping' and an area of 'shared objectives and standards.[34]

Although Britain's exclusion from a core group of states travelling what might turn out to be a fast track to European integration presented clear dangers to its international influence in general and its clout in Washington in particular, many in London felt that these risks were outweighed by American conversion to the possibility of European integration without Britain. This would, in their view, remove the single largest friction in US/UK relations and at last allow the special relationship to realize its full potential. For fear of seeming to sign up to a

European destiny and of creating self-fulfilling expectations that its future roles would only be regional in nature, the British Government had for the last two years resisted every move that contained the slightest implication that the UK was classifiable as a European power. A favourite phrase of Foreign Office documents of the time was that Britain should use every opportunity to 'insist that it was not just one more country in the European queue'. The result was that quite minor matters developed into full blown rows with Washington. To optimists in London, American policy now accepted the three-fold division of the Western world into North America, Britain and Europe, rather than a two pillar vision in which Britain would have to merge with the rest of western Europe if it was to have a role. As Eden put it:

> we wish to cultivate the idea of an Atlantic Alliance based on the three pillars of the United States, United Kingdom (including the Commonwealth) and Continental Europe. In such a community we can reconcile our world-wide commitments with our responsibilities towards Europe and the Commonwealth. This could not be done within the confines of a European federation.[35]

To the extent that Anglo-American relations could now develop on the basis of compatible expectations about Britain's place in the international system, the role of the Schuman Plan in consolidating a shift in America's European policy to tolerance of European integration without Britain was even taken by many in London to be a merciful release from a previous period in which the UK lived under threat of US favours being linked to UK participation in European unification.

5.   Exceptionalism constrained

If American opinion in 1950 was more than usually favourable to Britain's abstention from European integration, the British Government was guilty of exaggerating the status that the US would be prepared to accord the UK as a non-member of the Schuman Plan. This can be seen in two respects. First, there were inherent limits to which the US could afford to regard the British as 'special' amongst the European states. Second, the US Administration considered itself to have reached an understanding with Britain whereby the UK accepted important *constraints* on its freedom of action in return for not participating as a full member in a European Community.

British foreign policy-makers were quite accustomed to pressing their claims to a special relationship with the US in the face of denials that any such thing existed.

This reflected a belief that the US had little choice but to serve out an apprenticeship in foreign affairs, under Britain's tutelage, if it was to meet the challenge of sudden responsibility for the stability of the international system after two centuries of isolation. Hugh Gaitskell, Chancellor of the Exchequer and later Labour leader, felt that:

> they are curious people to deal with - nice, well intentioned, but, I think, often lacking in judgement. Whereas most high officials here are pretty shrewd judges of political interests, one has the impression that their counterparts in the American civil service are often very much at sea (Williams, 1983, p.196).

It was also thought to be a requirement of the structure of inter-state relations in the Atlantic area - and not a matter of choice - that the Americans should accord Britain a privileged status. However, all of this ignored one overriding reason why the US should not allow one ally to appear much more equal than others. Any suggestion that the relationship with the UK was of greater interest than others to the US was incompatible with the construction of the Atlantic Alliance. Bruce wrote from Paris:

> it is almost impossible to have an understanding of this nature with the UK without at the same time prejudicing our hopes of co-ordinating the free peoples of the Occident for a common purpose. Such special relationships cannot be kept secret. This is especially true when as is the case with the UK's one of its representatives are not on occasion averse to letting their continental colleagues know that they are favoured above others by us.[36]

If the Anglo-American relationship was to be given priority, this could be taken to mean that the US was not as serious about the defence of continental Europe as it was about protecting the UK in the event of conflict: that unable or unwilling to bear the costs and risks of a forward defence it had already compounded with the UK to withdraw across the channel in the event of a serious onslaught from the East. Such a suspicion would erode confidence in mainland Europe. 'Any overt distinction between allies could only have the effect of seriously upsetting the Continental countries, particularly France, adding to the ever present fear that both we and the British will abandon them in the case of an emergency'.[37] As some suspected that the US Administration may have prompted the invasion of South Korea by seeming to suggest that there were some parts of the Far East that it was more interested in defending than others, it was not about to repeat this mistake in Europe.

Not only was it imprudent to look to a special relationship with the US as some kind of compensation for non-involvement in an integrating Europe, abstention from the Schuman Plan also left British foreign policy much diminished in the eyes of many in Washington. Whereas two years before the US Administration had been prepared to back Britain in any bid for a leadership role in West Europe, the dominant view after Britain's abstention from the Schuman Plan was that it would have to accept a reduction of its influence on the continent and relinquish its veto on the pace and character of European integration. The deal - from Washington's point of view - under which Britain was 'excepted' from the process was that it would support integration from the outside, even though this would amount to a substantial limitation on its European policy; even though integration would probably be accelerated by Britain's abstention: even though it was not yet clear that British Governments really were happy to leave the continentals to integrate in any way they liked, provided that the UK did not have to be involved.

It is worth noting Franks' report from Washington in summer 1951 that Britain was seen as having let the US down in its role as 'principal lieutenant' when it came to the 'cherished ideal of European integration'. The French attitude was seen as 'resourceful' where that of the British Government seemed 'consistently reluctant and unhelpful'.[38] UK intentions towards the new European Community were no longer entirely trusted, for there was always a suspicion that its Government had a greater interest in keeping the continent divided to leave room for a British leadership role than in facilitating unity. Chapter 6 will show how far the US was determined to insulate the development of the new Community from any malign British influence, how this threw UK European policy on to the defensive and undercut the attempts of both Labour and Conservative Governments to develop the status of influential outsider, in the expectation of which they had originally assumed that it would be safe merely to associate without joining as full members.

Most in the US Administration also continued to view the overall pattern of British policy as unsustainable. Whilst acknowledging that there were constraints on any immediate switch from Commonwealth to Europe, they fretted that this would only sharpen the contradiction between resources and commitments that lay at the heart of British foreign policy. After all, the UK was putting itself in the relatively unfavourable position of bearing heavy security costs in relation to West Europe, Africa and Asia, while abstaining from a leading role in the management of markets in its own part of the world.

It may well be that the salience of security questions with the formation of NATO and the Korean War absorbed the attention of British decision-makers to the exclusion of the Schuman Plan, temporarily flattered perceptions of the UK's international importance and obscured the degree to which two different patterns of influence were emerging in relation to the main issue areas of western politics. If, in matters of security, the US Administration had to admit that Britain was the most reliable ally, while France was the awkward partner and Germany had yet to be rearmed, in economic questions Britain was much more exposed to marginalization. There was a danger to Britain that all of the major West European powers would come to enjoy a special relationship with the US, each bilateral contact special only in its peculiarities of character, not in its exclusiveness.

In arguing that the US should do nothing 'to save the British from any ill consequences which might follow from their comparative self-containment',[39] Bruce reflected a view that the US had merely agreed to differ with the UK; and that a fundamentally artificial situation could not be cured until Britain had been put through a learning process. In the meantime, the US should, according to this view, do nothing to undercut Britain's position, for that would provide an alibi in which something other than Britain's own delusions were seen as responsible for the failure of its policy; nor should it do too much to prop up the UK, as this would only retard the process of adjustment. Another possibility is that the US was also on a learning curve and far from retreating on British participation in Europe it was altering its policy in a way that was more likely to achieve that objective in the long run. After all, in an alliance of sovereign states, there were limits to how far the US could force the British to integrate against their will and limits to how far the UK could stop the Six from coming together as they wished. But the Six - with the support of the US - could subtly shift the costs and benefits of British abstention. States other than Britain were free to use their legitimately acquired and mutually recognized sovereign powers to put competitive pressures on one another. If this analysis is correct, the change of US heart on Britain's role in European integration was no long-term recognition of the rightfulness or practicality of Britain's aspirations to turn the Empire/Commonwealth into a discrete sub-system of world politics, or of Britain's character as a 'non-European' power. Where the UK saw the status quo as permanent, the US Administration saw it as temporary, sharing Jean Monnet's perception that the best way to proceed was through a two stage process in which a European Community was first insulated from British influence and then enlarged to include the UK. The question of whither Britain had only been postponed.

6.   Britain, West Europe and the Schuman Plan

There is little need to dwell for very long on the implications of the Schuman Plan for Britain's relations with the West European circle, as this is the subject matter of the whole of this work. It is, however, worth using this section to consolidate some of the foregoing analysis and to link it in with the remaining chapters of the book. The theme of this section is that the Schuman Plan was both a response to Britain's flagging leadership in West Europe and a catalyst for its further decline.

A group of independent states will only consent to the leadership of another in defining rules and institutions if this is broadly profitable to their own perceived interests and/or they cannot organize themselves to achieve preferable solutions. By 1950, the balance sheet of British leadership in continental affairs was increasingly questionable. After its initial success in organizing a European response to the Marshall Plan in 1947, the British Government had frequently obstructed measures that others felt necessary to their own recovery and to the construction of a European trading and monetary system with political guarantees against the instabilities of the interwar period. This was not the product of any malice towards the continental countries, but of something that was far worse for being less curable. Once British Governments had decided to treat West Europe as the residual arena in the three circles doctrine, they lacked the foreign policy resources to extend favours to their near neighbours. On the contrary, for reasons discussed in this and the last chapter, London found itself having to insist on positions that threatened the continentals with a lower level of economic welfare because it could not afford the knock-on costs to the UK's own domestic and Commonwealth policies that could flow from better arrangements for trade and payments in West Europe (Milward, 1984).

By late 1949, however, British policy threatened to go beyond a mere failure of leadership in West Europe to downright un-neighbourliness. Bevin argued that 'it should be our object to postpone as long as possible being faced with a choice between overstepping the limits of safety in European integration and appearing to abandon the ideas of the Council of Europe'.[40] As indicated above, the British Government did its best to obstruct negotiations for a Franco-Italian-Benelux free trade area, cold shouldered overtures for a Franco-British commodity agreement and, at one stage, held up negotiations for a European Payments Union for fear of the impact that Belgium alone could have on the UK's balance of payments position. The problem was that if Britain was going to head off experimentation with more integrationist alternatives it had to show that its own preferred method of informal and intergovernmental co-operation was capable of coping with the pressing problems faced by continental European states.

Given that lack of resources impelled the British Government to establish priorities that could not easily be kept secret, there was always a risk that the least favoured of the three circles would soon learn the nature of its status, discover that Britain did not have the economic leeway to maintain a leadership role that was profitable to all and seek a degree of self-organization. It was only a matter of time before at least some West Europeans broke away from British leadership in matters of political economy. As Milward explains, the opportunity presented itself between 1949 and 1950, when the countries that were to form the Six began to form a self-contained 'growth circuit' in which each fed the GNP growth of the other through the rapid development of import-export trade. Britain was not a part of this process. This meant that the disadvantages of forming an economic group that did not include the country with the highest *levels* of trade in the region were outweighed by the UK's comparative unimportance to *marginal* trade growth.

Although British Governments felt they could not announce an intention to integrate with any one circle if they were to preserve a position as trusted interlocutor between all three, active participation in West Europe remained essential to the three circles idea. Foreign Secretaries from both parties acknowledged that Britain's influence within each of the three circles was tightly interdependent and that the construct stood or fell as a whole (Lord, 1993, pp.10-6). Bevin, for instance, argued that British Governments should aim to level up their influence with the United States over time and that 'by virtue of their leading role in West Europe and the Commonwealth' they should seek 'to play a larger and larger role in the Western system'.[41] Even Eden, who is seen by many pro-Europeans as the prince of darkness who prevented a reappraisal of Britain's abstention from the Schuman Plan when the Conservatives returned to power in October 1951, is recorded as not taking 'the naive view that the Anglo-American relationship or the new Commonwealth provided alternative routes for Britain which would enable it to dispense with a close European association' (Shuckburgh, 1986, pp.17-8).

To see why continued political leadership in West Europe remained critical, we need to recall the ambitious aspirations that were wrapped up in the three circles idea and the commensurately resourceful foreign policy that would be needed to operationalize it. The goal was nothing less than to remain one of the leading players in the international system and the means was to compensate for Britain's reduced economic and military substance - and to obtain greater influence than was justified by the UK's inherent power - through the clever structuring of its external friendships.

A two circles diplomacy, centring only on Britain's involvement with the Commonwealth and United States, would have been quite insufficient to secure these outcomes. A key ingredient of three circles thinking was that Britain should have some *independent* power base that would allow it to approach Washington as an equal. Yet the problems of sustaining the Commonwealth only contributed to the development of a series of UK foreign policy dependencies on the US in the late 1940s and early 1950s. Dollars from Marshall aid were diverted to sustain the viability of the sterling area. The last attempt that the UK made to develop a Commonwealth security mission - in the Middle East - depended on US security infrastructures, it left British troops dangerously exposed without some guarantee of US support in the event of danger and it only involved Australia and New Zealand to the extent that the US was able to assure them of its protection in the Pacific. The State Department correctly observed that there were limits to the degree to which British Governments could afford to fall out with Washington - on issues such as European integration - if they wanted to hold the Commonwealth together. Here was the ultimate contradiction: the Commonwealth that was supposed to be Britain's independent power base in its dealings with the US could only be sustained with American support and the prospect of a de facto condominium in which individual members were likely to look to Washington as well as to London. And yet it was, in part, because Britain was supposed to have this private power base that it had been considered unnecessary for it to look to co-operation with its West European neighbours to give it a margin of manoeuvre independent of the US, should it find the inequality of the US/UK relationship oppressive.

In secret, the UK Government also showed concern at what it had agreed to in allowing the US to develop a series of bases on UK soil. Meanwhile, from the US itself, Franks warned that British representatives could only roam the corridors of Washington power, pressing their own positions with confidence and independence, in those rare moments when UK and Commonwealth finances were sufficiently secure for there to be no need to ask too many favours of various US agencies. Pointing to the economic consequences of Korea and the rearmament programme, he went on to caution, 'instead of economic independence, we envisage years of economic dependence on the US'.[42]

By contrast, if the US had shown any interest in the three circles model of Britain as interpreter of US intentions to others and organizer of coalitions amongst the more politically diffuse parts of the free world, this had been in relation to West Europe and not the Commonwealth. Even if the Commonwealth had been a more plausible base for sustaining an independent world role, it could have been argued that Britain's position in West Europe had to be preserved as an insurance policy against possibility that the UK would be no more successful than the other metropolitan powers in transforming its former Empire into a source of post-colonial influence. The Foreign Office was also aware that if it was neglected 'continental Europe' might 'bid for US support against the UK':[43] far from Britain acting as a pivot between the European and American circles, others could find it to their advantage to reach understandings and then present them to the UK as faits accomplis. Mallet suggested that it would be a mistake 'to take the line that the Commonwealth, the US and perhaps Germany are all that matter and write off the rest'; even the non-German part of West Europe was a vital interest to the UK.[44] Monnet also showed how the very assumptions of the three circles doctrine could be used to demolish the conclusion that the UK could remain indifferent to West Europe. He told Harvey that 'of the three (circles), West Europe is the weakest link' and without UK attention 'its weakness could endanger the other two' (circles).[45]

The contemporary rhetoric of not tying the UK to the defence of the continent beyond a point of no return coexisted uneasily with an understanding that it was precisely in West Europe that Britain's future security would be decided;[46] indeed, with a security policy that was committing Britain, by the month, more closely to just such an integrated defence of Europe beyond a point of easy return. On the economic side, there was, likewise, some awareness that if Britain's trading and financial links were more with the Commonwealth than Europe, this could be but a temporary and exceptional state of affairs, resulting from substantial disruption of the normal economic development of West Europe between 1914 and 1950, and ripe for reversal by precisely the initiatives in continental market integration that were now being proposed. Fussy quantifications of how little British industry need be affected by European initiatives usually ended with the caveat that there was a quite incalculable and long range threat of being on the outside of a vast and dynamic market, knit together by a whole series of further economic initiatives made possible by precisely that transformation of political relationships from which Britain was now abstaining. Even reasons for rejecting the Schuman Plan sometimes reflected the perceived importance of the European circle to British diplomacy. For example, reluctance to give up control over coal and steel exports that were a valuable source of British influence over other West European states. Bevin told the cabinet that 'coal is a most valuable counter in foreign trade negotiations' and that those countries, such as the Scandinavians, that were most dependent on UK coal were those 'with which we have the closest political ties'. British coal exports also prevented others like Italy from becoming absorbed into a German economic zone.[47]

However, the Schuman Plan did not shake the confidence of British foreign policy-makers in their claims to a leadership role in West Europe. Rather, they redesigned the claim to fit the new circumstances, even though this meant reversing the assumptions on which the European part of the three circles idea had rested before May 1950, thus revealing the intellectual ad hocery with which the premises of that doctrine could be adjusted to maintain its conclusions. Where it was previously held that a British leadership role would flow from the incoherence of European politics, it was now predicted that a tightly organized core of continental states would be more and not less dependent on a mediator with the US and that Britain, from its intended position of semi-attachment to the new Community, would be the natural provider of this service. A European club would contain sufficient dangers to the Atlantic Alliance for the formation of the Coal and Steel Community to make both the US and the Six even more dependent than before on a power that was close to the discussions of both without being exclusively identified with either; an intermediary that could anticipate problems, explain intentions, smooth misunderstandings and, if necessary, broker deals and even arbitrate differences. In early 1951, one confident Foreign Office view was that:

not only would the United Kingdom perhaps have more opportunities of acting as a bridge between West Europe and North America; the fact that continental Europe had come more closely together and that the United Kingdom was less directly concerned in its grouping than some other members might well lead to closer ties between the United Kingdom on the one hand and the United States and Canada on the other.[48]

Indeed, the Six would be unable to speak for Europe as a whole, requiring the British Government to undertake two forms of simultaneous brokerage: one between the Six and the US and another between European countries inside and outside the ECSC. In early 1951, the US Ambassador to London reported that the British Government remained confident that it could sustain the linked roles of European leader and transatlantic intermediator against all evidence that its 'prestige and consequently influence in West Europe is at a low ebb as a result of the consistently negative attitude they have adopted to European integration'. This was underpinned by a belief that Britain's 'long association and skill at handling the peoples of Europe exceeds that of the US'. In addition, the British were not yet convinced that the Schuman Plan had invalidated their claim that 'much of what is *practical* in European co-operation since the war has been achieved because of their contribution'.[49]

A further idea was that Britain's disproportionate contributions to NATO would offset its absence from the full membership of the European Community: that its role as a major regional security provider would more than compensate for its absence from a Community as yet only concerned with the management of two industrial sectors, coal and steel. To use some international relations jargon, security was thought to be the dominant factor in relations between states and the UK's power in this dimension would prove 'fungible' over lesser areas of policy-making (Keohane and Nye, 1977). In other words, it could always be used to prevent the Coal and Steel Community from developing in a manner prejudicial to British interests, providing the UK with an 'outsider's veto'.

The problem was that things could easily work the other way round, for any failure to get Britain's economic positioning right could invite 'military overstretch': a vicious circle of unsustainable military expenditures and economic decline. A policy-mix in which the UK contributed much to common security structures while abstaining from a major experiment in economic co-operation and market access may have meant accepting too many of the burdens while receiving too few of the prizes. Yet, such was the confidence of some British opinion in the invulnerability of its interests to exclusion from full membership of the Schuman Plan that there were even some who were prepared to tolerate a degree of commercial discrimination against the UK to get the Schuman Plan off the ground, remove the presumption that the formation of a European Community need involve Britain and secure a deal between France and Germany that was necessary to the construction of NATO:

> Any risk or loss to British economic interests from integration of the type
> under discussion must be weighed against the possibilities of gain and, in
> particular, the loss even on unfavourable assumptions would be a cheap
> price to pay for a stable and contented West Europe, which would be
> conducive to our own stability.[50]

This was, arguably, the reverse of a free-rider strategy with the UK providing a
disproportionate share of an international public good in the form of security, while
allowing others to eat into its economic position. Although this could have been a
rational course for a great power hegemon or economic leader, it was less
appropriate to a country which had three times been forced to the edge of
insolvency over the past five years.

7. Conclusion

The hard evidence provides little support for the insouciance of Britain's foreign
policy-makers and it is hard to avoid the conclusion that the Schuman Plan did
create problems for British pretensions to the leadership of West Europe. These are
fully discussed in previous and future chapters. However, it may be useful to the
reader to have a single summary list of all the ways in which it is claimed that the
Schuman Plan, and British reactions to it, weakened the UK's position in the
politics of West Europe. This is now provided by way of conclusion with cross-
references to chapters or sections where fuller exposition of the arguments can be
found.

1   The Schuman Plan promised Franco-German reconciliation. This would
undercut any need for a British referee between the two largest mainland powers,
make it unnecessary for smaller countries to look to the UK for protection against
collateral damage from the lumbering giants and reveal the extent to which
prospects for British leadership in continental politics had been dependent upon the
perpetuation of old patterns of Franco-German tension (Chapters 1 and 3).

2   Common commitment to building the new European Community raised the
prospect that France and West Germany would in some matters be closer to each
other than either was to the UK. The balance of relationships within the
quadrilateral of US, UK, France and West Germany, which was mainly responsible
for shaping postwar Europe, would be very different before and after May 1950
(Chapter 2).

3. Although only limited in its agenda in 1950, the Schuman Plan was a declaration of intent by its members to act as a unit of growing cohesion and ambition. So long as this project remained credible, a law of anticipated effects was likely to apply with both the Six and outsiders adjusting their behaviour to the expectation that the EC countries would be stuck with one another, and constrained to co-operate, for the foreseeable future. Amongst the Six, this would have an immediate impact on rules and practices of inter-state behaviour, and sharpen distinctions between insiders and outsiders (Chapter 6).

4. Where Franco-German frictions had previously set an upper limit to the possibilities of European integration, limiting the risk that full participation in European politics would involve British acceptance of unwanted institutional forms, the Schuman Plan required supranational structures to secure Franco-German reconciliation (Chapter 2). This threatened to freeze the constitutionally fastidious British out of the European core (Chapter 3).

5. Where the United States had looked to the British to explain their intentions to West Europe and to organize coherent political responses to collective initiatives, the Six now constituted an interlocutor on their own and Paris became an access point to West Europe politics that rivalled London (Chapter 4). The role of most reliable ally was henceforth split between France on matters of European integration and Britain on questions of security (Chapter 5).

6. Indeed, France emerged as a strong rival for the political leadership of West Europe as a result of the formation of the Six without Britain. West Germany's need to develop its external relations through multilateral frameworks and to reassure others that it was safely contained by organizations such as the new European Community would limit the degree to which it was prepared to upset France, so long as it remained the only other major European power in the EC, and provide an incentive to develop policies through prior consultation with Paris.

7. The Schuman Plan promoted competitive divergence between British and French diplomacy. The manner of its introduction, post hoc rationalizations for the different positions of the two governments and attempts to deal with unanticipated consequences of previous decisions left the two powers with substantial mutual suspicion as to the 'true intentions' of the other (Chapters 2 and 6).

8. The Schuman Plan exacted costs to the reputation and credibility of British policy. As the British Government itself acknowledged, Foreign Policy leadership was, in part, a product of consensually developed conventions between leaders and led. Yet the UK was already living off diminished political capital as a result of its

increasingly unneighbourly behaviour towards West Europe in trade and in monetary questions (Chapter 4).

9. The Schuman Plan proved that a small Europe was possible, creating a new confidence that continental countries could organize themselves without Britain, where before 1950 this had been doubted by many on both sides of the Atlantic (Chapters 4 and 6).

10. The development of the Plan over the period 1950-2 showed that there was still a role for an external leader in organizing West Europe and brokering deals, but this could be more plausibly played by the United States than Britain (Chapters 2 and 6).

11. British Governments were themselves becoming dependent upon US Administrations to deliver goals that were valuable to them. This allowed the US to enforce a deal that effectively liquidated Britain's leadership role in relation to the new European Community. In exchange for acknowledging that Britain was an exceptional case that could not be made to participate in the EC in the immediate future, the UK was expected to adopt a hands-off approach and support whatever the Six decided was best for themselves (Chapter 4).

Notes

1. 'Proposals for the Unification of Europe', memorandum by the Secretary of State for Foreign Affairs, 25 October 1949, PRO [C.P.(49)203].
2. Memorandum by the Minister of Defence, 1 July 1950, PRO [CE 3452/2141/181].
3. Memorandum by the Secretary of State for Commonwealth Relations, 3 July 1950, PRO [C.P. (50)153].
4. ' The Council of Europe', 9 November 1951, PRO [WU 10712/32].
5. *House of Commons Debates*, 1950, Vol 450, Col 1782-95.
6. 'European Unity', Draft Policy Statement, 12 July 1950, *Labour Party Archives*, Harvester Press, Microfiche 394.
7. Memorandum by Pierson Dixon, 23 August 1950, PRO [FO 800/517].
8. Proposal to the Secretary of State of Defence for large-scale emigration to the Commonwealth and Bevin to Attlee, 17 February 1948, PRO [FO 800/444].
9. 'European Unity', *cit.*
10. 'United Europe', memorandum by the Prime Minister, 29 November 1951, PRO [C(51)32].

11. Report of a Working Party of Officials on the Treaty constituting the European Coal and Steel Community, 31 December 1951, PRO [F.G.(W.P.)(51)43].

12. Gordon Walker to Commonwealth Governments, 30 August 1951, PRO [CE(W) 1543/424].

13. 'Feet on the Ground: a study of European Union', The Labour Party, 1948, *Britain and Europe since 1945*, Harvester Press, Microfiche 259.

14. Bridge to Compton, 14 December 1951, PRO [M 581/103].

15. Memorandum by the Secretary of State for Commonwealth Relations, 3 July 1950, PRO [C.P.(50)153].

16. Memorandum by Secretary of State for Foreign Affairs, 19 October 1950, [CAB 129/42].

17. Memorandum by Secretary of State for Commonwealth Affairs, 3 July 1950, PRO [CE 3451/2141/181]; Memorandum by Secretary of State for Foreign Affairs, 19 October 1950 PRO [CAB 129/42].

18. 'European Integration', Memorandum by the Permanent Under-Secretary's Committee, 12 December 1951, PRO [ZP 10/1 of 1952].

19. Annex B to Memorandum by the Secretary of State for Foreign Affairs, 13 May 1952, PRO [CAB 129/52].

20. 'Mr Boothby's Strasbourg Proposal, December 1951, PRO [MH 581/98].

21. Extracts from minutes of a meeting with M. Schuman, 2 October 1948, PRO [FO 800/460].

22. Memorandum by Secretary of State for Foreign Affairs, 13 May 1952, PRO [CAB 129/52].

23. Mr Boothby's Strasbourg Proposal, cit.

24. The Commonwealth Relationship, 21 June 1949, PRO [C.P.(49), 141].

25. 'India's future relationship with the Commonwealth', 31 December 1948, PRO [C.P (48), 309].

26. Memorandum by the Secretary of State for Foreign Affairs, 18 October 1949, PRO [C.P.(49) 208].

27. Ibid.

28. Summary of High Commissioners' reports on the Attitude of Commonwealth Governments towards the Schuman Proposals, 3 July 1950, PRO [C.P.(50) 181]

29. Attaché in the United Kingdom to the Secretary of State, 29 January 1951, *Foreign Relations of the United States*, Vol IV, 1951.

30. Franks to Morrison, 23 July 1951, PRO [ZP 18/17].

31. Minutes of the Seventh Meeting of the Policy Planning Staff, 24 January 1950, *Foreign Relations of the United States*, Vol III, pp.617-21.

32. *ibid.*

33. Essential elements in US-UK relations, 19 April 1950, *Foreign Relations of the United States*, Vol III, 1950, p.870.

34. *Ibid.*

35. Eden to HM Representatives Overseas, 15 December 1951, PRO [FO 953/1207].

36. The Ambassador in France to the Secretary of State, 25 April 1950, *Foreign Relations of the United States*, Vol III, 1950, p.64.

37. Essential elements of US/UK relations, *cit.*

38. Franks to Morrison, *cit.*

39. Ambassador in France to the Secretary of State, *cit.*

40. Memo by the Secretary of State for Foreign Affairs, 24 October 1949, PRO [C.P. (49) 204].

41. 'European Policy', memorandum by the Secretary of State for Foreign Affairs, 18 October 1949, PRO [C.P.(49) 208].

42. Memorandum by Franks, 27 September 1950, PRO [UE 11914/106].

43. 'Should Western Europe federate without the United Kingdom?', 13 February 1951, PRO [ZP 18/19].

44. Mallet to Strang, 19 December 1950, PRO [ZP 13/3].

45. Harvey to Morrison, 1 May 1951, PRO [CE(W) 1543/201].

46. Record by Mr Davies of a conversation with the French Ambassador, 8 November 1950, PRO [WU 10720/9].

47. 'The importance of Coal in the Foreign Affairs of the UK'. Memorandum by the Secretary of State for Foreign Affairs, 3 November 1950, PRO [C.P.(50)23].

48. 'Should Western Europe federate without the United Kingdom?' Memorandum by PUSC, 13 February 1951, PRO [ZP 18/19].

49. Ambassador in the United Kingdom to the Secretary of State, 20 January 1951, *Foreign Relations of the United States*, Vol IV, 1951, p.897.

50. 'Should West Europe Federate?', *cit.*

5 Not Beyond the Point of No Return: National Security and the Schuman Plan

The Schuman Plan was launched into a pattern of West European politics preoccupied with security. The previous year had seen an attempt to force the West out of Berlin and, in June 1950, the House of Commons would debate the Coal and Steel Community on the day after the invasion of South Korea. The war had left the Red Army two-thirds of the way between the Soviet border and the English Channel (Bullock, 1983, p.7). By 1950, the remaining third of the distance was still not regarded by Britain, or by many others, as credibly defensible. Eden later summed up the mood of vulnerability: 'in 1950, NATO still in the process of formation, could only muster 14 divisions with which to confront 175 Soviet divisions, not so gently poised in East Europe' (Eden, 1960, p.30). The grip of cold war thinking was equally decisive in the Labour Government and Party with the international committee of the NEC proclaiming that the 'Kremlin made no secret of its aim to enslave the world to its machinery of tyranny..half of Europe has been sucked into its Empire..it has organized fifth columns all over the world'; and, seeing the new challenge through the lens of the 1930s the report concluded, 'we know the suicidal stupidity of appeasement'.[1] All of this contributed to a perception of undifferentiated Communist threat, ruthlessly disciplined, monolithically directed, ready to exploit any moment or place of western weakness by any method from open aggression to domestic subversion.

Through the NATO pact of April 1949 the US, Canada and ten European states had committed each other to regard an attack upon each as an attack on all. But when the Schuman Plan was announced in May 1950, NATO remained an arrangement without definite substance. The British Defence Secretary, Emanuel Shinwell, told the Atlantic Council in September 1950, 'we must admit that the efforts we have made for 12 months and more to build up adequate defences had so far failed'.[2] Most of the hard questions about who was to contribute what, when and how - about who was to be armed and who was to command -lay in the future. Unless these were resolved, there was a danger that NATO could go the way of many other international agreements, remaining no more than an empty shell that was neither activated nor allowed to die - testimony only to what might have been and to the demoralizing intractibilities of inter-state co-operation.

All of this was of especial concern to the British Government. It was a basic axiom of British policy that there was no internal balance of power on the European continent. Stability could only be assured by an external guarantor. Britain's ability to perform this role on its own had ended on the Somme in 1916. Yet the task would have to fall to someone, for the European continent remained the centre of the international strategic system in the sense that even far flung countries could not allow it to be dominated by a single, unfriendly power. The pattern of twentieth century history suggested that European wars soon became world wars. Indeed, the period since 1914 could be regarded as a single crisis and, in 1950, British policy-makers were far from certain that the cycle of conflict had stabilized. The wartime alliance with the Soviet Union had arguably raised up a greater power than that which had been cast down. The First World War had at least ended with a peace Treaty, even if it was a flawed one. By contrast, it had been clear since 1947 that no settlement was negotiable even between the allies of just two years before: and that Europe faced a future without international agreement on the basic principles of its arrangement.

In all, British assessments of the Schuman Plan concentrated more on its implications for security than any other issue. This was true even before October 1950, when Schuman's scheme would come to be twinned with the Pleven Plan to create a European Army.

1.   From Bevin Plan to Schuman Plan, the changing nature of British security policy 1948-50

Two years earlier, in 1948, Bevin too had given his name to a plan. In what was, perhaps, to prove the high water mark between 1945 and 1961 of British preparedness to make a commitment to co-operation weighted towards the European side of the Atlantic, Bevin had toyed with the idea of a union between the British Commonwealth, other West European states and their vestigial imperial systems. This would be a defensive alliance, committed to the containment of communism and allied to the US. But it would also allow the 'middle powers' a margin of independence from the superpowers.

By 1950, the consensus view in the British Government was that the work on the

Bevin Plan had been useful, but mainly in serving to clarify how *not* to go about the task of defending West Europe. Indeed, the Plan now seemed quite inadequate in view of the further deterioration that had occurred in the security environment over the previous two years. 1948-50 saw the ruthless integration of East Europe into the Soviet bloc, confirming that the territory, men and industry of those countries would be fully available to the Soviet military; and, above all, that the Soviets' massive conventional superiority would continue to be deployed right up against the boundaries of Western Europe, leaving neither time nor distance to compensate the West for its seeming inferiority in military strength. 1949 brought a further shock when the USSR succeeded in exploding an Atomic bomb, years before the West had expected this to be within the reach of Soviet technology.

The lessons that the British drew were, first, that there should not be the slightest room for doubt that any Soviet probe into West Europe would immediately and automatically engage the considerable and reinforceable might of the US in the form of American troops already positioned in Europe[3]; second, that it was imperative that the US be persuaded to extend a nuclear umbrella over West Europe to provide a further guarantee and compensate for conventional inferiority; and, third, that North Atlantic Countries needed to construct an integrated defence of a kind that would be a revolutionary break with orthodox approaches to alliance-building. In place of a collection of separate armies, it would, in Bevin's words, be 'organically prepared' for international threats through a shared command structure and common defence planning[4]. The Bevin Plan had acknowledged that only an Atlantic partnership could provide the critical mass needed to defend West Europe. But it had not made the further conceptual leap to the idea of an integrated defence at the transatlantic level. Indeed, the whole purpose of the Plan had been to retain some room for manoeuvre in the international system for a British-led Western Europe. The US and West Europe would be allies in extremis, but short of a Soviet attack, there would be no need for identity in their foreign and security policies and plenty of room for a calculated ambivalence in their relationship. By 1950, the Whitehall view was that this would neither deter outsiders nor reassure insiders.

2.   The Schuman Plan and British fears of a Third Force Europe

It has been useful to begin the chapter with a survey of defence policy between 1948 and 1950, for British reactions to the Schuman Plan were divided between those who saw it as a regression to the now inadequate principles of the Bevin Plan of 1948 and those who, conversely, saw it as likely to facilitate the ability of the new NATO Treaty to deliver a truly integrated defence. The holders of the first view argued that, at the very moment that NATO faced the uneasy transition from aspiration to operational security system, Schuman's initiative would, as so often happens when hard decisions need to be made, encourage both sides of the Atlantic to succumb to wishful thinking that little needed to be done. The Permanent Under Secretary's Committee established in the Foreign Office to consider British reactions to the Schuman and Pleven Plans argued that:

> if a third world power, comprising the United Kingdom the Commonwealth and Western Europe would be unable to maintain its independence politically, economically or militarily, a power confined to West Europe could not a fortiori stand alone..even the mere suggestion that a third force was practicable would foster dangerous illusions and thus be undesirable in the present state of relations between the Communist and non-Communist worlds.[5]

As late as 1951, the Foreign Office, ever alert to signs of what it considered to be American naivety, was cautioning against the encouragement of forces in American politics that were responding to the anticipated costs and risks of a commitment to European defence by 'looking for a panacea' and finding one in unrealistic expectations of European integration. Indeed, there was a danger that the latter could provide a convenient meeting point for isolationist and internationalist opinion in the US.[6] The Permanent Under Secretary's Committee warned that far from easing the burdens that the formation of an Atlantic Alliance would impose on the US, Europe would be at its weakest 'during the transitional and experimental phase leading to full integration'.[7] Federation was, after all, a long and painful process, only achieved in the case of the US itself through a war of self-assertion and then a civil war.[8]

Those who argued in this vein considered it essential that a collective defence should be built on the firm foundations of existing nation states, rather than the treacherous sands of European integration. Only then would the resources of West European societies be fully mobilized to meet the new security challenges. Strang cautioned against the assumption that 'an integrated Europe would in some sense be stronger to resist Russia'. He argued that, on the contrary, 'the contribution of individual countries would be weakened if merged in a diffuse civilization'.[9] Hall-Patch warned that the movement towards European integration was grounded in despair. France, Germany and Italy had been unable to shake off the postwar malaise of 'weak and divided government'. This had in turn encouraged an experimentation with political integration that was reckless because the security threat had an immediacy that could only be met by existing 'national' structures, rather than the 'federal institutions' of fond and distant hope.

Holders of these arguments thus considered it essential that NATO should be constructed on a substratum of nation states with their established arrangements for taxation and military recruitment. By contrast, the formation of new Federal institutions was likely to be followed by an initial period of intense argument about the allocation of obligations and sacrifices. Far from being able to rely on established norms to facilitate consensus, all temporary solutions would be disputed for fear that they would harden into unchangeable precedents. Discredited though the nation state might be in much of Western Europe, it did not have to face the challenge of having to earn a modicum of authority and legitimacy from scratch; and with the added handicap in relation to each national society of being some distant and new-fangled transnational institution.[10] Bevin likewise tended to see European constitution-building as a nervous displacement activity. He argued that, until security structures were in place, there would be insufficient confidence to sustain the economic recovery of West Europe. Without economic recovery, Federal institutions would become as unpopular as existing states; with economic recovery, consent would as assuredly return to the nation states of Europe as to any Federal structures (Bullock, 1983, pp.617-8).

Integration might also tempt the Europeans to exaggerate their international strength. This could, for example, follow from the idle habit of adding up populations and national products to reach the conclusion that West Europe was a considerable power on its own: a way of thinking that was no more than a fallacy of aggregation so long as a Federal Europe lacked the political attributes needed to mobilize and combine resources with the same efficiency as nation states. A further possibility was that a federating Europe would attempt to define itself in contradistinction to the United States, picking arguments in order to assert its individuality and independence. Either boldness or hostility could then incline a European Community to adopt a middle position between East and West. Yet it would be fatal for continental Europe to eschew commitment for ambiguity in the cold war. As one Foreign Office memo put it, two days after the announcement of the Schuman Plan, 'History teaches that powers which seek to maintain their neutrality or to play a balancing role fall miserably between two stools unless they have the strength and coherence for such a policy'.[11] Without a well integrated Atlantic Alliance, West Europe would lack the security to pursue policies independent of the Soviet Union. The continent would be 'Finlandized', always having to respect the constraints placed on its evolution by the presence of an over-mighty neighbour.

There were, to be more precise, two different British fears of how a third force Europe might develop through the instrument of political integration: one in which France would be the pied piper leading the other countries out of a closely-knit Atlantic Alliance and another in which West Germany would play this role. The first version saw Paris as eager to exclude the US and the UK from a continental bloc. West Europe would then become a French sphere of influence that would allow France to pursue a profitable diplomacy of manoeuvre between East and

West. Although this would be a high-risk strategy given the preponderance of Soviet arms in Europe, it might allow the French only to call on 'Anglo-Saxon' defence resources when they were needed; to put the onus on the US and UK to demonstrate how their help in a crisis would be a more attractive option than the surrender or neutralization of West Europe; and to avoid the hard slog of rearmament, common security planning and compromised national decision-making that Britain was prepared to accept in its own plans for a defence Community that would be both integrated and Atlantic in scope. Above all, there would be no external pressure for German rearmament with all its potential to split French politics.

These anxieties about the true intentions of French policy emerge from a letter written by Kenneth Younger during his period in charge of the Foreign Office in June 1950. He asked Harvey to answer a series of questions about the Schuman Plan: were the French attempting to have it both ways, 'drawing away from the Atlantic Alliance', while at the same time 'preserving contact with the Atlantic Powers'? Were they leaving open the option of 'escaping the consequences of another war' by attempting at a 'suitable moment to deal with the Soviet Union'? In an interesting demonstration of the power of painful memory over present assessment, Younger revealed his fear that such a Europe could 'stand between the United States and the Soviet Union and endeavour to practise the same neutrality as was practised by Vichy'.[12]

In his reply to Younger, Harvey quite rightly insisted that the Schuman Plan was sponsored by those in French politics who were most committed to the Atlantic Alliance. However, the uncertainties presented by the 'revolving door' governments of the Fourth Republic meant that the fear of a Third Force Europe could never be entirely exorcized from British assessments of French policy. John Young's study of the period reveals how far NATO dealings could become hostage to the fine balance in French politics between supporters of a closely integrated Alliance and a more 'independent' Europe. The summer before the Schuman Plan had seen the fall and rise of four French Governments, two of which were more inclined to a cautious approach to the Atlantic Alliance (Young, 1984, pp.101-6). It appeared to many in London that European integration without the UK would necessarily put France in a better position to lead West Europe away from the Atlantic Alliance. The wish might then be father to the thought. What is more, France seemed to be fated to be the third and dissatisfied power of the Atlantic Alliance, always looking to strategies like European unification to alter its status, always prone to protest and awkwardness. Some British diplomats even acknowledged that the Atlantic Alliance could involve a distribution of risks which was unstable from the point of view of keeping the group together or allowing it to function with sufficient consensus for common defence planning. In November 1950, Harvey singled out for comment a prescient analysis by J.J. Servan-

Schreiber. This pointed out that the West would have to defend itself with nuclear bombs, given its inability to match the Soviets at the conventional level. But this would not involve an Alliance of equal and shared risks between the two sides of the Atlantic, as an atomic exchange would, in the current state of technology, still be confined to Europe. The West Europeans would thus always be much less willing to confront - and more willing to accommodate - the Soviets than the Americans.[13]

If Third Force Europe started as a French ambition, others suspected that it might ultimately become an instrument of West German power. The Permanent Under Secretary's Committee was concerned that the French were 'over-confident in their ability to handle Germany within a Federal Union':

> As for the attitude of Germany, given the size of her population and their capacity for hard work, the wealth of her resources and technical knowledge, the historical background of her national ambitions - and, perhaps above all, the knowledge that France wishes to restrict her scope- it is well-nigh certain that Germany would set out to become the leading partner in such a federation. If so, it is more than likely that she will succeed'.[14]

Kirkpatrick later argued that the choice of coal and steel as the starting point for supranational institutions could prove ill-advised, allowing the Germans to play to their industrial strengths and to establish an early primacy over the other participants. The problem with the philosophy of integration behind the Schuman Plan was precisely that its emphasis on the use of economic means to achieve political ends might end up creating a German hegemony rather than a European Union. A hegemony established through economic means could also be harder to detect or challenge than any based on naked coercion. It would be 'very hard to detect in its early stages' and it would be very hard 'to choose the precise point at which to call a halt'. Unlike 'political and military predominance' it would also 'tend to bind the union together, rather than set up a strain leading to disintegration'.[15] In other words, there would be a certain ineluctability to German foreign policy dominance of such a Europe, softened, yet made more effective, by the substitution of economic for military constraint on other countries.

Present intentions to sublimate German nationalism in an integrating Europe were thought to be genuine enough. But a unified Europe might provide a future German state with an instrument that it could use for its own purposes. The Permanent Under Secretary's Committee cautioned against presenting 'Germany with Federal organs of government all ready to manipulate', thus implying that such a constitution could magnify German power, rather than constrain it, as the French anticipated. Once re-endowed with the means to dominate, the will to do so might follow. Indeed, there was one very good reason why West Germany might strive to maximize its foreign policy resources, rather than accept the logic of self-effacement. The wish to reverse the division of Germany could well tempt Bonn to use any economic predominance of a European Union to 'capture' the grouping for its own foreign policy priorities. This could, in turn, lead either to the reckless appeasement of the East[16] or to a dangerously aggressive approach to the Soviet bloc. On the second, the Permanent Under Secretary's Committee warned that 'Germany might seek to involve her associates in some military adventure, perhaps a war, to recover the eastern territories' and pursue 'revanchist aims'.[17]

3.   The Schuman Plan and fears of a divided Alliance

Even if a Third Force Europe were no part of the intentions of the supporters of the Schuman Plan, some in the British Government viewed it as a dangerous precedent for the multiple fracturing of the West into groupings of varying membership. The formation of sub-groups could prevent the development of a sense of Atlantic solidarity, retard the full and free exchange of views, encourage mutual misunderstanding and complicate co-ordination between the economic and the military aspects of policy. One Foreign Office working party argued that 'a European Union was not a necessary stage in the establishment of a NATO Community'. It could, on the other hand, 'tend to rely too much on its own strength and consult less closely and less early than it should with the Americans and Canadians'.[18] In May 1950, the first interdepartmental review of the Schuman Plan argued that it was a 'broadside directed precisely against our policy of trying to get the Atlantic Pact to be the framework within which economic questions should be considered'. As an example of the problems that could be caused by a mismatch between economic co-operation on a European scale and security collaboration on an Atlantic scale, it was pointed out that the NATO programme would require the identification of spare capacity in the European coal and steel industry and its assignment to military production. Yet how could this be done, given that the High Authority envisaged by Schuman could not receive instructions from Governments?[19]

Indeed, it was important to avoid all sub-groupings that might cause tensions between the Atlantic Allies. When he became Foreign Secretary, Morrison warned that 'we should not allow ourselves to get into a situation in which the European continent sits on one side of the table and the North Americans on the other'.[20] Moreover, American support for the formation of a European Customs Union for Coal and Steel was in flat contradiction to the new international economic order that the US was also trying to promote. The strain that this could impose on the transatlantic relationship had been amply demonstrated when Schuman's initial exposition of the Plan was met by anxious enquiries from Acheson about the cartelization of European markets. Another US Secretary of State, Henry Kissinger, would later question how far commercial discrimination could co-exist with strategic alliance. Indeed, the Schuman Plan could easily become the first stage in the construction of a system of comprehensive trade preferences limited to the Six.

To its critics in the British Government, the Plan threatened a double fissure within the alliance: one between the two sides of the Atlantic and another between the Europeans themselves. The latter would be divided into insiders and outsiders, creating problems of hierarchies and core/periphery relationships. Thus Mallet warned that a 'continental bloc' of just some of the states of West Europe 'united economically in the Schuman Plan, politically in the Council of Europe and militarily in the European army' would 'conflict with the principle of the Atlantic Alliance as a free association of twelve equal, independent states and might constitute a serious disruptive element in the Atlantic Alliance'.[21] If Schumania came to be accorded privileged treatment by the US, other European allies would face an invidious choice between continued marginalization or involuntary acceptance of the supranational model of integration. This could further strain the cohesion of West Europe.

4.   The Western 'Defence Crisis' in 1950-1

It is a reasonable surmise that of the twelve states that had signed up to the NATO Treaty a year before the announcement of the Schuman Plan, four were essential to the ambitious plans that began to circulate for a common defensive system that would be unprecedented in its scale, its integrated planning and its construction in conditions short of actual hostilities. Without the full and willing co-operation of America, Britain, France or West Germany, the remaining three partners would have had to settle for a modest - and probably ineffectual- defensive system in comparison with that which eventually emerged.

Over the next few pages, we will see that as it became more obvious what NATO would entail, all of the four key states except for Britain came to require something akin to the Schuman Plan if they were to give their all to the common defence. That Britain was the exception, accounts for the scepticism recounted in the last section. That the Schuman Plan and NATO came to be parallel and interdependent bargains for the other three partners, explains why the successful negotiation of the ECSC came to be a part of Britain's own defence interest, in spite of the reservations explained above. The British Government had to recognize that if it wanted an ambitiously conceived NATO it would have to accept the Schuman Plan. The maximum of its foreign policy manoeuvre on ECSC consisted of refusal to take part itself - the further option of spiking the Plan was not available.

To set the context for this argument, we need to appreciate that American and British defence planners soon concluded that a forward defence would be essential: West Europe could only be credibly defended from what was to be known as the inner German border, not from the Rhine.[22] The latter would leave western defences strung out along extended lines: as a peripheral alliance of states without easy internal lines of communication. Younger thus concluded that 'it would be difficult to sustain a viable defence system from France and the Low Countries'.[23] Bevin reinforced the argument in a letter to Attlee about the dangers of a two-stage aggression in which the Soviets would first move against West Germany and then, fortified by the absorption of Europe's industrial heartland, extend its military domination to the rest of Europe: 'if Germany is left in a vacuum, the Russians will walk in and get resources which will be a tremendous gain in carrying on the conflict'.[24] Attlee agreed, later telling the French Prime Minister, 'if we cannot make effective strategic plans along the Elbe, we would effectively be handing over the whole of Germany to Russia.[25]

If NATO was not prepared to defend West Germany, the Soviets might not even have to fight to absorb it into their sphere of influence, as Bonn would come under enormous pressure to reach some accommodation with Moscow.[26] Even those who supported NATO in West Germany were only likely to continue to do so if it promised them a credible guarantee without the merest hint that there might be a hidden agenda to abandon Germany in the event of conflict. Acheson cautioned that the allies had to remove the 'attitude of defeatism and disintegration in West Germany'.[27] The British Cabinet was warned that the Germans remained 'sceptical of the willingness and ability of the West to defend them in an emergency'[28] and this was responsible for a 'dangerous attitude of lethargy on the part of the German population'. Bevin wrote to Attlee that even an emergency, a sense of international crisis short of physical hostilities, could lead to 'chaos in West Germany':[29] a Vichy-like sauve qui peut with West Germans rushing to make their peace with the East. Unless and until the allies put together a defensive system that commanded the credibility of West Germans, confidence in the future would be weak, economic and social stabilization would be precarious and publics and elites exposed to false offers from the East in exchange for some temporary psychological surcease.

Once the decision had been taken to use West Germany as the front line for Western defences, the allies needed to mobilize sufficient resources for a forward defence and to ensure that any arrangements they agreed were underpinned by a political consensus. In May 1950, it was agreed that the remaining restrictions on German heavy industry would have to be lifted to create sufficient industrial capacity for rearmament. In September, the US took the still more dramatic step of insisting that West Germany itself be rearmed as a precondition for the continued commitment of US troops to NATO Europe. Throughout the period, the growing *inter*dependence of America, Britain, France and West Germany in security matters was reflected in the very decision to create the new Federal Republic, discussion of its return to full foreign policy sovereignty and consideration of its formal admission to NATO. Leaving policy towards West Germany unchanged would have meant using its territory as a large scale military base while discriminating against the economic 'life chances' of its population, preserving symbols of both political inequality and war guilt, and excluding Germans from any participation in what was supposed to be their own defence.

The link between the Schuman Plan and the lifting of allied controls on German coal and steel was obvious. It has already been explored in chapter 2 and will be elaborated a little further here. Although slightly less direct, the connection between the Schuman Plan and German rearmament was no less vital. Indeed, the first recorded discussion of the Plan inside the British Government was provoked by the Chiefs of Staff, who informed the Cabinet on 10 May 1950 of their view that 'ultimately some form of German rearmament will be essential'. They then went on to observe that 'a necessary prelude must be a large measure of political and economic integration (of West Europe). The French proposal appears to be an extremely important step in that direction'.[30] Harvey reinforced this assessment: 'by this one step..the use of German manpower in connection with West European Defence would become not only possible but inevitable'.[31] Shinwell likewise advised the Cabinet, 'the potential of West Europe' could not be harnessed for a collective defence system 'until French fears of a resurgence of German armed power' were assuaged by the 'determination of safeguards which Germany must give for her good behaviour. The Schuman Plan might be helpful here. A full and effective control of the coal and steel industry of Western Europe might help to convince the French that they no longer need fear invasion from Germany'. It would bring 'nearer the day when it would be politically practical' to respond to the 'logic of events' with German rearmament.[32] There were even some in the French Government itself who were prepared to admit as early as 12 May 1950 that this could be one consequence of the Schuman Plan.[33]

As they edged towards economic equality for West Germany and some measure of German rearmament, the allies faced two options. They could either start drawing on West German output and manpower for the common defence without adjusting any of the institutional architecture of West Europe, or accept that the inclusion of West Germany in NATO efforts would only be possible in parallel with some wider rearrangement of inter-state relations, such as that proposed in the Schuman Plan. The next few pages will be concerned with explaining the advantages of the second approach and why it came to be a part of the lowest common denominator of agreement between the United States, France and West Germany.

Even before the attack on South Korea heightened perceptions of Soviet aggression, military planners in Washington came to the conclusion that an extra $30b would be needed over the next 5-6 years to bring NATO up to the strength necessary to sustain a defence of West Europe. But, if it was to succeed, rearmament would have to be compatible with the sustained recovery of the West European economy, the hard-won stabilization of West European governments and a new consensus in US politics that had so recently turned through one hundred and eighty degrees, in order to substitute an unprecedented peacetime involvement in the defence of another continent for an isolationist past. The challenge was to 'make West Europe physically strong while preserving her economic stability and not wrecking America's own economic strength'[34] and the obvious answer was to mop up any pool of spare resources that would avoid taxing Americans or disrupting European recovery. This would mean allowing German industry to return to full production and - eventually - looking to German manpower to make a contribution to an allied army. In keeping the German economy to artificial production limits, the allies had ensured that a country that was not a formal member of NATO was the only significant source of spare industrial capacity for rearmament.

In failing to make full use of West German industry or to bring it into the NATO system as a consenting partner, the West was thought to be foregoing its main comparative advantages of economic potential and politically legitimate systems of government. In what were otherwise gloomy assessments of prospects for Western defence, the US Administration predicted that for all its armour the Soviet bloc would lack the economic capacity or political cohesion for a sustained military assault on the West and that it would, therefore, only be able to prevail through Blitzkrieg. If the West could prevent the Soviets from achieving their objectives in the first days of an aggression, West Europe could be reinforced and the Eastern bloc might itself be the first to buckle in any conflict of attrition. What made this a plausible strategy was that the productive potential of West Europe alone was twice that of the Soviet Union. It was also superior in both quality and technology. Western planners also believed that their political systems could be a source of decisive advantage. Totalitarian structures might allow the East to appropriate a higher proportion of its productive surplus to military uses than was possible in any western democracy, but this only got the Soviets back to square one, for they started with a smaller productive base; and, in any case, they were expected in the event of conflict to have to divert a larger part of their military capability to internal policing than a Western defence system that rested upon consent.[35]

Not only was the West foregoing economic potential through controls on the German economy, it would be difficult to keep what was considered the industrial core of West Europe below capacity without risking cumulative movements away from macroeconomic equilibrium in allied countries. West Germany would no longer provide a powerful heart-beat, pumping out high levels of both demand and supply to the rest of West Europe, which would in turn be subject to a more erratic trade cycle as well a lower GDP. How could an alliance be constructed on such an economic base? Not only would it reduce the affordability of any common defence, increasing the dependence of the whole enterprise on American subsidy, but frustrated economic hopes would only fan social discontent and increase support in Western Europe for political parties that were either neutralist or actively sympathetic with the eastern bloc. Indeed, there were several allied defence planners who took the view that in spite of the size of the Soviet military establishment, the main risk did not lie in any military aggression; that East and West were locked in a novel form of power struggle in which the competition would in essence be one between social systems; that the main instrument of aggression would take the form of low-risk exploitation by the Soviets of any economic and social discontent to bring about political change in the West; and that the main means of defence would be for the West to marginalize any potentially pro-Soviet forces by running its economy at full-employment, incorporating all sections of the population into the status quo by developing welfare systems and excluding extreme parties from coalition politics.

With the invasion of Korea in June 1950, Britain, France and the US all increased their rearmament programmes to the very limits of what was politically and economically sustainable - and yet assessments remained pessimistic about the ability of the West to defend itself. Given that agreement had been reached in May to make full use of German industry, the only remaining source of slack was provided by the ban on West Germany recruiting troops of its own. The strain on Britain, France and America in the absence of German contributions was plain from assessments carried out by the UK Government. Franks reported from Washington in September 1950 that US defence expenditure would 'almost certainly now exceed 10% of national income'; and that it would look to the Europeans to 'match this effort', probably on a formula of '170% of the pre-Korean rate of defence expenditure. It was admitted that such a commitment of resources to rearmament could cost Britain its 'economic independence', put the country on a 'war footing'[36] and throw into doubt its whole 'future as a trading nation'.[37]

Meanwhile a special Foreign Office paper on France argued that its political system also faced strains from a failure to harness German resources to the common defence. In the absence of German contributions, NATO would have to look to France to provide the main pool of manpower, to increase its military spending to 60% of its government budget and 10% of national income and to divert resources from the increasingly beleaguered defence of its colonial positions. The third point would boost support for the right; the second would create economic and social tensions that would add to the support of the French

Communists who already commanded 25% of the vote. The first, in conjunction with any aggravation of the 'political instability endemic in the fabric of the Fourth Republic', would mean that a large proportion of the population that would have to be mobilized in an emergency would be Communists, or right wing opponents of the Republic; and that the Communist Trade Union movement, the CGT, might be in a position to practice 'industrial sabotage in the event of war'.[38]

Whatever their anxieties about placing Germans under arms, the British and French Governments had to admit that it made little sense to place heavy manpower constraints on their own recoveries when there were many unemployed who could be used for military recruitment, if only in supporting rather than mainline combat roles. Indeed, the fear of German industrial competitiveness, ever present in both Paris and London, had to be weighed against that of German rearmament. There was a certain insanity in freeing West Germany from all defence burdens, while transferring the cost of its defence to its major industrial competitors. This could -once again - just be an alternative, economic route to German domination of West Europe.

The British delegation to the New York meeting of the Atlantic Council in September 1950 identified a further reason why the West's defence plans required it to change its policy towards West Germany. If this was to be where NATO would make its stand, the allies would make themselves peculiarly dependent upon the support of the German people: 'it carries with it the inescapable fact that the battle will be fought in Germany itself. It is, therefore, reasonable to ensure that in such a contingency, we shall have the active support and sympathy of the Germans themselves'.[39] Germany's role as the key territorial unit where any collective defence would be based would require all kinds of practical, everyday acts of co-operation from the Federal Government, Lander and general public. The German Department of the Foreign Office warned that any regime to guard against German reassertion would have to be accepted voluntarily if America, Britain and France were not to find themselves having to 'use force indefinitely' to keep the Germans down at the same time as they were trying to keep the Soviets out.[40] On becoming Foreign Secretary, Morrison noted that 'we can only carry Germany with us willingly and by consent..the policy on which we are now embarked will seriously increase the psychological burdens of Occupation'. He spoke of the need to give the West Germans a 'contractual' rather a 'subordinate' relationship and argued that even the 'cumulative effect of hesitations' in treating the Germans as equals could be fatal to the interests of the West.[41]

As these quotations suggest, any prospect of sustaining discriminatory limitations on West Germany died the moment that the West decided to defend itself on the inner German boundary rather than the Rhine. Likewise, the attempt to defend the Federal Republic without the use of German manpower was probably forlorn after the invasion of Korea in June 1950. To recreate the fears of the time, it is necessary to appreciate that the Soviets were busy forming 200, 000 East Germans into a force known as the 'Bereitschaften' and that Germany was seen as an analogue to Korea. Both were nations that had been divided into communist and non-communist halves. This seemed to leave the Soviets with the low-risk option of using a satellite state to foment an aggression by proxy; of disguising an annexation as an act of national unification. As Mallet minuted in September 1950,

> Korea opened our eyes to the danger that the Russians will use the Bereitschaften to stage a civil war in Germany for the avowed purpose of reuniting the country and freeing it from foreign occupation. It is doubtful whether the allied forces, as presently constituted, would be able to hold the western sectors of Berlin against the Bereitschaften by the end of the year, or whether they would be able to hold Western Germany by the end of next year if the Bereitschaften continue to develop as they are doing.[42]

So long as there were no West Germans under arms, the only German combatants in the event of an East/West conflict would be from the East. This could leave the West Germans - in the allies' rear - confused as to their loyalties. Bevin spoke of his fear of 'being made to appear as fighting Germans to prevent the reunification of the country and its liberation from occupation'.[43] At the very least, the allies were concerned that so long as the East was able to portray NATO as an army of occupation, rather than one of protection, the Soviet propaganda campaign would make sufficient headway to prevent the transformation of West Germany into a credible defence glacis. The best solution to this seemed to be to allow German troops to take their place alongside the NATO allies.

5.   The Schuman Plan and NATO as parallel bargains: binding Germany and reconciling France

Even if the allies did agree to return West Germany to full sovereignty and to include it in its new security system, this would just be the beginning of their problems. For fear that it would seal the division of the German nation, the main opposition party, Kurt Schumacher's Social Democrats, over whom Adenauer had only a precarious majority, questioned any integration with the West. Moreover, the interaction of Soviet and NATO strategic concepts implied that Germany - and West Germany at that - would be the main battleground in the event of any hostility between the two blocs. This could leave the West Germans as exposed to the temptation of Soviet offers to join in the neutralization and demilitarization of Central Europe as any failure of the West to assume responsibility for their defence in the first place. It will be seen in a moment, that the acceptance of such offers would be fatal to NATO - but not to the survival of the Soviet bloc.

By September 1950, Schuman's approach on the Atlantic Council seems to have been to recognize the inevitability of some German rearmament: he 'acknowledged it was not possible to accept a situation in which allies had to defend Germany without the Germans making a contribution to the common cause'..he 'believed that French opinion might accept German rearmament when France itself was stronger'. However, Schuman was equally eager to point out the enormous risks of such a course: 'any agreement now would only be rejected by the French Parliament..(rearmament) would come as a shock to the peoples of Europe and could provide a dangerous backlash against the whole European defence effort'.[44] By December, his pessimism had deepened: there was, in his view, 'no prospect of the French Parliament ever voting to admit Germany as a member of NATO' and if the original US proposal of September 1950 for German rearmament had been put to the vote it would only have attracted the support of 10 Deputies.[45]

In all, German rearmament was a traumatic episode in French politics and other NATO countries had to consider French domestic reactions a shared problem and do all they could to bend their plans to take them into account. To understand why, it is necessary to recall that the governments of the Fourth Republic were squeezed between two 'non-system parties', the Gaullists on the right and the Communists on the left, both of whom were opposed to the very institutions of the Fourth Republic. Administrations could only be formed by bringing together parties of the centre into grand coalitions, an arrangement that only threatened the further radicalization of politics as moderate parties vacated the role of opposition to the Gaullists, Communists and various 'surge parties' which were able to ride successive waves of disillusionment with the closed elite politics of the Fourth Republic (Macrae). Throughout the period, the seepage of support from the Centre was closely correlated with foreign policy pressures - including those associated with German rearmament. These pressures contributed to a cumulative degradation in the coalition politics of the Fourth Republic. As mainstream parties lost more votes, individual coalitions became more exposed to the withdrawal of support by just one faction within just one party, very probably on a foreign policy issue; as the revolving door process of government of the Fourth Republic became more vertiginous, the system was discredited, more votes drained away from the main parties, which found it even harder to deal with the massive foreign policy problems of the period.

It was not difficult to understand why so many in France expected their Governments to fight for constraints on Germany - and not to agree to measures that could one day allow another German Government to mobilize its industry and manpower for conflict. French Defence Minister, Moch, who burst into tears when Acheson first proposed German rearmament, reminded his colleagues at the

Atlantic Council in September 1950 that France had been invaded by Germany once a generation for each of the past three generations. On two of these occasions it had been defeated, on one it had been occupied and on another it had lost more than a million dead. A country that was connected to such a neighbour by a land boundary was also bound to be more wary than allies separated from Germany by a channel or even an ocean. Various Foreign Office reports suggested that a tendency to see Germany as a threat to France was 'habitual' and equally grounded in both collective and personal experience: 'reluctance to welcome Germany back into the family of nations was not a matter of historical grudge but of the recent personal experience of practically every Frenchman'. While to others in France, the Soviet Union was not even a primary threat: it remained a potentially useful ally against German reassertion.[46]

It was Bevin himself who told the Atlantic Council in May 1950 that NATO could only work in parallel with Franco-German rapprochement. He argued that the peoples of West Europe had recently 'done their best to destroy one another' and this had 'sewn seeds of suspicion and prejudice which must be overcome if solidarity is to be achieved'.[47] So long as France was undecided as to whether Germany or the Soviet Union represented the greater threat, it would want to retain a substantial proportion of its defence capacity to meet a challenge from its immediate neighbour. Moch claimed that any bungled German rearmament would put French Governments under pressure to form two divisions to supervise each new German division created, or to pull its troops out of West Germany altogether, so that they could be used to defend the national territory (Bullen and Pelly, 1989, p.104n). None of this would be compatible with integrated defence planning or maximizing the availability of scarce resources for resisting the Soviet Union. Continued schizophrenia in French security thinking could even present operational difficulties in the event of conflict. One US assessment asked how, in the absence of Franco-German reconciliation, would it be possible to look to French troops to fight with full morale and determination in the event of a not improbable NATO mission to save West Berlin, so recently the capital of the Reich that had defeated and occupied the French?[48] In the UK, the Ministry of Defence concluded that French fears of Germany would have to be allayed before the potential of West Germany could be harnessed to the defence of the West.[49] One Foreign Office view was that short of Franco-German reconciliation there was not even a possibility of a 'coherent western policy towards Germany', for France would always be in a position to 'undo the work' of the UK and US, maybe singlehandedly driving Germany into hostility, neutrality or a link with the East.[50]

An effective military alliance also seemed to presuppose a healthy political economy and, in particular, some mechanism for avoiding any recurrence of the interwar trade wars that had developed between France and Germany. Acheson noted that US pressures to lift production controls on West Germany coal and steel could be extremely dangerous if not accompanied by the creation of some Franco-German framework to control over-production in these two industries. Without this, one of the two countries could dump its surplus on to the other, provoking a rerun of the interwar period with all its dislocation, unemployment and political destabilization. West Germany might even turn to the East in search of new markets, further straining the cohesion of NATO.[51] From the British side, the soon-to-be Chancellor of the Exchequer, Hugh Gaitskell, was also impressed by the point that 'if there was to be co-operation in the military sphere, there had to be a good feeling. This could not exist in the face of economic warfare' (Williams, 1983). Observations such as these implied that spill-over arguments were not confined to theologians of European integration. The demands of constructing a common defence in NATO also linked into the need for stable systems of trade and payments, nested in institutions that ensured political commitment to the consensual resolution of economic frictions between neighbours.

As it became obvious that Franco-German reconciliation was a precondition for a common defence, the Schuman Plan enjoyed a peculiar status over alternative means to achieve this objective, for it was a route to rapprochement that had been chosen by the protagonists themselves, in direct communication with one another and without the mediation or imposition of outsiders. Both London and Washington considered and quickly dismissed the option of avoiding the problems of Franco-German reconciliation by pressing ahead unilaterally with the rearmament of West Germany and then leaving it to the French to decide whether they were prepared to collaborate fully with the collective defence. There were broadly two problems with this. First, the UK and US needed France as much as the other way round. If West Germany was needed to provide a front line, France was needed for defence in depth. Without transit rights through French ports, land communications and airspace, the job of resupplying NATO forces from across the Atlantic would be vastly complicated. If the goal really was to ensure that this time round Europe would be 'defended rather than liberated', the lesson of 1940-4 was that, once France was lost, the task of reintroducing allied forces to Europe would be hard and hazardous. The Foreign Office paper of August 1950 on France calculated that without West German troops - and it would be a long time before proposals for German rearmament would anticipate sizeable contributions from that quarter - NATO would need to look to France to provide 40 divisions, or four times as many forces as were then available. Failing this, Britain and the US would have to provide the same level of forces as in October 1944, a mobilization that had only been achieved after four years of intensive preparation and with what was probably an unsustainable pre-emption of manpower from the domestic economy.[52] Second, without full French participation, German rearmament would have to be even more extensive. This would be an enormous provocation to the East. It would also strain West German politics where there was a strong tide of opinion in favour of making a decisive break with a militaristic past. And, according to some in the UK, it would turn West Germany into a massive military satellite of the US, removing any prospect of a balanced Atlantic Alliance, let alone a special relationship between Washington and London.

The goal of reconciling France to allied plans for the new West Germany was, of course, intimately related to that of binding the Federal Republic to various policy commitments and codes of international behaviour. As the British Chiefs of Staff implied, Germany could be fully sovereign or fully rearmed, but not both.[53] Binding, in fact, meant two quite different things: restraining Germany from any aggression against its western neighbours and preventing it from ignoring the West altogether by redirecting its ties towards Eastern Europe. However, the lessons of the interwar period suggested that binding would only work if it was based on some mechanism of constraint that was acceptable to the Germans themselves.

Schuman's Plan gave an answer of startling novelty to this old problem. It was the following section of his announcement on 9 May 1950 that caught the public imagination: 'the solidarity in production thus created would make all war between France and Germany not only unthinkable but *materially impossible*' (Bullen and Pelly, 1986, p.3). The choice of coal and steel as the industries to be pooled was, of course, deliberate, as these were the very activities that would need to be mobilized in the event of conflict. From now on, they would not be readily available for any unilateral aggression by one European Community country against another; for, say, a West German threat to France. But they would be available to a collective defence of West Europe, for example, through NATO. The Schuman Plan was thus a decisive step towards converting West Europe into what Karl Deutsch has termed a security community: an area in which force ceases to be a thinkable instrument of political change, even if it remains a credible means of defence against outsiders (Deutsch, 1968). In his memoirs, Adenauer points out that, at the very least, a European Coal and Steel Community would make the aggressive plans of any one country transparent to its neighbours. In order to mobilize the two industries for war, any member state would have to start diverting production from an intimate network of transnational trading contacts. It might even have to disentangle itself from the Authority. This would function as an early warning system (Adenauer, 1966).

However, the coal and steel of the Ruhr would be put beyond the reach of any future German militarism not through restrictions on the *level* of production but through the *internationalization* of that production: through the combination of a supranational regulatory structure and the complex web of input-output dependencies between different types of coal, iron and steel that were expected to develop with free trade between the Ruhr and Alsace-Lorraine in particular. A logic of specialization and divided efforts would be substituted for the logic of self-sufficiency needed for a self-contained military-industrial complex, capable of supporting unilateral nationalistic ambition. Unlike the old physical limits on German production, the new security guarantee would no longer work through economic discrimination against German producers and restrictions on the life chances of millions of German citizens. Nor would they mean holding the whole European economy at less than full capacity with attendant risks of economic and social instability and under-resourced defence and welfare programmes. Indeed, the new arrangements would be a source of economic opportunity and growth, in so far as they encouraged free trade and rationalization in production.

But this was not all. If the sovereignty of the West German state was to be limited by participation in the ECSC, so would that of France and all other members of the Plan. If the Schuman Plan was specifically aimed at the constraint of the Federal Republic in intention, its restraining effects were not limited to West Germany, like some permanent emblem of war guilt. The Plan did not imply that just one West European state would, on account of its past, be less sovereign than others in the future. It was a shared divestiture of sovereignty, a loss of absolute but not of relative sovereignty, or, perhaps, not even the former in the precise circumstances in which West Germany found itself in 1950. The Head of the Foreign Office's German Department advised that it was because the Schuman Plan reconciled constraint with political equality that it was the first French scheme that 'had a chance of being acceptable to the Germans': that would be 'acceptable to Germany in the long term precisely because it places it on the same footing as France or any other participating country'.[54]

Indeed, the divestiture of sovereignty was asymmetric in West Germany's favour to the extent that it was in the happy position of being asked to give up freedoms that it had not yet recovered. In a sense, it was more and not less sovereign as a result of the Schuman Plan. As a direct consequence of the Plan, it was no longer tied to production limits, even if it had to accept the possibility of supranational intervention in the regulation of its coal and steel industries; as an indirect consequence, it was eventually allowed to form an army of its own, even if this was accompanied by whole series of safeguards. The allies were themselves quick to recognize the value of the Schuman Plan in building up the political authority of the new West German state. There was some concern at the time that the new Federal Republic could too easily be portrayed as a bastardized political entity: a puppet state of the occupying powers run by collaborators in the political and economic oppression of West Germany: a provisional entity, pending the reunification of the German nation. It was also noted that democracy would not decisively supplant the political perversions to which Germany was still considered to be susceptible unless and until Federal Governments were considered to be self-determining and politically responsible. For these reasons, it was British and American policy in 1950 to allow Bonn to make its own foreign policy; and to encourage the Federal Republic to join as many International Organizations as possible.[55]

The beauty of the Schuman Plan was that foreign policy sovereignty could be returned to Bonn in the knowledge that it would be less likely to use it to make some Faustian bargain with the Soviet Union. The day after the publication of the Schuman Plan, Acheson, apparently with West Germany in mind, told senior members of the British Cabinet of his fear that 'if the Western powers were not sufficiently strong and well organized, some of the weaker and more exposed members might, when a crisis arose change sides'.[56] Having created the new West German state, both the US and UK saw themselves in 1950-1 as engaged in a race against time to prevent it from being tempted or threatened into neutrality, maybe even alignment with the East. The view of the US State Department in 1950 was that the Soviets had identified Germany and South East Asia as pressure points on the West; and that they were likely to wage a psychological campaign on West German opinion, alternately alarming it with further attacks on West Berlin and alluring it with the bait of reunification. They might even withdraw their own troops from East Germany as a pretext for demanding that West Germany should also be demilitarized as a step towards reunification.

Tempting though these offers might be to West Germany, they would upset all prospects for an East/West balance. They would leave the ability of the Soviet Union to project force little changed, while depriving NATO of territory needed to construct a concentrated defence in the heart of its sphere.[57] For reasons mentioned above, West Europe would be indefensible without West Germany. But the East would remain a formidable military bloc even without East Germany. Younger minuted at the beginning of 1951 that the obvious course for the Soviets was to offer the reunification of Germany in exchange for its demilitarization. This would spike the formation of NATO.[58] However, any refusal of the offer expected from the Soviets might itself precipitate a political crisis in West Germany, given the 'yearning for reunification' and the reluctance of many Germans themselves to see 'Germany rearmed'.[59]

The Schuman Plan helped to assuage Acheson's fear that NATO would build up West Germany as a defence glacis only to find it uncertain in its allegiance to the West, for any pooling of its coal and steel industries would tie its economic base to that of its western neighbours and create a 'community of fate' in which the security of the whole of the west was vital to the Federal Republic's own prosperity. Ambiguity between East and West would thus come to be as 'materially impossible' for the Federal Republic as any threatening behaviour towards its western neighbours. The US Ambassador to London thus wrote, 'Through the pooling of basic production in Germany, France, Benelux and Italy, the plan would tend to *weld* Germany to the West and make it more difficult for Germany to play off West against East'.[60] Enmeshment would, according to the State Department, be sugared by consensus, as 'Germans would judge their real acceptance by the

West, not only upon political equality but upon equal opportunity to develop markets within the West' - precisely the benefits that would come from the Schuman Plan.[61]

It was also hoped that European integration would be an attractive project of political creativity that would amply absorb West German attentions and divert energies from dangerous schemes of German reunification, which could only be secured at the price demanded by the Soviet Union. Acheson thus concluded that the US should 'welcome a French proposal' that discouraged 'West Germans from thinking always of eastern Germany'.[62]

As for the Soviets themselves, it had been noted two months before Schuman's announcement that the great diplomatic prize would be to re-unite Silesia and the Ruhr in a single industrial complex, or at least to deny the resources of the latter to western defence.[63] The more that the Ruhr was meshed into its own distinctive transnational regime, the less plausible this objective became. The Schuman Plan would not only dampen German receptiveness to Soviet proposals for reunification and neutralization. It would also reduce the determination with which such offers were pressed and bring forward the day when the USSR would turn instead to an exclusive concentration on the integration of its own sphere.

As the months passed, it became still less likely that the British Government would get the kind of NATO it wanted without the successful completion of the Schuman Plan. To see why, it is useful to summarize remaining doubts felt by both the US Administration and Congress in 1950-1, who were unwilling to assume the unprecedented military risks and responsibilities implied by NATO plans unless they could limit their liability in three respects. First, it was necessary to stabilize politics within and between West Europe states: to ensure that the US could concentrate on a defence against the USSR and avoid the burdens of peacekeeping between countries that were meant to be allies, or even a morass of domestic policing roles that could undercut the legitimacy of the American security commitment to Europe. It was essential that American troops should not be squeezed between internal protest and external threat, or find themselves under attack from the East while West Europe crumbled behind them. Second, the US needed guarantees that it would not get itself involved in an organic defence that depended upon each state playing its part, only to find that some allies showed insufficient commitment, diverted resources to other ends, or even defected, perhaps as a result of a victory for left-wing parties brought about by social and economic discontents. Third, the financial burden would have to be minimized with any disproportionate US contribution tapering off after a once-off injection to get European economies and military forces up to full capacity. Any possibility of the Europeans 'free-riding' for their defence on the US would have to be removed.

With these points in mind, it is unsurprising that at the September 1950 meeting of the Atlantic Council in New York, the 'Americans..refused to give their final agreement' unless and until the French accepted the principle of German rearmament.[64] The US line was that if an integrated defence were to be undertaken at all, it had to be done properly. It had to be resourced in a manner that reflected the strength of the opposition - the demands of deterring Soviet forces - and the sums could not be made to add up without including German manpower in some shape or form. Truman laid it on the line to Attlee that it was 'vital to convince Congress that there was a real hope of defending Europe effectively'.[65] Acheson likewise insisted that there was no question of 'committing US troops' until there was agreement on a 'programme, which taken as a whole, offered success'.[66] On the other hand, Schuman argued that simple acceptance by the French Government of German rearmament would probably only command ten votes in the National Assembly. The September 1950 meeting reached deadlock and for a while it looked as though the entire NATO initiative would fail.

The French view of what be necessary to break the impasse came a month later with the announcement of the Pleven Plan for the creation of a European army in which troops would be integrated at battalion level. Universally unloved, and eventually to be strangled in the country of its origin, the Pleven Plan would, for all its faults, be essential to the delicate consensus that allowed the allies to inch forward with the creation of Nato between 1950 and 1954. The allies could neither afford to bring to a head any final decision on the shape of German rearmament nor risk practical delays either in their own mobilization or that of the West Germans. With this in mind, General Spofford proposed a compromise in November 1950 that made use of the Pleven Plan to keep the construction of NATO on the move, pending final decisions on European security. Contingency plans for the raising of German troops would proceed and, in the meantime, the French would convene talks on the creation of a European army. If they talks were successful, any German troops raised by NATO would be integrated in the manner suggested by Pleven. German rearmament would be rendered safer by lagging behind American, Britain and French programmes. However, the West Germans would know that their own participation was being taken seriously. Against this background, it became even more difficult for the British Government to contemplate the failure of the Schuman Plan. The Pleven process was temporarily necessary if there was to be US/French consensus on the construction of NATO,[67] a collapse of the Schuman talks would have cast doubt on the supranational model on which the Pleven Plan was also constructed and successful completion of the ECSC had, in any case, been stipulated by the French as a condition for proceeding with Pleven Plan.

Notes

1. Report of the international sub-committee of the NEC, 27 September 1950, *Labour Party Archives*, Harvester Press, Microfiche 396.
2. Jebb to Attlee, 23 September 1950, PRO [C6109/27/18].
3. Jebb to Younger, 16 September 1950, PRO [C5900/27/18].
4. Bevin to Franks, 14 August 1950, PRO [FO 800/517].
5. Memorandum of the Permanent Under-Secretary's Committee, 13 February 1951, PRO [ZP 18/19].
6. 'The American attitude to European Integration', Brief by the Foreign Office, 20 December 1951, PRO [WU 1005/1 of 1952].
7. Memorandum of the Permanent Under-Secretary's Committee, 13 February 1951, cit.
8. 'American attitude to European Integration', cit.
9. Minutes of a Meeting of the Permanent Under-Secretary's Committee, 29 March 1951, PRO [ZP 18/1].
10. Sir E. Hall-Patch to Mr Eden, 8 July 1952, PRO [M 551/88].
11. 'The French Plan from the Political Point of View', Memorandum by Kirkpatrick, 11 May 1950, PRO [CE 2330/2141/181].
12. Younger to Harvey, 12 June 1950, PRO [CE 3068/2141/181].
13. Harvey to Bevin, 23 November 1950, PRO [WU 10711/58].
14. Memorandum by Permanent Under-Secretary's Committee, 13 February 1951, cit.
15. Memorandum by Permanent Under-Secretary's Committee, 12 December 1951, PRO [ZP 10/1 of 1952].
16. Kirkpatrick to Morrison, 28 May 1951, PRO [ZP 18/14].
17. Memorandum by the Permanent Under Secretary's Committee, 9 June 1951, PRO [ZP 18/20].
18. 'Schuman Plan: Foreign Policy aspects', 30 April 1951, PRO [CE(W) 1543/188]; also Mr Wilson to Butt, 5 May 1951, PRO [CE(W) 1543/198].
19. 'Political Problems in the Schuman Proposals', 31 May 1950, PRO [CE 2820/2141/181].
20. Statement by the Secretary of State for Foreign Affairs to the Committee of Ministers in Strasbourg on 3 August 1951, Annex 1 to PRO C.P.(51)236 [WU 1079/105], 16 August 1951.
21. Memorandum from Mallet to Strang, 19 December 1950, PRO [ZP 13/3].
22. 'Defence of Europe and German participation', 6 October 1950, PRO [C.P.(50) 223].
23. 'Proposed Four-Power Meeting'. Memorandum by K. Younger, 26 January 1951, PRO [C.P.(51) 33].
24. Bevin to Attlee, c 14 September 1950.

25. Meeting with the French Prime Minister and Minister for Foreign Affairs, 2 December 1950', 2 December 1950, PRO [FO 800/465].

26. Morgan Phillips address to Comisco, 21 October 1950, *Archives of the Labour Party*, Harvester Press, microfiche 398.

27. Second Meeting of the Foreign Ministers in New York, 13 September 1950, *Foreign Relations of the United States*, Volume III, 1950, p.1208.

28. 'Policy towards Germany', 26 April 1950, PRO [C.P.(50) 80].

29. Jebb to Attlee, 23 September 1950, PRO [C 6106/27/18].

30. 'Franco-German Steel and Coal Control'. Notes by the Chiefs of Staff, 11 May 1950, PRO [CAB 130/60].

31. Harvey to Bevin, 19 May 1950, PRO [CE 2342/2141/181].

32. Memorandum by the Minister of Defence, 1 July 1950, PRO [C.P.(50)154].

33. Acheson to Acting Secretary of State, 12 May 1950, *Foreign Relations of the United States*, Vol III, p.698.

34. Executive Director of European Co-ordinating Committee of Mutual Defence Assistance Programme to Deputy Director, 29 March 1950, *Foreign Relations of the United States*, Vol III, 1950. 'A proposal for strengthening defence without increasing appropriations', 5 April 1950, *Foreign Relations of the United States*, Volume III, 1950.

35. The United States Delegation at the Tripartite Preparatory Meetings to the Secretary of State, 4 May 1950, *Foreign Relations of the United States*, Vol III, 1950, pp.961-4.

36. Memorandum by Franks, 27 September 1950, PRO [UE 11914/106].

37. Jebb to Younger, 12 September 1950, PRO [UE 11914/58].

38. 'France'. Memorandum by the Foreign Office, 13 June 1950, PRO [WF 1019/15].

39. UK delegation to New York to Ministry of Defence, 21 September 1950.

40. Memorandum by Kirkpatrick, 11 May 1950, PRO [CE 2330/2141/181].

41. 'Policy towards Germany', *cit.*

42. Minute by Mr Mallet, 12 September 1950, PRO [C6004/3333/18].

43. Bevin to Harvey, 5 September 1950, PRO [C 5541/27/18].

44. Atlantic Council, September 1950, *cit.*

45. 'Meeting with French Prime Minister and Foreign Minister', *cit.*

46. Memorandum by Harvey, 6 May 1950, PRO [C 7309/96/18]; Memorandum by Kirkpatrick, 11 May 1950, PRO [CE 2330/2141/181]; Harvey to Morrison, 4 May 1951, PRO [ZP 18/8].

47. Acheson to Acting Secretary of State, 15 May 1950, *Foreign Relations of the United States*, Vol III, 1950.

48. Meeting of US Ambassadors in Rome, 22-4 March 1950, *Foreign Relations of the United States*, Vol III, 1950, p.812.

49. Memorandum by the Minister of Defence, 1 July 1950, PRO [CE 3452/2141/181].

50. Mallet to Gainer, 30 October 1950, PRO [WF 1023/36].

51. *Ibid.*

52. 'France', *cit.*

53. Annex 1 to Minutes of a Meeting held in the Prime Minister's Room, 11 May 1950, PRO [CAB 130/60].

54. Memorandum by Kirkpatrick, 11 May 1950, PRO [CE 2330/2141/181]; Harvey to Bevin, 1 March 1951, PRO [CE(W) 1543/49].

55. Mallet to Bevin, 5 September 1950, PRO [C 5712/20/18].

56. Record of a meeting at No 1 Carlton Gardens, 10 May 1950, PRO [ZP 2/149].

57. 'Meeting of US Ambassadors at Rome', *cit.*

58. 'Proposed Four-Power Meeting', *cit.*

59. *Ibid.*

60. The Ambassador in the United Kingdom to the Secretary of State, 6 June 1950, *Foreign Relations of the United States*, Vol III, 1950, p.722.

61. The United States Delegation at the Tripartite', *cit.*

62. Secretary of State to acting Secretary of State, *cit.*

63. Meeting of US Ambassadors, *cit.*

64. Memorandum by the Secretary of State for Foreign Affairs, 6 October 1950, PRO [CAB 129/42].

65. The Prime Minister's visit to Washington, 4 December 1950, PRO [COM 50/17].

66. 'Atlantic Council', September 1950.

67. Franks to Morrison, 23 July 1951, PRO [ZP 18/17].

6 With but not Of: Britain and the Schuman Negotiations, 1950-2

We left the narrative in chapter 2 with the decision of the Labour Cabinet on 1 June 1950 not to take part in the negotiations that would lead to the creation of the European Coal and Steel Authority. However, it is the theme of this and the next chapter that this was by no means seen as a parting of the ways. Over the subsequent two and a half years, both the Labour Government and the Conservative Administration that would replace it in October 1951, worked to become a substantial influence in relation to the Europe of the Six, albeit from what they considered to be the vantage point of not being a formal member of the new Community.

Churchill would call this a policy of being 'with but not of Europe'. The conclusions of the last four chapters would seem to underpin the rationality of such a middle course. Direct membership seemed to be precluded by the constitutional features of a Community that immediately conceded the principle of supranationality and ultimately committed its membership to full political integration. Such a level of commitment to West Europe was also considered incompatible with a diplomacy of manoeuvre in which Britain would maximize its influence in reduced circumstances by holding itself out as the trusted interlocutor of the three circles of the free world, a role that clearly could not be maintained if the UK was perceived as owing its prior loyalty to any one circle.

On the other hand, the three circles doctrine made it equally important to British Governments that they should avoid any outcome that would leave them with insufficient influence in West Europe. Over a longer period, there was also a danger that the new coal and steel authority could become the basis of a formidable new competitive entity in the international political economy; and that it would thus challenge many of Britain's own markets, unless, that is, UK producers were adequately placed to participate in some of the benefits of the new collective entity, even without the UK itself being a member.

1.   Avoiding 'the utmost political odium': why the British Government
        did not oppose the Schuman Plan outright

While examining how British Governments attempted a complicated diplomacy of
becoming an influential non-participant, we need continuously to ask why they did
not adopt an alternative course of opposing the new Community outright or, more
subtly, giving it verbal support while seeking all the time to convert it into
something quite different and more acceptable to Britain. Faced with the cross
pressures delineated in the last paragraph, it might seem surprising that they did
not work harder for a European entity more to their own liking: a Community of
which they could become a full member, providing a more secure basis for their
instincts to influence processes from within.

If they had the motive for such a stance, British Governments arguably also had
the means. British reservations about the Schuman Plan were shared by many
across the Six who were strategically placed in official decision-making processes,
coalition and party politics or amongst directly affected economic interests. Indeed,
the new Community only struggled into existence after a difficult and protracted
negotiation and in a form which was substantially different to that originally
anticipated. The responsibilities expected of Britain in relation to West European
security under the new Atlantic Alliance might also have been used as a source of
leverage: as a means of insisting that the economic and political organization of
West Europe should be more in keeping with the UK's interests if it was to commit
itself to the degree expected to the collective defence of the continent.

Indeed, Britain's exclusion was in a sense everyone's problem, raising as it did
a dilemma that was to recur throughout the subsequent history of European
unification. On the one hand, there would seem to be little justification in allowing
the reluctant to veto the plans of the integrators, particularly, if this leads to the
adoption by default of what is, in fact, only a minority view of how Europe should
be structured; or, if it leads to a logical tangle in which supporters of state
sovereignty seek to impose restrictions on how other states seek to use their
sovereignty. On the other hand, integration takes place in a shared space of
economic and security interdependencies that extends well beyond those states who
feel able to subscribe to a particular model or initiative and there are limits to
which some inner group can pursue European integration to the exclusion of
outsiders: the effects of their actions do not stop at their boundaries, they may find
themselves having to co-operate with outsiders in other spheres and international
organizations, the gap between themselves and the outsiders may widen instead of
converge and, finally, the cumulative cost of exclusion may eventually compel the

outsiders to make an application for membership not because they have in some way been converted to the goals of the club but because continued exclusion is seen to involve unacceptable costs.

The possibility of outright opposition was, indeed, considered from time to time within the British Government. In July 1950, the Foreign Office asked,

> Is the Government prepared to allow West Europe full rein to organize itself on federal lines without the participation of the United Kingdom, leaving the United Kingdom to associate itself with whatever bodies or organizations emerge from this process, or are the risks of such a hands off policy so great that it is necessary to intervene to arrest this process?[1]

In the same month, Plowden suggested that Britain should either 'put a block on the Schuman Plan and other negotiations or participate in them'.[2]

It was acknowledged that as a champion of the sovereignty of states, Britain could scarcely object to the decision of others to use - and even relinquish - their sovereignty as they saw fit: 'it would be a heavy political responsibility for the United Kingdom to prevent closer forms of association which were generally desired by other Western European countries, simply on the ground that we ourselves could not participate in them'.[3] Makins would later add, 'our attachment to the intergovernmental system should be not be allowed to stand in the way of the free development of some other system acceptable to West European countries'.[4]

However, the main reason why a supranational six was not opposed outright was that many saw this as in Britain's own interest, so long as it happened without the UK itself. This was essentially for reasons discussed in chapter 5: the stabilization of West European politics through Franco-German reconciliation was considered to be a condition precedent of the construction of NATO and thus of the successful containment of Communism. The Ministry of Defence felt that 'any failure to give effect to the Schuman proposals would amount to a setback in the cold war'.[5] The Foreign Office agreed that a collapse of what could be the last chance to 'reconcile German revival with French security..would increase those feelings of inferiority and isolation which make the French so hard to deal with', while the West Germans would be 'bound to feel grave doubts about the sincerity of the west in professing to want them reinstated as equals..this might have grave consequences as they become more independent of the occupying powers and have to make their choice between eastern and western orientation'.[6]

A perception that the success of the Schuman Plan could be vital to the political coalition that the UK was attempting to put together in NATO was picked up in the observation that 'if we are going to allow ourselves to appear to be the deliberate enemy of the closer union of continental countries, we shall find ourselves knocking down with one hand the European structure which we are trying to set up with the other (Bullen and Pelly, pp.292-3n). Indeed, the Permanent Under Secretary's Committee concluded that a united Europe could add to the deterrent value of the NATO: in place of a diffuse and fractious set of West European states, the Soviet Union would be made 'to pause' by being confronted with the 'combination of a united Europe, the United States and the British Commonwealth.[7]

By mid June, the Foreign Office had developed the interesting position that West Europe could have stumbled by accident into the best possible outcome: a Europe limited to the Six would give France and Germany the supranational institutions necessary to their reconciliation and the UK would be able to escape participation in a pre-federal political system it could not accept.[8] British membership, by contrast, might only have impeded a desirable process. The German section of the Foreign Office thus advised that a supranational authority may serve to 'cement Franco-German relations more firmly than any authority with weaker powers which we could join'.[9] Makins commented that it 'might well be that the advantages of anchoring Germany to the West via the Schuman Plan may outweigh any risks there may be for us in what is mainly a Franco-German arrangement'; and, in another note, he remarked that there could be more logic in Monnet's supposed efforts to exclude Britain than Massigli's tireless campaign to change the Plan to suit the UK, 'I am not sure that the French Government are not right in thinking that the real importance of the Schuman Plan is in the field of Franco-German relations and, consequently, that the French Embassy are not wrong in thinking that the most vital thing about the Schuman Plan is to get us in' (Bullen and Pelly, 1986, p.224n).

However, the most important constraint was that, as seen in chapter 4, outright opposition to the Schuman Plan would have put impossible strain on UK/US relations, as the US Administration was only inclined to accept Britain's abstention from European integration on condition that it was supportive from the outside; and, on the assumption that the disadvantages of a smaller European Community would be balanced by the advantages of more integrated, supranational institutions. As Makins admitted, 'We did not think we should intervene to prevent progress towards a West European Federal system...we should incur the utmost political odium were we to do so'.[10]

There were some jitters at Britain's exclusion from the talks, but on the whole outright opposition to the formation of a European Community without the UK seemed unnecessary as well as undesirable. The dominant assumption was that UK interests would be well protected *whatever* the Six decided between themselves. Broadly speaking, it was assumed in summer 1950 that there were, as follows, four possible outcomes to the negotiations and the British Government could afford to be indifferent between them:[11]

1. The talks would succeed but on a very different basis to that on which they had started, in which case the UK might be able to join after all. This could happen if the Six realized the limitations of the supranational principle and the problems of operationalizing it into an agreement acceptable both to states and vested economic interests.

2. The talks would fail and Britain would be called upon to make proposals to save the initiative. In case of such an eventuality, the Attlee government even started on a detailed British draft for a European Coal and Steel Community. Such tenuous support as the supranational scheme enjoyed might not survive the two-stage obstacle course presented by the need to negotiate a detailed Treaty and then secure its ratification by each of the parliaments of the Six.

3. The talks would proceed smoothly and a supranational structure would emerge which the UK could live with for reasons discussed above. But the absence of political and economic self-sufficiency of the Six would be understood by all and the need for an association agreement with the UK would be anticipated in each clause of any Treaty that was negotiated. The talks would thus proceed in full but informal consultation with the British government.

4. In constructing a supranational system, the Six might prefer to sort things out on their own, but even this would do nothing to lessen their interest in a meaningful association with the UK, which would constitute the first business of any new European Coal and Steel Authority.

The belief that underlay each of these four assumptions was, of course, that the UK would remain a dominant factor in shaping West European institutions, even as a non-participant. This could take the form of continued British leadership of a European Community from the outside, but it could equally work through the purported need of the Six to adjust of their own volition to UK interests and the rules of other international organizations. As the working party on the Schuman Plan was to put it at the very end of 1951, 'even as non-members our bargaining power and goodwill would be considerable. If GATT could be made to function more effectively, some of the advantages of membership could come to us without being a member'.[12] One view expressed on the Permanent Under-Secretary's Committee was that the Six would not be able to 'put their federal ideas into practice without at least the blessing and probably the active participation of the UK.[13] By choosing the coal and steel industries as the starting point for their integration, the Six had, apparently, made things easier for the British government by selecting two sectors in which the UK seemingly had an evident and effortless preponderance. Bevin thus told Massigli of his full confidence that Britain would be able to negotiate its own preferred solution of 'two systems to operate and if possible be complementary', even if it placed itself at the comparative disadvantage of only beginning to talk after the Six had agreed everything between themselves: 'when they had agreed, we as a country with a great steel and coal industry would meet the new European organization, whether this took the form of a supranational or governmental authority'.[14]

2.   Lying doggo

From June 1950 to March 1951, government policy was that the UK could best secure any of the four outcomes that it considered acceptable by doing and saying nothing. Makins called this 'lying doggo'.[15] Those who believed that a supranational authority without Britain could contribute something useful to the new West European architecture felt it better that opinion amongst the Six should begin to adapt to the probability that British participation would be limited to an association agreement. Likewise, lying doggo appealed to ministers and officials who felt that the supranational experiment would ultimately fail, requiring Britain to put Humpty-Dumpty together again with 'more practical' proposals for a European coal and steel authority. However, Britain could only re-enter the process of European integration reinforced in its leadership role by a clear demonstration of the impracticality of any alternative to the intergovernmentalism after supranational possibilities had been fully exhausted. It was also necessary that blame for any failure should be unambiguously attributable to the inherent shortcomings of the Schuman approach and that no alibi should be available in the form of British meddling. Thus Harvey wrote:

> it may prove that after the present line of advance has been thoroughly explored (and it is perhaps better than it should be explored by those who already accept its principles), the difficulties may prove too great for final acceptance to be achieved..The opportunity would then present itself for His Majesty's Government again to enter the scene with their own version of the plan, in which they themselves would be willing to take part.[16]

By contrast, the main danger to the British position seemingly lay in responding too soon while Schuman had momentarily caught the imagination of the world with a supranational scheme that would only be revealed as impractical with time: It was simply no use coming out in public with an immediate British counter-proposal, as

Schuman felt that he had the 'public opinion of the world behind him' and would prevail both inside the French Government and world counsels, if a public show of strength were forced at this moment.[17]

Bevin also felt that the British and French governments were playing for very high stakes in relation to the Schuman Plan, that only one could emerge as the winner from the episode and that timing would be of the essence in determining who that would be. On the one hand, he inclined to a black and white view of the non-combinability of supranational and intergovernmental structures. On the other, he felt that things had been so mishandled since 9 May 1950 that the Schuman proposals had, regrettably, pitched the two countries into a conflict to maintain the reputation of their foreign policies. By seeming to 'push the British around', Schuman had focused the eyes of the world on a trial of diplomatic strength between the two countries and assured that any flicker of British interest could be interpreted as a capitulation. He had also prevented consideration of a coal and steel community on its merits, decoupled from the more general and conflictual issue of where Britain and France stood in the hierarchy of Western powers. Bevin thus warned of 'allowing ourselves to be classified by the French as a Luxembourg'.[18] Even Harvey accepted that Britain and France were, to a degree, engaged in 'rivalry for leadership of Europe' (Bullen and Pelly, 1986, p.175n). The lesson which Bevin drew was that the British government should, at all costs, avoid anything that could be taken as even tacit acceptance of supranationalism and that it should maintain this stance until the original scheme collapsed into its intergovernmental opposite, or the French were prepared to 'remove the impossible conditions for our participation'.[19] Well after 1 June 1950, Bevin continued to reiterate the position that 'on no account must H.M. Government come into an arrangement providing for an Authority independent of Governments'.[20]

Bevin was thus determined that Britain should have nothing to do with the Schuman talks until the original demands that it should accept the supranational model had been fully and publicly recanted. In taking this position, Bevin was confident that he had Schuman's measure: 'The Secretary of State has frequently had occasion to follow Monsieur Schuman's methods in negotiation. His tendency is to start strong and to come down later to get agreement'.[21] Schuman and Monnet were, in Bevin's view, 'gambling' (Bullen and Pelly, 1986, p.156n) by attempting to bluff Britain into accepting the supranational principle, knowing full well that they by no means had a solid basis of support for this amongst the rest of the Six or in French domestic politics. Younger thought that Schuman was hoping to 'rush the Germans over a number of fences'.[22] Reports received by the Foreign Office also suggested that the Dutch remained 'very much concerned about the French ideas for a supranational authority', while the Belgians 'did not regard themselves as in any way committed by the signature of the communiqué'.[23] At base, Bevin believed that the French state was in a parlous condition,[24] and that as long as the UK played matters long and cool the internal contradictions of a supranational scheme would become apparent. The attempt by France to wrest foreign policy leadership from the UK would be revealed as a try-on and the natural order of things whereby French policy had to be propped up by the UK would soon erase all traces of Schuman's preposterous attempt to 'dictate to us'.

However, lying doggo may not have been the sign of strength that it was taken to be. It was never entirely clear that the UK really could afford to remain indifferent between all possible agreements that the Six might make between themselves. Indeed, this conflicted with many other opinions that were expressed from within the British government, such as a Foreign Office view on 16 June 1950 that 'it is in our interest to see that the Schuman Plan is set up along practical lines not liable to prejudice unduly the interests of non-participant countries'.[25] The Permanent Under Secretary's Committee likewise concluded that federal Europe 'might take several forms, none of which would accord with British interests'.[26] On 14 July 1950, the Permanent Secretary to the Treasury brought together a remarkable cross-section of Britain's top mandarinate. Concern was expressed at the way in which the Schuman Plan had provoked a proliferation of other schemes for the economic organization of West Europe: the Stikker, Pella and Petsche Plans. Some felt that unless the UK took the initiative with counter-proposals of its own, it would, 'be dragged along by the others' and then frozen out of its leadership of the OEEC, which was the focus for its bridging role between West Europe and the US in economic matters.[27]

Indeed, the decision to lie doggo may, first, have said more about the constraints on the British Government's position after June 1950 than its ability to steer outcomes and sustain its claims to leadership of West Europe from outside the Schuman talks. It may, second, have been a miscalculation that led to the neglect of such diplomatic options as remained to the UK. And it may, third, have been the product of indecision. Faced with some very difficult choices, both domestic and diplomatic, the Foreign Office preferred to do nothing and rationalized this as a cunning strategy. The next section will examine the first and second of these weaknesses by looking in detail at the failure of the UK Government to publish any counter-proposals to Schuman. The section after that will relate all three weaknesses to repeated failures by the Foreign Office to clarify what would be entailed in an association with the Schuman Plan, even though pursuit of such a status had been government policy ever since 1 June 1950.

3.   A time for British counter-proposals: June-July 1950?

It was not until April 1951 that the Six finally agreed a treaty for the new Coal and Steel Community. A further eleven months would then be needed for the parliaments of the Six to complete ratification of the Treaty. It is difficult to read the extensive collection of official papers that cover Britain's dealings with the nascent ECSC without a perception that it was hemmed in by a mixture of it own concern to avoid anything that could be taken as even tacit acceptance of supranationalism and a suspicion of others that it was out to wreck the new Community. Although they would receive many invitations to get more involved in the politics of operationalizing the Schuman Plan, British governments would repeatedly hold off through an almost obsessive fear that the slightest slip on their part would be met with accusations of sabotage. It was for this reason that British counter-proposals to the Schuman Plan were drawn up in utmost secrecy and, in the event, never even tabled. Thus Bevin confessed:

> we were sure that if..we started putting in any new plan, we
> should create the suspicion that we were only doing it to try to upset the
> work that they had already done. We were not going to put ourselves in
> that position. They could go on with the absolute assurance that we would
> not interfere with their discussions.[28]

On another occasion, he suggested that if 'our proposals did not go as far as people hoped', Britain's hard-won abstention from supranational Europe might not survive 'another round of attacks in the Council of Europe and in America'. The UK would soon find itself 'in a position like the Dutch are in', sliding towards membership of institutions they did not want for fear of external disapproval.[29] Bevin likewise ruled out discussions with other non-participants, such as the Scandinavians, in case the 'French and other delegations' claimed that the British had 'intrigued to sabotage the Schuman proposals'.[30] The Cabinet in a rare admission that Britain's influence as a non-participant might not after all be the same as it would have been as an active negotiator, warned 'there would be some disposition to blame the UK for the breakdown if it had put forward alternative proposals from outside the conference'.[31]

There were, however, those who felt that Bevin and the Foreign Office were wrong, that opportunities for convergence between Britain and the Six would not disappear until the end of July 1950, and that these were only neglected through an overly fastidious attachment to the policy of non-involvement. According to this view, the state of French domestic politics and overtures from the Six themselves suggested that British counter-proposals would have been well received. Many felt that Bevin underestimated the degree to which the rest of the French Government was already on the verge of rebellion against Schuman and Monnet. On his return from convalescence, Cripps called on his counterpart in Paris, Michel Petsche. He was surprised to find the French Minister for Finance 'open his heart on the Schuman Plan'. Cripps was left with the impression that Petsche, the Minister for

Justice, René Mayer, and the Head of the Government, Georges Bidault, would form a powerful triumvirate opposed to 'placing French industry under a supranational authority' and excluding Britain from any plan for coal and steel. They had not been consulted about the Schuman Plan and would provide strong support from within the French Cabinet for steering the whole initiative in a different direction to that originally intended. As Harvey pointed out, the Cripps-Petsche meeting suggested that Britain's position had support from right across the governing coalition in France. Bidault represented the alternative tendency to Schuman's within the Christian Democrats; Petsche and Mayer the Radicals; and the Socialists were known to favour British participation on the grounds that this would provide further reassurance against German domination, while bringing in a Labour Government that would prevent a coal and steel authority being run as a cartel that would favour big business.[32]

The fall on 24 June 1950 of the French Government that had proposed the Schuman Plan - and a subsequent three week crisis in forming a new Administration - was seen by some as offering a fresh start in Anglo-French relations. Harvey reported from Paris that even the old cabinet had been 'stampeded' into accepting the Schuman Plan and that it was 'far from certain' that it 'really regarded itself as committed to the details of the Plan'.. any new Cabinet would not necessarily support 'Monnet's proposals in all their purity'.[33] According to Clappier, even Schuman was separable from Monnet with the former only interested in supranational institutions so long as no-one could show him a safer route to Franco-German reconciliation (Duchêne, 1994, p.205). The French Ambassador himself urged the British Government to seize the initiative and fill the policy vacuum in Paris by coming forward with its own detailed alternative to the Schuman Plan. Thus he told Younger, 'One of the first questions which a new President would ask would be: what were the British views? That would be the moment at which people in Paris would be most open to influence from Britain'.[34] Massigli went on to argue that this was precisely the moment at which Monnet and his circle were at their most vulnerable: they had hijacked French foreign policy and developed an initiative towards which the French 'Foreign Ministry were thoroughly hostile'.[35] Now they suddenly found themselves over-extended, given the likelihood that any new government would want to reappraise policy. Bevin's answer to all of this was that those who saw an opportunity in the change of government in France to press a British alternative to the Schuman Plan misunderstood the nature of French coalition politics: the new government would be 'much the same as before'.

Also in June 1950, the British Government was offered a far more intimate relationship with the Schuman talks than any that eventually developed or any that suited its own view of its role as hors du combat. At one stage, the Dutch hinted that they might be prepared to act as advocate within the negotiations for any

British position, if 'given advance information' of what the UK wanted. At another, the Dutch signalled that 'if there is the slightest chance of so conducting the negotiations that the UK can be brought in to the plan they would very much press for this'.[36] However, of far greater significance was that Schuman himself repeatedly implored the British to abandon the policy of silence and to present both reactions and counter-proposals to the detailed discussions that were being held between the Six. He told Younger that he was 'most anxious to see Britain taking part in the Schuman Plan..that he hoped the liaison arrangements for keeping us informed would work efficiently, and that he was particularly anxious that the information.should not merely be allowed to become dead when we had got it..he would welcome our comments at any stage'.[37]

There was, indeed, much concern that the British Government could not solve the dilemmas of its European diplomacy through silence; that this would be interpreted as hostility or indifference, not as self-restraint; and that the UK risked losing the confidence of the Benelux and Scandinavian countries, which had previously been most receptive to the notion of a British leadership role. Thus Cripps wrote to Bevin, 'I don't see how it is possible for us to refuse to give our friends some indication of the sort of authority we envisage as being acceptable to us.[38] In early July, Harvey cautioned that the French Government would be legitimately aggrieved if Britain did not act soon to clarify its position on the Schuman proposals. If the UK had an alternative, it should be stated; if, as seemed to be the case from Cabinet discussions, the UK position was that it would be prepared to 'pool their coal and steel industries into a combined authority, but on condition that there should be no supranational authority and no federal principle involved' then this should be made public. It was by no means obvious to continental opinion. Schuman and his colleagues in the French cabinet had the right to be appraised of the British position, so that they could make up their own minds as to whether they really favoured the original Monnet scheme over a wider but looser authority.[39] Indeed, full and frank disclosure of information and intentions between governments represented precisely the approach to European co-operation that the British were eager to champion, as an alternative to the creation of new non-state organizations.

According to the view that opportunities for convergence were lost, the greatest tragedy was that the unpublished counter-proposals of the British Government showed some flexibility and imagination, just when the Six in their own talks agreed that the Coal and Steel Community should have some intergovernmental dimension that was lacking in Monnet's original conception. A Committee of Ministers, set up under Cripps, to work out the detail of a British counter-position, recommended on 1 July 1950 that so long as 'there is a suitable chain of responsibility to Ministers, it would in our view be *acceptable to delegate a considerable amount of control*' (to the High Authority). This can be seen as an attempt to make what was a substantively similar set of arrangements to those being discussed by the Six acceptable to British opinion by shifting the focus away from the rhetoric of supranationalism to a practice more familiar to British politics, the delegation of technical functions to an official body. It was thus a continuation of Cripps' own thinking in cabinet discussions the month before. It is instructive to look at the considerable scope that the ministers were prepared to allow to the High Authority, albeit with the ultimate sanction of a Council of Ministers and accountability to such a body. Five points emerge from the draft British position: the High Authority i) would be independent and thus supranational as proposed by Schuman[40] ii) it would have 'wide powers of initiative and recommendation'; iii) it would be 'responsible for all ordinary matters of operation and execution'; iv) it would be made up of 'industrial statesmen' and not 'mere technicians'. In other words, these would be individuals with substantial status in their own right; v) it would be accompanied by an Advisory Council of workers and employers[41].

In comparison with British positions in relation to constitutional proposals for the OEEC and Council of Europe over the previous two years, this all represented a substantial shift towards supranationalism. Quite apart from conceding any role at all to an independent authority, points i) and ii) were not far distant from the compromise between supranationalism and intergovernmentalism that would eventually lie at the heart of the Treaty of Rome: a compromise whereby a supranational authority would initiate and recommend, whilst governments represented on a Council of Ministers would decide. Points iv) and v) neatly reversed previous British objections to 'supermen' independent of governments, or to representative bodies that could ally with supranational actors against governments.

At the time of the Cripps proposals it was, meanwhile, known in Whitehall that the Six had added a Council of Ministers to their own plans on the grounds that it would otherwise be impossible to co-ordinate policy between the national and European levels. Both sides had moved closer to the other and, on 5 July 1950, Schuman signalled once again that none of the Six, not even his own Government, were committed as yet to the work of their own negotiators.[42] Another option for convergence came from the Cabinet Office, which suggested that it might be possible to have a 'loose' coal and steel authority for the whole of West Europe without 'crabbing the French desire for a close association for particular countries'.[43] The Six would join the wider authority as a collective entity, while others would join as individual states. This possibility was not pursued by the UK in 1950, but it would become important in 1951-2, when its problems also became more apparent.

On the other hand, the Cripps paper also showed the limits of convergence. Whilst it envisaged that a supranational body might have a veto over new investment, the full Cabinet preferred that this should be left to the Council of

Ministers.[44] Opposition to a compromise with Schuman's schema would seem to have hardened as drafts were passed up the hierarchy of decision-making, officials and specialist groups of ministers being prepared to consider supranationalism where it might be of advantage to the UK, whilst the Cabinet was more concerned to oppose it in principle. Thus, in suggesting that the High Authority might be allowed to veto investment plans, the Committee of Ministers argued that 'in practice this should tend to work to the advantage of the United Kingdom, whose development plans for coal and steel have, in many cases, been completed, and are in many cases more realistic than those of other potential members'.[45] The Foreign Office would later hint at a certain difficulty in getting ministers to consider gradations of supranationalism or sophisticated ways in which this might be traded off against an intergovernmental approach; anything that contained an element of the former risked peremptory dismissal 'however careful Ministers might have been on past occasions to keep the door open'.[46]

Such possibilities there were for convergence also had to contend with forces making for further divergence after 1 June 1950. Traces of what foreign policy analysts have called 'cognitive mirroring' could already be discerned in British and French diplomacy. This is a syndrome in which two parties form stereotypes about one another that are self-confirming both in the sense that all new moves are interpreted through fixed preconceptions and to the degree that each party adopts an attitude towards the other likely to provoke the very behaviour of which they complain (Jervis, 1976). In addition, both sides now had to provide public justifications for the positions they had taken in the lead up to the Anglo/French split and, in their efforts to do so, they inevitably articulated their differences more clearly and sharply than before, cutting off lines of retreat and embedding rationales for a small Europe without Britain in the standard operating assumptions, and inherited folklore, of bureaucracies and political parties. These problems can be illustrated through two happenings in June 1950. First, in spite of an agreement to co-ordinate communiqués in order to minimize public unease at their failure to reach agreement, the Foreign Office went public with the fact that the Quai had offered a ministerial conference to discuss UK participation only to withdraw the suggestion. Indeed, it now adopted the idea as its own. This was clearly done to minimize criticism in the House of Commons. However, to outsiders it looked like an attempt to 'wean the other continental powers away from the French proposal..a challenge to the renaissance of French leadership on the continent'.[47] Second, the publication of *European Unity*, hastily adapted to relate the Cabinet's decision to stay out of the Schuman talks to basic tenets of Labour party faith, accelerated a transition for some on the continent from an old belief that Europe could not function without Britain to a new belief that it could not be constructed with the UK.[48] Most significantly of all, it split what might otherwise have been the strongest constituency for British inclusion - the French Socialist party - into groups for and against UK participation.

4.   Association: an elusive status?

By the end of July 1950, the Foreign Office was receiving advice from the Paris embassy that the 'time for putting forward an international authority on the lines hitherto considered by London is past'.[49] Over the next months, the Six would disagree on many things, and many of the ECSC's successes would ironically derive from Monnet's failure always to get what he wanted (Gillingham 1991). But the supranational framework would not on the whole be a bone of contention. Indeed, it grew in importance as the glue that held the Schuman process together, for the Korean war lessened the industrial incentives for German participation, leaving acknowledgement of political equality in a supranational framework as the main pay-off that Bonn could obtain by persisting with the ECSC. In August, the Paris Embassy reported: 'we understand that in this insistence on the federal character of the scheme the German delegation have gone even further than the French'.[50]

In keeping with the decision of the British cabinet on 1 June 1950 to join a coal and steel authority if it was to be intergovernmental and to associate if it was to be supranational, the Paris embassy drew the obvious conclusion that the time had come for London to consider the forms that association might take. There was, it was claimed, an urgent need 'to be ready at very short notice with our views so that we can put them forward at the time most convenient to us'.[51] Yet remarkably little progress would be made towards defining and agreeing a policy of association between July 1950 and the fall of the Labour Government on 26 October 1951, leaving it as a paradox of that Administration that it should have given more thought in one month to unpublished terms on which it might have sought full membership than it ever gave over the next fifteen months to what was considered the more likely outcome of association.

The main reason why the British Government found it so hard to agree firm plans for association was that back in June 1950 it had been too glibly invoked as a cure-all, as a solution that mysteriously and miraculously split the difference between membership and exclusion in the spirit of 'with but not of'. In reality, association was incapable of doing none of these things, for it merely replicated many of the dilemmas that were entailed in the original choice between joining and not joining. These dilemmas were of four kinds.

Choices of institutional structure. Some attempts were made to define precisely what the UK might want from any association. The Permanent Under Secretary's Committee suggested that Britain should seek 'an influence for moderation in

Europe...while also keeping... wide freedom of action outside Europe...and selecting points of association most advantageous to ourselves economically'.[52] The Cabinet Office and Treasury wanted an association that would guarantee a great deal of influence over any further development of the Community beyond coal and steel: 'In the narrow sense of making bargains on coal and steel matters, we could probably get on well enough outside. But if we wish the Community to develop on the right lines..we need to establish *as close relationships as possible*'.[53] In a suggestion that implied some entanglement of the UK with the ECSC might even contribute to Commonwealth cohesion, the New Zealand Government asked that 'the special form of association would put the UK in a position to moderate economic policies evolved by the authority which would be to the disadvantage of the UK or other members of the Commonwealth' (Bullen and Pelly, p.700n).

On occasions, the Foreign Office conceded that the association mechanism would have to be fairly substantial if the Six were to be persuaded to 'limit their own plans' to take 'the views of His Majesty's Government into account'.[54] But it was thought that even if the Six took their own decisions in a supranational framework they could deal with the UK on a classic intergovernmental model of voluntary co-operation between two veto holding parties; and that, regardless of any problems with this institutional mix, common incentives to collaborate and the importance of the UK would ease the mutual adjustment of British and ECSC positions. It was thus suggested that there might be '*consultation* and *co-operation* in research; *interchange* of information about investment programmes; *consultation* about steps to deal with conditions of shortage or surplus; general co-operation in pricing policy and avoidance of dumping; and *consultation* on commercial policy'.[55] In short, dialogue without institutional commitment would be enough.

Others were less confident. Makins asked, 'do we really know what we mean by a close but non-committal association or by the procedure for putting forward our own views within the councils of the Schuman Authority?' (Bullen and Pelly, pp. 518-9n). The Foreign Office wondered whether it really was possible to 'contemplate association for certain economic purposes without becoming involved in the political machinery?' (Bullen and Pelly, p.519n); and went on to ask what would happen if specific acts of 'functional co-operation' proliferated as anticipated, only to be tidied up and formalized at some point under a single political authority with unified democratic control. There was a risk that the 'UK position could then become embarrassing. Continued association would be harmful, but withdrawal would be difficult'.[56]

In other words, association might either be meaningless, or sweep Britain back on to the shoals of supranationalism that it had sought to avoid in the first place. There was, first, a problem of reciprocity. Some in Whitehall admitted that the Six would not always allow the UK the advantages of membership without the disadvantages, the rights without the obligations. Given that the UK and West

Germany were the two industrial cores of West Europe, the inter-departmental working party on the Schuman Plan suggested that it would be worth seeking an association agreement that would 'retain some influence and control over German industry', but it went on to warn that the UK would have to concede 'loss of freedom in relation to our own industries' if it was to have a say in continental industrial policy (Bullen and Pelly, p.482n). In like vein, the Cabinet Office complained about the naive view of the Ministry of Supply that the UK could 'admit up to half a million tons of European steel but thereafter shut it out with a hefty tariff'[57] and the Foreign Office argued that the Six would hardly allow the UK priority access to their coal and steel in times of shortage, unless a like obligation was to bind the UK, overriding its preference for supplying these commodities to the Commonwealth.[58]

Having spun a delicate web of obligations between themselves, in which confidence in supranationalism was central if others were to consent to the revival of West Germany, the Six were unlikely to encourage any of their number to believe that they could take an à la carte view of their commitments, opting in and out of the Treaties, or attempting to defect in times of economic or political difficulty to some easy option of association, established to accommodate the UK. If anything, they wanted to move in the opposite direction of tightening the obligatory force of the new institutions so that further acts of collaboration, which had previously seemed unprofitable in the absence of safeguards against cheating, could be safely nested in the new supranational context.

A second reason why an association had the potential to bring the UK under the shadow of a supranational process of which it was not even a member concerned the likely bargaining relationship between the ECSC and the UK. The Foreign Office conceded that the Six would not want Britain 'so far in' that it would be in any position to 'drag its feet';[59] nor would they want the UK to be able to play divide and rule games. They would, therefore, insist that associates deal only with the High Authority and only discuss matters already agreed in ECSC processes. From such a position, UK Governments could find themselves concluding worse deals than if they were full members; first, because the High Authority would have no mandate to consider the UK in its agenda-setting roles which would critically shape the first round of bargaining before the Six moved on to talk with Britain; second, because the Six would in the proposed bargaining format constitute a ready-made alternative coalition, primed to go ahead on their own, even if the UK was not prepared to co-operate; third because the UK would have inferior information as to the real preferences and likely alliances of other players and it would, therefore, be more vulnerable to 'strategic misrepresentation' in bargaining; and, fourth, because the Six would be unwilling to renegotiate terms concluded between themselves, as this would involve costs of 'recontracting', diminished confidence in bloc solidarity and reduced credibility of group agreements.

2. Choices of market relationships. If the UK was to associate by moving towards freer trade with the Six in coal and steel, the 'sluice gates' between the British and West European economies would be lowered in relation to these key industries. If UK Governments really were going to practise Keynesianism through subsidy of these commodities and variation in investment programmes for coal and steel, a greater proportion of demand injections would leak abroad, even assuming that such measures would be allowable under the terms of the association agreement. If the autonomous operation of markets produced input-output interdependencies with European coal and steel, industries vital to the UK's defence capacity could be meshed beyond a point of easy return, no less than if they had been subject to directions from a supranational authority. On the other hand, if association did not include some market integration, British coal and steel would not be a part of the improved international division of Labour, or enjoy the economies of scale, which the official working party warned could turn the Six into a formidable industrial combine and long-term competitive threat to the British economy.

3. Choices of timing. Was association to be a temporary or permanent arrangement? Monnet's dictum on this question has become notorious: 'there is one thing you British do not understand, an idea. There is one thing you do understand, a fact. We will form the Community without you and then when we have shown you that it can work, you will join us'. What is less well known is that, at times, he even seemed to suggest that British membership could follow straight on from the formation of the ECSC and that association could, therefore, be but the briefest of interludes, possibly even emulating in its detail some of the transitional arrangements that the Six would allow themselves before the Treaty operated in full, and thus minimizing any 'catching-up' that the UK would have to do on full accession. For example, Monnet told the Six-power meeting on 21 June 1950 of his hopes that the British Government would be able to participate as soon as it had seen the 'project and especially the plans for democratic control'.[60] By contrast, the dominant view in London was that the UK would not progress beyond association. It could even regress, if association also proved entangling. It was certainly to be a vehicle for continued British influence over European integration, possibly an option to exit altogether from that process, and definitely not a way station to full membership.

4. Choices of negotiating strategy. Were membership and association talks to be sequential or parallel? Here the dividing line between the UK and the Six was to be somewhat surprising with the British Government repeatedly rejecting invitations to begin discussing the nature of an association at the same time as the Six negotiated and ratified the main ECSC Treaty between themselves. In September 1950, Schuman suggested that the optimal moment to discuss Britain's association would be after the Six had finished their own deliberations but before they had cast them in stone by drafting the text of a Treaty.[61] After April 1951, the French, German and American Governments all called on the UK to make an opening bid for association before the Treaty itself went before the parliaments of the Six. Monnet suggested that some announcement be made on the 'creation of a standing joint council between Britain and the High Authority, even before the Treaty comes into effect'.[62]

The Foreign Office resisted each of these invitations and stuck throughout to the position that it would not discuss association until all the parliaments of the Six had ratified the ECSC Treaty. Various reasons were given for this: a wish to avoid 'the laborious and perhaps fruitless task of negotiating and confronting some of the awkward choices delineated above, only to find that the Plan was not going to proceed after all';[63] an anxiety to protect Britain's bargaining hand by avoiding any approach to the Six which would 'imply that we are more worried about being left out of the Schuman authority than we in fact are';[64] a continued fear that British involvement would be mistaken for an attempt to sabotage the plan; and a concern that the UK might lose control of the terms on which it would associate, if one of the governments or parliaments of the Six threatened only to ratify once satisfied with the agreement between Britain and the Six, as well as that between the Six themselves.[65] The blame for any failure could then be transferred to the UK, which could come under enormous pressure, from the US in particular, to accept a form of association that failed, for instance, to insulate it from all supranational modes of decision-making. Even the offer of a bilateral Anglo-French meeting after the terms of the Treaty had been successfully concluded was turned down for fear that it might encourage the French to 'over-rate the part that His Majesty's Government may play in the future'.[66]

Little of this squared well with self-confident claims to the leadership of West Europe and much of it amounted to a crippling complex of inhibitions. Indeed, it was questioned from both within and without the Foreign Office. Younger queried with Bevin whether the decision to rule out 'commitment' to association before ratification precluded all 'consideration' of the Plan.[67] The Paris embassy thought that a request for more contact would only be met with enthusiasm and that London was really being 'excessively coy' about even asking 'a few pointed questions', when there was really very little chance of the French suspecting the British of either mischief-making or insecurity in their dealings with the Six.[68] The Cabinet Office thought it was absurd that there should be no dealings with the Six until everything was 'signed, sealed and delivered'. After all, Schuman himself was anxious for British comments, the Plan was wide open to influence and the UK only risked being confronted with faits accomplis if it did not respond to invitations to state its position. It also questioned the right of the Foreign Office to decide Britain's tactics unilaterally and without convening the full inter-departmental working party that had concerned itself with the Plan.[69] In response, the Foreign Office even admitted that it had allowed itself to get into something of a tangle: 'the main difficulty.. was that our Secretary of State has at different times used rather different formulae about the timing of any talks on our association with the Schuman Plan' (Bullen and Pelly, p.307n).

The risk was that Britain's bargaining position would deteriorate, and not improve, the longer its government cultivated an air of studied aloofness. The arguments for abstention had a certain self-reinforcing logic. Although it was itself responsible for the initial decision to lie doggo even on questions of association, the Foreign Office was the first to argue that, as agreements between the Six firmed up, it would be harder to demand changes to accommodate British interests; and that the UK was even more likely than before to incur the charge of sabotage the longer it waited to press a position of its own, as the whole fragile web of understanding between the Six would become increasingly vulnerable to the uninformed and belated interventions of an outsider of Britain's stature. Indeed, the French Government conceded that Schuman's offers to show the UK draft texts might not amount to very much, as there would be only limited opportunities for changes to be made.[70] By 30 September 1950, Clappier suggested that any comments from Britain 'would not bear on the substance of the proposals but only the manner in which we would co-operate with the consortium'.[71] The Six were already moving towards a position that would become familiar in its later dealings with outsiders. As a condition for any relationship, non-members would have to accept what would one day be known as the 'acquis communautaire' - all decisions already made by the Community - in full and unamended. There seemed little alternative given the difficulty of unstitching the elaborate and interdependent bargains by which member states embedded their interests in the construction of the Community. The principle also seemed to follow from a wish not to allow informal extensions of Community membership by allowing outsiders as privileged a position within the decision-making process as that enjoyed by full members.

A further problem was that the Schuman talks represented a shared learning experience in which the UK was not participating. While the Six would progressively deepen their knowledge of the mutual adjustments they could make to their common gain, the same would not be true of dealings between Britain and the Six. With the passing of time, some figures in the British Government became progressively more insecure about their own ability to make rational, or even calculable, moves in relation to the Schuman process. By November 1950, the Foreign Office concluded:

> we are in the awkward position of having to consider a text without having taken part in any of the discussion and bargaining that led up to it. This difficulty affects not only our understanding of what the text

means, but also our estimate of the concessions and other adjustments which participating governments have made in order to arrive at agreements. We shall have to deduce for ourselves..the implied understandings with which some of the articles..are to be read.[72]

As the talks progressed, there was, indeed, a deterioration in information flows between the Six and London. At the end of September 1950, Clappier presented the British Embassy in Paris with 'two immense documents showing the present stage reached in the Schuman Plan discussions'.[73] By November, however, there were complaints that the 'French have volunteered little information on the progress of the discussions lately'.[74]

From British diplomats in Paris and Bonn, the Foreign Office, conversely, received warnings that the policy of silence was decreasing the probability that the relationship with the Schuman authority would be co-operative and increasing the danger that it would be conflictual. From Paris, Harvey wrote that even in a world of good intentions and perfect information, there were limits to 'absolute philanthropy' and a tendency for insiders to prefer their own interests and protect them at the expense of third countries. Unhappily, current British Government policy put the UK in the still worse position in which its intentions were misunderstood and its 'hostility' assumed. The result, he feared, was that the new Community might be organized in a manner that was designed to 'defend' the project against the UK, rather than maximize the possibilities for fruitful association.[75] From Bonn, Kirkpatrick wrote that Adenauer simply lacked 'sufficient knowledge of the fundamental motives underlying British policy towards European integration' and this made it hard for him to resolve two conflicting trends in Germany's own European policy: one that was anxious to leave the Community as open as possible to contact with Britain, another that saw Britain as conveniently excluded, given its status as Germany's 'principal (economic?) rival in Europe' and a preference of some for a small bloc of predominantly catholic continental states.[76]

With the publication of an agreed Treaty in summer 1951, and its likely ratification over the coming months, the Labour Cabinet, now in its last months in office, had to prepare itself for the probability that it would itself become a negotiating partner with the new Community. The draft Treaty suggested a possibility of partial membership that no one had considered before and, on closer reflection, association could mean as much as membership in all but name or as little as the accreditation of a junior and insignificant diplomat to the High Authority.

In June 1951, the official working party presented the Cabinet with the rather startling advice that it should seek partial membership at the most and a *formal* association at the least. Their reasoning - similar to arguments above - was that little had really been decided in the formal negotiations since June 1950. The Treaty was a mere framework that could develop in many conceivable directions. Britain should be involved as intimately as possible to make sure that the ECSC was complementary to the Atlantic Community and not the vehicle of a Third Force Europe. There should also be sufficient economic co-operation and exchange with the new Community for the economies of Britain and the Six to benefit from each other's development. Economic competition with the Six was not in itself to be feared - quite the opposite. It was the protectionist, predatory and capacity destroying practices that might develop between two great industrial combines, subject to different political management structures, that worried those who wanted an intimate relationship with the Six. For the Treasury, Pitblado argued 'if we wish the Community to develop on the right lines - expansive rather than restrictive, planned rather than cartelistic - we need to establish as close relationships as possible.[77] For the Cabinet Office, Hall argued that what was about to be decided in Britain's absence over the next three or four years was nothing less than 'the whole economic future of the Continent'.[78]

As discussion moved out of the Working Party into the wider process of Government, the cumulative impact of individual contributions was to whittle away Britain's concrete options for a relationship with the new Community to the point at which it becomes hard to say that the Government had any substantial European policy when it left office on 25 October 1951. The Foreign Office objected even to the term 'formal' association and persuaded ministers that all that was needed was a relationship akin to that between the US and the OEEC. In other words, the appointment of a 'delegation to reside permanently' at the High Authority. No substantive policy agreements should be made in advance. They should only be decided as 'our relations with the Community developed'.[79] Remarking that the Foreign Office now desired that association 'should mean nothing', the Cabinet Office suspected an attempt to postpone serious consideration of the ECSC indefinitely and that the problem would not be solved until the Foreign Office resolved its own internal differences on Britain and Europe.[80]

5. An influential outsider?

Quite apart from the looming issue of association, it became increasingly difficult for the British Government to lie doggo after the beginning of 1951, for completion of the Schuman Plan talks meant decisions had to be taken about the transfer of allied controls over Germany to the new Coal and Steel Authority. The consent of the British Government was required, giving it a technical veto on the new Community, even if that veto was hard to exercise for political reasons. The evolution of UK policy on the International Authority of the Rhine would prove peculiarly erratic during 1951, in some ways confirming the argument of the last section that detachment diminished the UK's capacity to pursue a wise and informed diplomacy in European affairs; in some ways revealing still further constraints to earlier confidence that British Governments could either be insouciant towards the new Europe or dominate it from the outside; in other ways, suggesting that it still had some important leverage, at least in the peculiar circumstances of 1951.

As it became obvious in the Spring of 1951 how far the US was emerging as a key player in the Europe of the Six, the Foreign Office had to decide what it felt about others moving into its own purported foreign policy role of prime mover in West Europe politics.[81] Reactions were various. There was some concern that the British Government had not followed through the logic of its own analysis, for if West Europe was so dependent on external leadership, Britain's own decision to lie doggo had been responsible for the vacuum into which the US had now moved. Others thought it was not too late for the UK to emulate the US by changing to a policy of constructive engagement with the ECSC, though it had to be admitted that it was easier for the US to assume an air of impartial outsider, for, unlike the UK, there was no prospect of it becoming a member in the future. Others felt that, even if the UK had distanced itself too far from the Schuman process in 1950, it was too late now to change this stance. Not only would the British Government run an even greater risk than before of being charged with sabotage, it would be 'feeble sabotage' - a sign of ineffectuality that would further undercut the credibility of Britain's position in West Europe.

Nonetheless, the Foreign Office had neither complete control of British policy itself, nor of the manner in which it was perceived by other countries. During 1951, its heavy investment in reversing the perception that it was, at base, hostile to the Schuman Plan was thrown into doubt, first by a major miscalculation of its own and then by the partial 'capture' of European policy by domestic ministries. The mistake was to fret that the US was interfering in the Schuman talks in an attempt to impose an industrial settlement that would negate West Germany's return to political equality. This, it was believed in London, would only stiffen the will of those in France who wanted to turn the Schuman Plan back into an iron cage of political and economic discrimination against Germany. Grumbling that the US Administration had a 'childish' and 'doctrinaire' fascination with anti-trust laws[82] suggested that many in Britain continued to believe that direct US leadership in West European politics, unmediated by UK partnership, would be hamfisted, inexperienced and likely to attempt a misguided social engineering of other countries in the image of the US.

In fact, the US was all this time manoeuvring with consummate skill to bring about a compromise, and the main risk of failure was one of being caught between a refusal of German industrialists to cooperate with everything necessary for the detailed implementation of the Schuman Plan and a refusal of the French Assembly to ratify unless the High Authority inherited some of the commitments to the deconcentration of German industry that France had been promised in 1948. In the end, the solution was a mixture of French concession to the principle of industrial self-organization (but on a more transnational basis than before), pressure on German industrialists to give priority to the politics of Franco-German reconciliation, and a perhaps unlikely alliance of the German Christian Democrats and Trade Unions against the Social Democrats and more recalcitrant West German coal and steel interests (Duchêne, 1994, pp.215-23). It was the UK, and not the US, which ran the risk of complicating Adenauer's domestic position and scuppering Franco-German reconciliation by encouraging German industrialists to believe they could hold out for a near complete removal of all constraints. Indeed, the Foreign Office soon realized how close it had come to blundering. The German Section warned that information was power and that the effect of 'knowing less about the contents of the treaty than the French, the Germans or the Americans' was that British contributions to inter-allied discussions in West Europe were beginning to appear off beam.[83] Absence from just one multilateral context meant that the British were beginning to make embarrassing mistakes in others.

And yet problems remained for London. There were some concern that the lifting of production limits would allow West Germany to mount a formidable competitive challenge to the British economy. At a Cabinet meeting in April 1951, there were reservations about

> relaxing Allied control before it was known precisely how the Schuman organization would operate and what implications it would have for the United Kingdom Coal and Steel Industries. The Schuman Plan might give German industrialists extensive control over the coal and steel resources of West Europe, and they might use their power ruthlessly at the expense of this country.[84]

There was little doubt that some of the inputs needed for British steel making - such as Swedish iron ore and German scrap - might also be harder or more costly to obtain, if more steel was being produced in Germany. On the market structure of German industry, the Cabinet toyed with a complete reversal of its position of a few weeks earlier that the Federal Republic should be free to organize its production as it liked. It now expressed concern at reports that German steel companies would be able to own up to 25% of the national coal industry. Vertical combines such as these had been a principal feature of the interwar cartelization of heavy industry in Western Europe. Kirkpatrick, accordingly, advised UK abstention in any inter-allied vote on cross-ownership of Coal and Steel Companies. At this stage, the Foreign Office took a firm line that restrictions on German production could not be governed by Britain's commercial interest, for that would be a form of covert protectionism, even discrimination against German industry and it would be easily identified as such by the US. The IAR had been imposed solely for reasons of security and it followed that its restrictions ought to be lifted if the USSR was now to be judged a greater threat than a thriving West German economy that could contribute to the common defence.[85] Even abstention on changes to inter-allied agreements necessary for the Schuman Plan to proceed was thought to be beyond the freedom of manoeuvre of British European policy. Morrison advised the Cabinet that Britain would 'come under strong pressure to consent to solutions already agreed between the Americans, French and Germans' and that the price of not doing so would be that 'our relations with the French and United States Governments would undergo a serious strain'. He went on to predict that 'we would be subject to bitter and pertinacious propaganda'.[86]

Suspicion that the UK was secretly hostile to the Schuman Plan still seemed to demand that it should use every occasion to prove its support. Thus a vote for the new arrangements on cross-ownership would be taken as a 'touchstone of our sincerity'. Lord Henderson, then a Junior Minister in the Foreign Office, concurred: 'the only reason for our giving away and not fighting the matter out is that our action would be cited as hostility to the Schuman Plan'.[87] Indeed, the only way in which the British Government felt that it could recapture the initiative for its own priorities was to join the Schuman Plan bandwagon. It was thus suggested that concessions on the deconcentration of German industry should be made subject to the eventual ratification of the Plan, as this would provide an added incentive for the Bundestag to accept the Coal and Steel Community.

On the other hand, there was a palpable frustration at how little influence the UK had secured over the negotiations. A sense that Britain needed to assert its rights of participation - and its claim to a role - strained up against the judgement that, having once decided to absent itself from the Schuman process, it was hard, and possibly dangerous, for the British Government to muscle its way back in. In matters in which the UK had some jurisdiction, the British Government was faced with faits accomplis, most blatantly in April 1951 when the French Government wrote a letter to Bonn envisaging that the allied High Commission would, in the future, exercise no functions 'by itself'.[88] The British Cabinet felt that it had no choice but to support the French line, even though it had not been consulted as a fellow occupying power and felt that it had been 'bounced by the French, had little idea of what the Schuman Plan was all about' and continued to feel that it had 'essential interests' in ensuring that the existing control machinery was replaced by something adequate.[89] It turned out that the French had acted precipitately in order to avoid an embarrassing delay to the signing ceremony for the draft Treaty. Adenauer had threatened not to turn up unless he received the assurances that were eventually given in the French note. The task of keeping the Six together was proving an absorbing exercise that left little room for consideration of London, which was in danger of ceasing altogether to be a party to decisions on the future of Germany. The lesson of the talks was that the Six would tend to be a self-preoccupied group with reduced scope to accommodate outsiders. And this would be for reasons of internal complexity, which no-one could do much to change.

Nonetheless, Britain did develop a more assertive relationship with the Schuman negotiations under Morrison's Foreign Secretaryship from March to October 1951. A foretaste came with a peculiar attempt by the British Cabinet, at Morrison's behest, to insist that none of the new arrangements for the European coal and steel industry should prejudice the right of the Federal Government and Parliament to decide on the future ownership of German industry. This can be seen as a stirring of an old Labour hope that Britain's main industrial rival in Europe should also nationalize its heavy industries, opening the way to international planning on Socialist priorities. However, Morrison himself admitted the improbability of any such nationalization: 'even the Social Democratic Party and the Trade Unions in Germany have concentrated far more on attaining joint control of policy (Mitbestimmung)..they may in consequence be content with something considerably less than full state or public ownership'. Indeed, he went on to concede that the UK would almost 'certainly be outvoted' by the French and Americans, but suggested nevertheless, that Britain should be ready to provoke a row by taking the matter out of the hands of the High Commissioners for Germany and insisting on a direct negotiation between the allied Governments'.[90] However, it made little sense to risk precarious attempts to cultivate an air of support for the Schuman Plan for a demand that was unlikely to be realized and it is, therefore, unsurprising that attempts to protect German freedom to nationalize were quietly dropped.

When the UK did briefly adopt a collision talk with the Schuman process, the initiative came from the domestic economic ministries. For several months, there had been some concern that the recovery of the German economy would mean that scrap iron that had been promised to Britain under an informal agreement would be absorbed in domestic production in the Federal Republic. For all the familiar reasons, the Foreign Office warned strenuously against establishing any linkage between scrap deliveries and the giving of British consent to any changes in inter-allied restrictions needed for the Schuman Plan to go through: 'we shall render ourselves liable to obstructing the ratification of the Schuman Plan and will inevitably be outvoted by the Americans and the French if it comes to a show-down about the removal of Allied controls'.[91] If the Bundestag failed to vote for the Schuman Plan because British obstruction over scrap meant that assurances on the lifting of industry controls were not forthcoming, 'we would land ourselves in political difficulties of the first magnitude, and in particular might well affect very seriously Anglo-American relations'.[92] A further point was that everything changed with the prospect of Franco-German reconciliation in a grouping without

Britain. Harmonious Anglo-German relations could no longer be assured by a perception that it was France that was hostile to the reconstitution of the German state. On the contrary, it was Britain that was most open to suspicion on account of its uneasy relationship with the very framework that West Germany needed if it was to recover an equal sovereignty to that enjoyed by its neighbours.

The Foreign Office also estimated that Britain had 'very little bargaining power' in the matter. The situation on the ground was that the role and authority of the IAR was crumbling of its own accord.[93] There was little point in getting too far out of line with Paris and Washington, only to be left bargaining unilaterally for scrap with the Germans: 'the Germans will inevitably know that the French and Americans are opposed to our attitude'.[94] Nor was it particularly clear what Adenauer could do to meet British demands without complicating West Germany's own recovery and interfering in private contracts.

Although scrap was in many ways a minor issue in relation to the stakes involved in the successful conclusion of the Schuman Plan, it had all the conditions for a swamping of foreign policy by domestic priorities: issue salience, the involvement of concentrated domestic interests, the electoral problems of a government with short time horizons and the temporary wounding of Foreign Office credibility by other events. The Foreign Office thus lost its fight in Cabinet and for the remainder of the 1945-51 Government UK consent to the lifting of allied controls was tied to the conclusion of a satisfactory agreement on scrap. By May 1951, the Ministry of Supply was in something of a panic. It estimated that imports of German scrap were running so far short of what had been promised that British Steel production for 1951 could be as low as 15 3/4m tons, compared with a target of 16 3/4m tons. Given the priority of rearmament, the shortfall could have a serious effect on the export drive or limit domestic consumption, and all this when a government with a neuralgic fear of industrial dislocation, dating back to the crisis of 1947, was preparing for a knife-edge election campaign. Morrison and the Foreign Office may also have been weakened in Cabinet by their mishandling of the Abadan oil crisis in the Middle East, and there is evidence that Morrison, always something of a domestic politician at heart, did not consistently fight to protect his foreign policy from capture by the economic ministries. In one exchange, he seemed to be relishing the conflict with the German Government and to have reversed his earlier assessment that Britain had no bargaining power: 'We have got the whip hand over the German politicians..fight it through'.[95]

The attempt to use Britain's residual leverage over the conclusion of the Schuman negotiations did, in fact, produce a detailed agreement with the Federal Government on scrap, which was approved by Attlee in September. The United States also showed willing to forego some of its own entitlement to German scrap, if this was necessary to secure British agreement to the lifting of allied controls on German industry and keep the ECSC on course. It is hard to appraise the significance of the scrap over scrap. Did it prove that there was scope all along for a more assertive British policy towards the Schuman Plan, or just that the UK had a once-off source of leverage, given the need to obtain its agreement to the transfer of inter-allied controls on Germany to the ECSC? Did the Government do further damage to its relations with the Six and the US on issues of European integration, or was the slate wiped clean when, on 26 October 1951, the replacement of Labour by the Conservatives offered the opportunity for a fresh start?

6.   The Churchill Government and the Eden Plan

As Churchill had done so much to inspire the movement towards European unification in the 1940's, his return to Downing Street raised hopes of a reappraisal of Britain's abstention from the Schuman Plan. However, the Foreign Office advised against any significant policy change[96] and the Prime Minister made his own attitude abundantly clear in a memo to the Cabinet:

> I am not opposed to a European Federation..But I never thought that Britain or the British Commonwealth would become a part of the European Federation..I never contemplated Britain joining the Coal and Steel plans on the same terms as our continental partners. Our attitude is that we help, we dedicate, we participate, but we do not merge and we do not forfeit our insular or Commonwealth character.[97]

Nevertheless, a change of government brought a once off opportunity to demonstrate that Britain was not inherently hostile to plans for European unification. It, conversely, carried the risk that a second disappointment of continental hopes would prove fatal to notions of British leadership of West Europe. At the turn of 1951-2, the Foreign Office picked up signals that friends amongst the Six felt betrayed by the British Conservatives, and it also began to fret that Churchill would be unable to achieve his primary foreign policy goal of an intimate relationship with Washington without at least appearing to move closer to the Europe of the Six. It was argued that calls for European integration were no longer just an 'embarrassment', they were a 'menace', which threatened to become a 'disruptive element in the Atlantic Alliance (Bullen and Pelly, pp.804-5). American policy-makers, it was suggested, were only just beginning to understand the scale and permanency of the burden they had assumed in agreeing to support West Europe. They were, as a result, inclined to regard European integration as a 'panacea' and British refusal to involve itself more closely as a 'scapegoat' when European unification did not come up to their expectations. Without some preemptive move on Britain's part, the US Administration or Congress might even attempt to insist on a more positive attitude towards Europe as a condition for future dollar aid.[98]

At home, a simple perpetuation of Labour's European policy was further precluded by the new balance of forces in both cabinet and parliament, brought about by the change in governing party. Churchill's own crusade for a united Europe, and use of the issue in opposition to attack the Labour Government, had mobilized a group of Conservatives - the Strasbourgers - eager to negotiate a meaningful association agreement, which would provide some assured institutional basis for the UK to guide and encourage the process of integration and to indicate beyond peradventure that Britain supported a supranational Europe, even if it could not join it. The group was not large, and its representatives in the Cabinet were awkwardly positioned away from the main levers of foreign policy-making, with Harold Macmillan at the Ministry of Housing and Maxwell-Fyfe at the Home Office. However, the Government's majority of just seventeen was slender, and what the Strasbourgers lacked in numbers, they made up for in their determination to remind Churchill and Eden of the promises they had made in opposition to adopt a more positive attitude to the Europe of the Six (Young, 1988).

By January 1952, the Cabinet had persuaded itself that it would have to take some initiative. Churchill, who was not prepared to see his Government 'succumb to the Socialist Party hostility to United Europe', agreed that the British Government could do more to 'give a lead within the limits it had set itself' (Bullen and Pelly, pp.779-81). The last Administration had, in his view, been quite wrong to regard insistence on intergovernmental modes of co-operation as precluding a positive and active attitude towards the new EC. There would be no question of lying doggo. The new Government would seek a constructive engagement with any European Community, even if it was indistinguishable from the last in its preconditions for full British participation.

The Eden Plan proposed that the European Coal and Steel Community and the European Defence Community should make use of the Secretariat and Assembly of the Council of Europe. This would provide the constitutional structure - or political union - which the two Communities were widely expected to have to develop. The Council would operate according to supranational rules when dealing with the affairs of the Six and intergovernmental ones when concerned with co-ordination of the policies of the Six with all fifteen countries of West Europe. At first, Eden and the Foreign Office seem to have conceived the Plan as a means of appearing to be positive about European integration, whilst, in reality, withdrawing from the process. One paper pointed to the hope of 'transforming' the Council of Europe while 'taking the opportunity ourselves of beating a decent retreat from Strasbourg' and of 'killing the Council of Europe in its present form'. The Secretary of State predicted that the group of fifteen would prove too cumbersome to function intergovernmentally and that everyone would soon accept the monopolization of the Council's institutions by the Six, scarcely noticing that this would amount to a de facto withdrawal of the UK from Strasbourg.[99]

However, the British Government was forced into an abrupt reconsideration of whether it really wanted to use the Eden Plan to effect a graceful withdrawal from the Council of Europe, when in June 1952 the French Government came forward with its own proposals for a Political Community. Schuman suggested that the Assembly of the ECSC should function as a Constituent Assembly, drawing up proposals for an institutional structure, which would then be agreed unanimously by an EDC/ECSC Council of Ministers. Although Schuman promised that the Six would do all of this within the context of the Council of Europe, consulting the Council's other nine members as they went along, he had in a sense exposed the fundamental weaknesses of the Eden Plan by coming up with a proposal that was all too much in keeping with its original spirit of vacating the Council's institutions to the Six. Having planned only weeks before to use his Plan to effect a disguised withdrawal from the Council of Europe, Eden now fretted about British isolation from European institution building. He soon found himself defending a Council of fifteen against proposals that would have allowed the governments of the Six and the 'Assembly of the Coal and Steel Community' to 'work quite independently'[100] of everyone else. By July 1952, the Foreign Office was insisting that 'the evolution of a European Political Authority' should take place 'within the framework of an organization in which we play a full and active part'[101] and Harvey was instructed to tell Schuman that mere consultation with the wider Council of Europe would not be enough.[102] By September, Eden was warning against decisions which would not allow the UK

> to maintain the closest possible association with the ministerial and parliamentary institutions of the European Community. The application of our Council of Europe proposals..would have serious consequences for the policies of HMG and the whole intricate relationship of the United Kingdom, West Europe and the United States.[103]

If the 'first Eden Plan' of January-June 1952 showed that splendid isolation was sustainable only so long as the British Government did not want to join in the Six's discussions, the 'second Eden Plan' from July 1952 onwards illustrated the difficulties of institutionalizing the access of a mon-member state to Community deliberations. Monnet, supported by the German and Italian Governments, fiercely resisted what he considered to be an attempt to capture the supranational institutions of the new Community and place them under a 'higher mandate' of an intergovernmental organization in which decisions would only be made by the fifteen members of the Council of Europe, acting unanimously. There were also some signs that Monnet believed that it was better to associate both the US and UK with the European Communities through some Atlantic alliance machinery.[104] This would allow US Administrations to curb any British hostility to European integration. By contrast, use of the Council of Europe as a site for co-ordination, would allow Britain to place itself at the head of intergovernmental Europe and mobilize a group of outsiders against the plans of the Six.

Even Schuman, who was more eager than Monnet to find some way of operationalizing Eden's proposal, stressed that the ECSC should make use of the institutions of the Council of Europe, but neither body should belong to the other, and there should be 'no question of the nine countries who are not members being able to debate a political authority the Six might want to create'. He also emphasized, once again, that a Soviet offer on German reunification could come at any moment and that the task of binding the Federal Republic into the West had to proceed immediately and within the context of a political process that was already well advanced; or , as he put it, within a 'Union which already possesses a cohesion and a reality sufficient for Germany to feel itself properly integrated and that has the support of the US'.[105] In sum, the Eden proposals were coming late in the day. They offered only a diffuse setting that would be useful for little more than limited co-ordination between the Six and the Fifteen. The Six were already beginning to feel confidence in their own solidarity and the US Administration would not want them to compromise the integrity of their new Community.

Back in the Foreign Office, the problems of attempting to gain influence over the European Communities without full membership were revealed in two somewhat bizarre internal discussions. In an attempt to refute Monnet's point that it would be impossible to join supranational and intergovernmental modes of rule-making, the Foreign Office came round to arguing that the Schuman Plan was not all that supranational after all. Meanwhile, the originator of the Eden Plan, F.G.K Gallagher, suggested that it would be hard for Britain to secure more than the access of one foreign power to the decision-making of another, so long as it only had associate membership of a European grouping:

> Our association with the political authority would have to follow international usage. It would be like dealing with another state. We could not insist that UK observers should take part in the ministerial and parliamentary institutions of the authority, any more than we could ask for similar facilities in the US. There would also be awkward questions of reciprocity. Would we be willing to allow observers from foreign countries to take part in House of Commons Debates or Cabinet discussions.[106]

The Eden Plan had not resolved dilemmas of UK/EC relations. It had crisply defined every contour of the predicament. The role of influential outsider was hard to operationalize because it was so difficult in the early 1950s to bring intergovernmental and supranational practices together into a single framework without adherents of both approaches fearing that this would be but a device to subordinate their own preferred method of international cooperation to a dreaded alternative. On the other hand, the role of complete outsider was not acceptable to British Governments either.

Conclusion: all things not being equal

This chapter has attempted to suggest that the British Government was wrong to believe that it could be indifferent between all options for European construction in the best spirit of 'lying doggo'; that its preferred half-way house solution between full membership and exclusion was likely to prove elusive; and that with time it was more likely to drift apart from the Six, for the following reasons:

1. The phenomenon of sunk political costs. The political investment that the Six made in establishing their Community - in terms of foreign policy recantations, economic adjustments, interest group accommodation, consensus building, public persuasion and the general restructuring of domestic politics to give European integration a firm basis in winning coalitions in each member state - was a once off, sunk cost. For Britain, on the other hand, all of these costs lay in the future and constituted a barrier to entry to the club, whether that entry was to be full membership or a meaningful association. The barrier to entry could also rise with time, as the next points will show.

2. The phenomenon of synergistic linkages. Agreement on collective action was likely to be difficult even between Six countries. One possible response was to proceed by package dealing - omnibus bargains that would give all members something of what they wanted. But this could lead to rapid task expansion and multiply the number of fronts over which any latecomer would have to adapt its own policies. The Treaty of Rome of 1957 would clearly have elements of this approach (The Customs Union, Euratom and the Common Agricultural Policy). However, there were warning signs in 1950-2 with the proliferation of Plans on the Schuman model for other policies or sectors.

3. The phenomenon of externalities. The Six might also be tempted to make their bargains at the expense of outsiders. By imposing negative externalities on outsiders, they could increase their collective 'rents' from collaboration, ease distributional conflicts between themselves and thus maximize the over-lap between

European policy regimes and 'win-sets' in their own domestic politics.

4. The phenomenon of regime formation. The Six were likely to enjoy increasing returns from their acts of collaboration. In addition to converging around specific deals, they might also start to evolve shared rules of political behaviour and begin to socialize their understanding of how economies and societies work. This would lower the transaction costs and risk premia involved in making further deals and shorten the 'discovery time' needed to identify mutually advantageous bargains. Not only would the UK be outside all of this, the Six would have every incentive to 'nest' further collaborations in their new Community, rather than other fora. This would allow them to benefit from any normative order established there; to ensure that no government could cheat without calling into question the whole portfolio of its interests in a European Community; to make use of the opportunities offered for frequent and intense communication, as well as mutual understanding and transparency of their domestic societies; and, of course, to maximize the possibilities for 'synergistic linkages'.

5. The phenomenon of cognitive mirroring. There was a danger that divergence could become politically embedded in standard operating assumptions and political rhetoric: that the Governments of the Six and the UK would form self-perpetuating preconceptions of one another. For example, the perception that Britain was intrinsically hostile to European integration was, according to some, one of the principal dynamics the construction of a small but supranational Community of the 1950's, as it provided an incentive to hurry the project along before British entry (Camps, 1964).

6. The phenomenon of role-attribution. As seen, the formation of the Six without Britain threatened a series of new role attributions which further challenged old notions of UK leadership in West Europe: the development by the US of the role of external federator (Duchêne); the notion of French initiative in European integration and Franco-German reconciliation; and the idea that deviation from French and US preferences would henceforth set the main parameters of West German policy, given that these were now the main powers in the two international organizations in which the Federal Republic was most interested, the ECSC and NATO.

Notes.

1. 'Memorandum on the consequences of contemporary movements in Western Europe towards forms of economic integration having federal implications', 19 July 1950, PRO [WU 10711/22].
2. Makins to Strang, 12 July 1950, PRO [WU 10711/22].
3. 'Memorandum on the consequences', *cit.*
4. Makins to Franks, 17 July 1950, PRO [CE 3718/2141/181].
5. Memorandum by the Minister of Defence, 1 July 1950, PRO [CE 3452/2141/181].
6. Younger to Strang, 2 June 1950, PRO [CE 2773/2141/181].
7. 'Should Western Europe federate without the United Kingdom?', 13 February 1951, PRO [ZP 18/19].
8. 'Constitutional problems involved in a supranational authority as envisaged by M Schuman', Note by the Foreign Office, 16 June 1950, PRO [CAB 134/295].
9. Stevens to Younger, 20 June 1950, PRO [CE 3170/2141/181].
10. Makins to Strang, 28 June 1950, PRO [CE 3353/2141/181].
11. Note of a meeting in Sir E. Bridges's room, 14 July 1950, PRO [T 232/194] and Makins to Franks, 17 July 1950, PRO [CE 3718/2141/181].
12. 'Working party report', 31 December 1951.
13. Minutes of a Meeting of the Permanent Under-Secretary's Committee, 29 March 1951, PRO [ZP 18/1].
14. Bevin to Hayter, 31 August 1950, PRO [WF 1051/13].
15. Makins to Strang, 28 June 1950, PRO [CE 3353/2141/181].
16. Harvey to Younger, 6 June 1950, PRO [CE 2804/2141/181].
17. Harvey conversation with Bevin, 3 July 1950, PRO [CE 3422/2141/181].
18. Dixon to Makins, 13 June 1950, PRO [CE 3355/2141/181].
19. Note by Hall-Patch of a conversation with Bevin, 30 June 1950, PRO [CE 3385/2141/181].
20. Dixon to Makins, 13 June 1950, PRO [CE 3355/2141/181].
21. Harvey conversation with Bevin, *cit.*
22. Younger to Robertson, 12 June 1950, PRO [POWE 41/72].
23. Hall-Patch to Younger, 17 June 1950, PRO [CE 3078/2141/181].
24. Strang to Harvey, 6 July 1950, PRO [WF 1019/32].
25. 'Constitutional problems', *cit.*
26. 'Should Western Europe Federate'..*cit.*
27. Note of a Meeting in Sir Edward Bridges' room, *cit.*
28. Bevin to Hayter, 31 August 1951, PRO [WF 1051/13].
29. Bevin to Younger, 21 June 1950, PRO [CE 3274/2141/181].
30. Hall-Patch conversation with Bevin, 30 June 1950, PRO [CE 3385/2141/181].
31. Cabinet conclusions, 4 July 1950, PRO [CAB 128/18].
32. Harvey to Younger, 10 June 1950, PRO [PREM 8/1428].

33. Harvey to Younger, 24 June 1950, PRO [POWE 41/72].
34. Younger to Harvey, 28 June 1950, PRO [CE 3310/2141/181].
35. Strang to Harvey, 27 June 1950, PRO [CE 3313/2141/181].
36. Nichols to Younger, 6 June 1950, PRO [CE 2787/2141/181]; and Hall-Patch to Younger, 17 June 1950, PRO [CE 3078/2141/181].
37. Younger to Harvey, 19 June 1950, PRO [CE 3165/2141/181].
38. Cripps to Bevin, 1 July 1950, PRO [PREM 8/1428].
39. Harvey to Younger, 1 July 1950, PRO [CE 3356/2141/181].
40. Annex 1 to 'Integration of Western European Coal and Steel Industries', 20 June 1950, PRO [CAB 129/40].
41. 'Integration of Western European Coal and Steel Industries', 1 July 1950, PRO [CAB 129/40].
42. Harvey to Younger, 5 July 1950, PRO [CE 3430/2141/181].
43. Butt to Pitblado, 17 July 1950, PRO [T 229/750].
44. Cabinet Conclusions, 4 July 1950, PRO [CAB 128/18].
45. 'Integration of Western Europe', *cit.*
46. Wilson to Pitblado, 4 December 1950, PRO [T 229/751].
47. Douglas to Acheson, *Foreign Relations of the United States*, 1950, Vol III, pp. 718-9.
48. Harvey to Younger, 15 June 1950, PRO [WF 1051/10].
49. Hayter to Younger, 25 July 1950, PRO [CE 3785/2141/181].
50. Hayter to Bevin, 11 August 1950, [CE 4048/2141/181].
51. Hayter to Younger, 25 July 1950, PRO [CE 3785/2141/181].
52. Memorandum of Permanent Under-Secretary's Committee, 18 June 1951, PRO [ZP 18/20].
53. Brief by Pitblado, 20 July 1951, PRO [T 229/753]. See also Plowden's note of approval on this brief (Bullen and Pelly, p.656n); also, Butt to Robertson, 15 September 1951, PRO [T 229/753].
54. Morrison to H.M. Representatives in Western Europe, 16 April 1951, PRO [ZP 18/1].
55. Gordon Walker to Commonwealth Governments, 30 August 1951, PRO [CE(W) 1543/424].
56. Memorandum for the Permanent Under-Secretary's Committee, 9 June 1951, PRO [ZP 18/20].
57. Butt to Hall, 4 July 1951, PRO [T 230/182].
58. Memorandum by Mr Wilson, 4 July 1951, PRO [CE(W) 1543/366].
59. Memorandum by Mr Wilson, 4 July 1951, PRO [CE(W) 1543/366].
60. Harvey to Younger, 22 June 1950, PRO [CE 3182/2141/181].
61. Hayter to Bevin, 12 August 1950, PRO [CE 4067/2141/181].
62. Hayter to Stevens, 25 June 1951, PRO [CE(W) 1543/347].
63. Memorandum by Wilson, 30 April 1951, PRO [CE(W) 1543/188].

64. Stevens to Hayter, 7 December 1950, PRO [CE 5894/2141/181].
65. Younger to Jebb, 14 September 1950, PRO [POWE 41/16].
66. Younger to UK delegation (Ottawa, 15 September 1951, PRO [WF 1051/9].
67. Younger to Jebb, 14 September 1950, PRO [POWE 14/16].
68. Hayter to Stevens, 12 December 1950, PRO [CE 6203/2141/181].
69. Butt to Hall, 14 September 1950, PRO [T 229/751].
70. Younger to Jebb, 11 September 1950, PRO [POWE 41/16].
71. Hayter to Stevens, 30 September 1950, PRO [CE 4902/2141/181].
72. Wilson to Hood, 25 November 1950, PRO [CE 5735/2141/181].
73. Hayter to Stevens, 30 September 1950, PRO [CE 4902/2141/181].
74. Hayter to Stevens, 27 November 1950, PRO [CE 5894/2141/181].
75. Harvey to Morrison, 4 May 1951, PRO [ZP 18/8].
76. Kirkpatrick to Morrison, 28 May 1951, PRO [ZP 18/14].
77. Brief by Pitblado, 20 July 1951, PRO [T229/753].
78. Butt to Robertson, 15 September 1951, PRO [T 229/753].
79. Minutes of the Economic Steering Committee of the Cabinet, 9 July 1951, PRO [CAB 134/264] and Turner to Robertson, 31 August 1951, PRO [T 229/753].
80. Butt to Robertson, 15 September 1951, PRO [T 229/753].
81. Wilson to Pitblado, 28 November 1950, PRO [T 229/751].
82. Wilson to Pitblado, 27 February 1951, PRO [CE(W) 1102/117].
83. Stevens to Makins, 6 February 1951 PRO [CE(W) 1543/29] and memorandum by Wilson, 30 April 1951, PRO [CE(W) 1543/88].
84. Cabinet conclusions, 16 April 1950, PRO [CAB 128/19].
85. Younger to Strauss, 21 February 1951, PRO [FO 1013/1192].
86. 'Memorandum by the Secretary of State for Foreign Affairs', 19 March 1951, PRO [CAB 129/45].
87. Wilson to Morrison, 19 March 1951, PRO [CE(W) 1543/83].
88. Morrison to Harvey, 17 April 1951, PRO [CE(W) 1543/108].
89. Wilson to Porter, 24 April 1951, PRO [CE(W) 1543/160].
90. Memorandum by Secretary of State for Foreign Affairs, 20 March 1951, PRO [CAB 129/45].
91. Wilson to Rogers, 16 May 1951, PRO [CE(W) 1541/83].
92. Gainer to Rowlands, 6 June 1951, PRO [CE(W) 1543/384].
93. Brief for the Secretary of State, Foreign Office, 17 May 1951 PRO [CE(W) 1541/95]; also see Cabinet Conclusions, 5 June 1951, PRO [CAB 128/19].
94. Gainer to Rowlands, cit.
95. Henderson to Morrison, 5 July 1951, PRO [CE(W) 1541/129].
96. 'European Integration', Brief for the Secretary of State, 31 October 1951, PRO [WU 10712/49].
97. 'United Europe', Memorandum by the Prime Minister to the Cabinet, 29 November 1951, PRO [C(51)32].

98. 'Future of the Council of Europe', memorandum from Dixon to Eden, 30 January 1951, PRO [WU 10733/3].
99. 'Record of a meeting in Mr Nutting's room, 21 January 1952, PRO [WU 10733/1]; Dixon to Eden, cit.
100. Eden to Mallet, 23 July 1952, [WU 10744/37].
101. Brief by Dixon for the Secretary of State, 7 July 1952, [WU 10744/13].
102. Eden to Harvey, 8 July 1952, PRO [WU 10744/13].
103. Eden to Harvey, 4 September 1952, PRO [WU 10733/155].
104. Hayter to Dixon, 18 July 1952, [WU 10744/28].
105. Memorandum by Schuman, 9 July 1952, [WU 10744/21].
106. Gallagher to Hood, 20 September 1952, [WU 10733/242].

7 Conclusion

Alan Milward has laid bare the paradoxical character of schemes of European integration in the 1950s. Initiatives that were presented as first steps in a federating process often won the support of national governing elites by demonstrating how they could contribute to the survival, reconstruction and better functioning of the very nation states whose sovereignty the prophets of European integration intended to erode (Milward, 1993). And yet there was always a certain logic to this. Governments in a condition of interdependence are not self-sufficient policy providers and may quite rationally look to transnational, and even supranational, frameworks to improve their own 'problem solving' capacity (Moravscik, 1993).

The implication is that nation state and European Community may not stand in a zero-sum, or competitive, relationship. On the contrary, the two may be simultaneously strengthened, one by the other; and those governments which fail to realize this and to avail themselves of the 'state supplementing' services of European integration may find that the effectiveness of their policy-making declines relative to those who make best use of transnational political frameworks to their own ends. Was this the fate of British Governments who rejected participation in the Schuman Plan? In order to see whether this critique has any application, it is worth concluding the book by relating the decision to abstain from the Schuman Plan to two academic debates on the quality of British governance since 1950 and a third on the precise timing of any mistaken decision, if any, not to join in the early stages of European integration: the first debate concerns the role of external policy in Britain's postwar economic under-performance; the second is the 'Frankel critique' of postwar foreign policy as an out-dated strategy for obtaining international influence; and the third is the 'Bullock debate' on whether it was the decision to stay out of the Schuman Plan or the Treaty of Rome that represented a real parting of the ways between Britain and the Six.

1.   The Schuman Plan and the debate about economic under-performance

1950 was a pivotal year in Britain's postwar economic development. Between 1945 and 1950, Britain had, as Stephen Blank argues, been the 'first economic miracle' in the long postwar recovery of West Europe that would last until 1973 (Coates, 1994). From 1950 to 1973, on the other hand, the UK economy would splutter and falter around a long-run growth rate of 2.5 per cent, whilst the economic motor of the rest of West Europe would hum consistently with growth rates twice those of the UK, the average for the Six, for example, scarcely deviating even for one particular year from a rate of expansion of 4.5-5.0 per cent.

There is, of course, much debate as to when the relative decline of the British economy began and why. However, this does not have the effect of disconnecting the issue of Britain's relationship with West Europe since 1950 from the debate about economic decline, for any historically complete account of the latter cannot be confined to initial causes. It must also locate moments when there may have been brief opportunities to reverse the process of decline and explain why these may not have been taken. A strong case can be made that there was such a window of opportunity between 1945 and 1955 and that this was missed in good part on account of the very foreign policy decisions that are the subject of this book.

It is true that Britain came out of the war weighed down with external liabilities and stripped bare of the international assets that had previously covered its precarious balance of payments. Just when it needed to pay fully for its way in the world out of current output, it found that much of its physical capacity had been worn down by the demands of war, or converted to military production, thus complicating the challenge of rebuilding a competitive civilian economy. Nonetheless, the UK also enjoyed many economic strengths in 1945. The structural problem with its economy had essentially been one of over-commitment to old product lines and technologies. However, the interwar period had seen a painful process of readjustment in which the nation's factors of production came to be more concentrated on 'rising' industries such as cars, aircraft, engineering and chemicals. What is more, what mattered to Britain's competitive position was not the level of wartime dislocation in these industries in the UK, but whether that dislocation was relatively greater or less than in neighbouring economies. In many respects the war had even catalyzed growth of the new industries in the UK (Hennessy, 1992, pp. 87-109). Not only was the loss of production and capacity far more serious on the continent, it also has to be remembered that France was not yet a fully modernized and industrialized economy. Only Germany could rival the UK for its spread of industries, accumulated skills and ability to achieve 'early mover advantages' in new product sectors. Germany, however, was to be constrained by political uncertainty and production controls until the early 1950s.

It has recently become fashionable to distinguish exogenous and endogenous approaches to the economic growth. According to the first, markets find an optimal development path on their own, driven by changes in technology, methods of economic organization and shifts in consumer wants: factors that are all considered beyond political intervention. Endogenous theories, on the other hand, argue that the ability to absorb technologies, to adapt economies to organizational change, and even consumer tastes are shaped within the political and social systems: different kinds of state and society facilitate or debilitate different kinds of economic development and are thus a key variable in explaining relative economic performance.

From an 'endogenous' point of view, two related issues were wrapped up in the UK's rejection of the Schuman Plan: the domestic developmental capacity of the British state itself and the nature of the institutional interface between the UK economy and the external trading and payments systems. In preferring Commonwealth over European markets, the British Government demonstrated the power of 'more or less defunct economists' over policy-making. Old comparative advantage theories suggested that international trade was most likely to prosper between unlike economies. The exchange of primary products from the developing countries of the Commonwealth for the finished manufactures of the UK thus seemed to represent an ideal trading relationship and Britain's peculiar ability to sustain a post Imperial politics that put it at the centre of a family of developing countries seemed to account for its extraordinary over-representation in the whole process of international trade. The problem was that the postwar period would reverse these old verities. Trade growth would be fastest between countries that were economically similar in their consumption patterns and geographically close. In other words, the formula chosen by the Six would be more successful than that selected by the UK. The thinking that lay behind abstention from the Schuman Plan was thus part of a mistake by which the UK tied itself to inappropriate markets; to trading partners that British manufacture could too easily dominate with out-dated product lines, rather than markets of increasingly prosperous and critical consumers who would put continuous pressure on the UK to modernize its labour and capital, to sort out the sociology of its workplaces and, above all, to embed the latest information on consumer tastes in a continuous striving for product innovation and improvement. This last would be especially important to sustaining international competitiveness in trade between affluent societies. If, for any of these reasons, the balance of payments suffered over the next twenty years, government hostility to integration with West European markets in the early 1950s must be considered partially responsible for the stop-go cycle of 1950-73, thought by some to have been especially disruptive of the investment that was needed for the steady modernization of Britain's productive capacity.

A further step in our analysis might be to combine Milward's critique that Britain abstained from a self-sustaining 'growth-circuit' of market integration and productivity improvement in West Europe with David Marquand's argument that postwar British Governments failed to establish a developmental state appropriate to an advanced economy. While France developed indicative planning, and West Germany the Mitbestimmung system of negotiated economic adjustment, British Governments held fast to Keynesian macroeconomics, a conveniently aloof system of demand management that did not require them to dirty their hands with either the microeconomics or sociology of production (Marquand, 1988). By abstaining from European integration in the 1950s, British Governments lost the opportunity to watch, share and imitate these continental experiences. Some attempts were made between 1961 and 1974 to Europeanize Britain's political economy, but it was, by then, too late and, in any case, it was not yet in conjunction with full market integration with West Europe. The latter was key, for it was external competitive pressure that allowed the French and West German governments to act as modernizers and brokers without becoming captive to producer interests. It was also the export-led growth of 1950-73 that allowed the Six to make massive economic adjustments and develop ambitious welfare states without distributional conflicts. By contrast, such flirtations British Governments had with economic development or social brokering had to be abandoned because they were not embedded in an external context that ensured a healthy trading account and pressured the domestic economy to use its resources efficiently and mediate its social relationships harmoniously. The state could not use international market disciplines to preserve an adequate margin of independence in relation to producer interests and thus avoid pluralistic stagnation. It also became overloaded with distributional frustrations resulting from attempts to combine guarantees of full employment and a tax-hungry welfare state with a slow growing economy.

If valid, this hypothesis does, indeed, have ironic implications for those who rejected British membership of the Schuman Plan. For the Six, the developmental state and European economic integration stood in a subtle and mutually empowering relationship. For the UK, the attempt to preserve undivided sovereignty over domestic economic and social development may even have lowered the effectiveness of domestic policy-making. At the very least, membership of the ECSC was rejected on the basis of a false analysis in so far as it was predicted that Britain would be condemned to a less ambitious domestic policy inside Europe than out. The investment plans of British coal and steel would not, in the event, be used as instruments of Keynesian pump-priming state, although the need to keep them in national hands for this purpose had been a prime reason for refusing membership of the Schuman Plan. Contrariwise, membership of the ECSC would not stop France from developing indicative planning, nor would it set the boundaries between the private and public sectors of any of the Six economies in stone, nor would it prevent the Six from developing welfare states which were, by the 1960s, indistinguishable from Britain's in terms of government take of GNP. We must, however, treat this thesis with some caution, for while it is useful to mix the Milward and Marquand critiques, the truth may incline more to the first than the second. Indicative planning in France, for example, was always something of a façade - an exercise of doubtful economic effectiveness that was largely of political significance in sustaining a reassuring illusion of state-led development in a culture that did not care to admit that modernization was really being driven by the marketization and internationalization of French society (Hayward). Given this, the real error of British policy in the early 1950s may have been fear of markets and competition and, in particular, the assumption that West German economic competition would flatten British producers, rather than encourage convergence of productivity and a mutually profitable division of labour. France, which started off far behind the UK - indeed, as a country that had only partially industrialized - took a gamble on its economy being dragged up and not downwards by competition with West Germany: a gamble that it won (Milward). The real significance of integration was not that it changed German economic leadership of West Europe, but that it swapped France for Britain, and possibly even Italy for Britain, in second and third places respectively.

2. The Schuman Plan and the 'Frankel critique' of postwar British Foreign Policy

In his critique of postwar British Foreign Policy, Joseph Frankel memorably accuses Governments of 'cognitive lag': of believing that the future would be much like the past, of misreading the international environment and of trying to run the external affairs of a middling state in reduced circumstances on assumptions more appropriate to a previous age when the UK was a dominant, imperial power in the world order. To Frankel this was no harmless conceit. On the contrary, Britain's retreat was made more precipitous by a failure to admit the fact of decline. A small domestic economy had to sustain inflated international pretensions and suffer post-imperial 'over-stretch', just when the UK required the opposite solution of a foreign policy supportive of internal re-development. Great power delusions, and a false belief that Britain could lead West Europe from the outside, meant that in abstaining from the formation of the European Communities, British Governments allowed its neighbours to monopolize the formation of institutions and rules that would become key management structures in its own economic life, even as a non-member; to get a head start in the development of bilateral friendships that would often determine the distribution of influence and initiative in the new Community (Wallace, 1984); to enjoy Britain's costly contribution to the NATO security umbrella without giving the UK full access to EC markets; and, arguably, to confirm their own economies on higher growth paths than the UK by maximizing for themselves the benefits of the once-off conjunction between European integration and the dynamics of postwar recovery. By the early 1970s, F.S. Northedge would conclude in his study, *Descent from Power*, there was 'nowhere else for Britain to go but into the Europe of the Six..had the Six realized it, they could have made the fee for British entry even higher than they did' (Northedge, 1974, p.328).

Much of this book would support Frankel's critique. Nonetheless, his analysis needs to be both qualified and amplified in the particular instance of British abstention from the Schuman Plan. The obvious problem with Frankel's approach is that it assumes a *given* international environment to which foreign policy-makers adapt, if they are rational. An alternative view is that the main players are creative as well as adaptive actors. They are continuously reordering and renegotiating the structures, institutions and rules to which they must eventually adhere. Indeed, the Schuman Plan came at a peculiarly protean moment and it is hard to criticize British Governments for failing to adapt to new realities in the organizational structuring of postwar Europe when it was precisely these that were still up for grabs. Given the intensity of their preference for an intergovernmental order, it may well have been perfectly reasonable for them to have tried options such as association with the nascent European Community before concluding that there was no real alternative to full membership. What is more, rational choices could not be based on existing rules of the inter-state game in West Europe; they required guesses as to what these rules would be in the future and these could only be made on the basis of necessarily tentative and insecure expectations as to the emerging forms of postwar West European politics.

In fact, British Official Papers on the Schuman Plan, collated by Roger Bullen and M.E. Pelly leave the impression of a government machine that was, at least in the meticulousness of its methods, close to the ideal of a rational foreign policy actor (Bullen and Pelly). Almost all the consequences that were in the event to flow from the formation of the European Coal and Steel Community were anticipated by someone in Whitehall. Conversely, many politicians of the Six were only accidentally right about the Schuman Plan, supporting it for reasons that were either contradictory or which bore little relation to the real benefits that would eventually flow from the new Community. Indeed, early theorists of European integration made much of the unintended consequences of political action - of integration absent-mindedly achieved by those engaged in far more prosaic acts of problem-solving. This was one piece of thoughtlessness of which British Governments could not be accused.

Psychological resistance to change proceeded not only from the amour propre invested in past glories but also from a more forward-looking sense of foreboding at the enormous *transitional* costs that would be involved in reorientating Britain's foreign and economic policies towards West Europe. The degree to which British economic interests were embedded in Commonwealth markets, a sense of political responsibility for smooth transition from Empire to Commonwealth and a demanding domestic programme with little financial margin would have made even a government endowed with perfect knowledge of the future balk at the costs of an abrupt switch to West Europe in the early 1950s. Cynics might even argue that from the point of view of Governments determined to maximize their own interests subject to a five year electoral cycle - rather than some concept of a national interest defined over a longer period - the rational course was precisely the one adopted. The optimal solution was to muddle through, to decline the invitation for full membership, to search out some middle way between exclusion and non-participation, and to wait and see whether Schuman's Europe was really going to work before incurring the substantial political and economic costs of any adjustment to it.

Yet the rationality gap cannot be conjured away altogether. Indeed, the Frankel critique can be sharpened by labelling some kinds of foreign policy misperception as 'fundamental' as opposed to 'marginal' and 'transient'. An obvious candidate would be persistent error as to the very nature of political forms, relationships and bargaining patterns in the international system, as well as deficient understanding by a government of its own capabilities and the roles that other states are prepared to ascribe to it. Even in an experimental phase in which the full rules of the game have yet to be defined, it is important - indeed doubly important at such formative moments - for governments to have a clear understanding of their raw bargaining power and, as the rules do begin to firm up, governments must also be open to learning and to change in their policies, if they are to correct for previous miscalculations. Anything less amounts to a dysfunctional 'state adjustment strategy' (Ikenberry, 1986). While acknowledging their interdependence with West Europe, British Governments repeatedly assumed that they could play a leadership or a veto game in relation to whatever political construct emerged there; and that, in defining Britain's European policy it would, accordingly, often be sufficient for them to consider only their own preferences, rather than regard themselves as in a condition of 'strategic interaction' with their neighbours in which successful game play would depend as much on anticipating the wishes and moves of others, as on being clear about what Britain itself wanted. The freedom to adopt such an attitude might be characterized as representing the difference between a superpower and a middling power and, as Frankel has argued, it was, indeed, the US, rather than

France and Germany, that would for much of the 1950s be considered by British Governments to be the analogue power to the UK. By wrongly assuming that they were in a position of policy leadership - and that the continental Europeans would ultimately have to fit their new Community into the interstices and gaps left by the UK's own power in West Europe and in the wider international system - and by misclassifying themselves amongst the various categories of state actor, British Governments made more than systematically erroneous moves. They also lost a say in designing the game itself.

British Governments of the time may also have failed to understand the full force of the case that was being made for a new, more supranational approach to international institution-building and rule-making. They were too blinded by the rhetorical claims that were being made on behalf of supranationalism to appreciate that it was likely to be a durable innovation in the practice of international organization, precisely because it was well grounded in the needs of postwar Europe. It was facile to dismiss it as mere federalist fancy. In the absence of political guarantees of good neighbourliness, it would be hard for West European Governments to combine ambitious welfare models at home with a move away from the closed economies of the interwar. Without this, even limited economic interdependence could be unstable; with this, economic interdependence could, to a degree, be consensually managed to avoid conflicts of domestic objectives. A supranational structure would speed the identification of mutually advantageous compromises, and lock governments in to the steady development of interdependence, shoring up the confidence of both neighbouring governments and private economic actors. Given the history of 1914 to 1950, confidence in collaboration was fragile and it was, therefore, entirely logical for governments to tie themselves to the mast of European integration, in order to underpin confidence that the opening of their economies would not be reversed at some future date. If this cost them a degree of sovereignty, it also enlarged their opportunities.

International organizations for a new West Europe would also have to be socially constructed and could not rest on the ideal preferences of any one government. In other words, they would have to correspond to shared understandings of how international organizations ought to be used to embed states in their immediate environment. Although the structure of political preferences was such as to impose inherent limits on how far British, French and German views of international organization could be reconciled, the French Government between 1948 and 1950 arguably showed greater understanding than the British of the need for creativity and flexibility if it was to devise new norms of international behaviour that could be shared by West Germany. The ultimate reward for what at the time seemed to be a sacrifice of important foreign policy positions on the part of the French Government was the emergence of the Franco-German relationship as the dominant bilateral friendship in West Europe. By contrast, British Governments missed such an opportunity to stoop to conquer.

The final issue we need to consider is whether British foreign policy assumptions showed openness to learning and adjustment in the event of the supranational model being more successful than anticipated, or association failing to meet minimum expectations of continued British involvement in West Europe. Unhappily, Chapters 4 and 6 have shown that there were many ways in which foreign policy assumptions were being framed for the postwar period in a manner that was likely to prove 'learning resistant'. They were often structured in a way that would allow Britain's foreign policy-makers to carry on believing them regardless of subsequent outcomes and evidence, including flagrant contradiction of the premises that had given rise to the original beliefs. (Jervis, 1976). Although, we have seen that many of the problems that abstention would bring were noted, they were rarely brought together in one overall assessment. Still less did they reach Cabinet level en bloc, where consideration of the Schuman Plan was desultory after June 1950. Above all, it was always assumed that problems of exclusion could be 'managed' if and when they arose. In this regard, the possibility of association with the Schuman Plan acquired a damaging status as false panacea: an unworked out half way house between membership and exclusion that served to postpone choices under the guise of solving them.

3.   The 'Bullock Debate': when was the parting of the ways between Britain and the European Community, 1950-2 or 1955-7?

The arguments reviewed in the last two sections all connect with Alan Bullock's plea that we should be precise in locating any possible moment of error in Britain's European policy. The UK did not have the overwhelming interest in participation in the Coal and Steel Community of 1952 that it would arguably have in avoiding exclusion from the Common Market of 1957. What is more absence from the first by no means limited the willingness of the Six to negotiate Britain's inclusion in the second (Bullock, 1983). In between times, British policy-makers arguably had time to observe the over-estimates they had made of their bargaining position in the postwar world; to conclude that some kind of European integration was going to form a structural feature of their own immediate environment; to notice some shift of UK economic interests to West Europe and the overall dynamism of those markets; and to reflect on just how substantial had been their pretensions in the early 1950s to lead West Europe from a position of mere association with the ECSC.

The contrary argument, however, is that 1950-2 and 1955-7 were not really two distinct phases in the evolution of UK/West European relations: that the interweaving of interests and habits of co-operation built up between 1950 and

1957 were already beginning to mark the Six off from outsiders and give them a certain collective personality; that Britain's underestimate of the probability that the Common Market negotiations would succeed was the direct result of the detachment of its elites from the sense of political commitment and open exchange of information that was building up amongst the ECSC Governments; and that it was no coincidence that it was the same six states that formed the ECSC that went on to form the EEC - indeed, one of the motives that they had for this second initiative was precisely the need to restore credibility in their commitment to integration if member states were not to 'renationalize' their coal and steel policies, and turn away from the ECSC, in the crisis of confidence that followed on from the failure of the EDC in 1954. In classic 'spill-over' mode, a second initiative seemed to be necessary to protect the first (Duchêne).

Bibliography

Acheson, Dean (1969), *Present at the Creation: My Years in the State Department*, Norton, New York.

Adenauer, Konrad (1966), *Memoirs 1945-53*, Weidenfeld and Nicholson, London.

Addison, Paul (1977), *The Road to 1945: British Politics and the Second World War*, Quartet Books, London.

Alford, B.W.E (1988), *British Economic Performance, 1945-75*, Macmillan, London.

Austin, Dennis (1988), *The Commonwealth and Britain*, RKP/RIIA, London.

Berstein, Serge, Mayeur, Jean-Marie and Milza, Pierre (1993), *Le MRP et la Construction Européenne*, Éditions Complexes, Bruxelles.

Bosuat, Gérard (1992), *La France, l'aide américaine et la Construction Européenne 1944-54*, Comité pour l'histoire économique et financière de la France, Paris.

Bullen and Pelly (1986), The Schuman Plan, The Council of Europe and Western European Integration 1950-1952, *Documents on British Policy Overseas*, Series II, Volume I.

Bullen and Pelly (1989), German Rearmament, Documents on British Policy Overseas, Series II, Volume II.

Bullock, Alan (1983), *Ernest Bevin: Foreign Secretary 1945-51*, Heinemann, London.

Cain, P.J and Hopkins, A.G (1993), *British Imperialism: Crisis and Deconstruction 1914-1990*, Longman, London.

Cairncross, Alec (1985), *The Years of Recovery: British Economic Policy 1945-51*, Methuen, London.

167

Cairncross, Alec (ed) (1989), *The Robert Hall Diaries 1947-53*, Unwin Hyman, London.

Camps, Miriam (1964), *Britain and the European Community: 1955-64*, OUP, London.

Claude, Innis (1956), *Swords into Ploughshares: the Problems and Progress of International Organization*, Random House, New York.

Coates, David (1994), *The Question of UK Decline: The Economy, State and Society*, Harvester Wheatsheaf, London.

Dalloz, Jacques (1992), *George Bidault: Biographie Politique*, Harmattan, Paris.

Darwin, John (1988), *Britain and Decolonization: the retreat from Empire in the postwar world*, Macmillan, London.

Deutsch, Karl (1968), 'The Impact of Communications upon International Relations Theory' in Abdul Said (ed), *Theory of International Relations: The Crisis of Relevance*, Prentice Hall, NJ.

Diebold, William (1959), *The Schuman Plan: A Study in Economic Co-operation*, Praeger, New York.

Duchêne, François (1994), *Jean Monnet: The First Statesman of Interdependence*, W.W. Norton, London.

Eden, Anthony (1960), *Full Circle*, Cassell, London.

Frankel, Joseph (1975), *British Foreign Policy 1945-73*, RIIA, London.

Fursdon, Edward (1980), *The European Defence Community: A History*, Macmillan, London.

Gallagher, John (1982), *The Decline, Revival and Fall of the British Empire*, CUP, London.

Gamble, Andrew (1985), *Britain in Decline: Economic Policy, Political Strategy and the British State*, Macmillan, London.

George, Stephen (1990), *An Awkward Partner: Britain in the European Community*, Clarendon Press, Oxford.

Gilbert, Martin (1988), *Never Despair: Winston S. Churchill 1945-65*, Minerva, London.

Gillingham, John (1991), *Coal, Steel and the Rebirth of Europe, 1945-55*, CUP, Cambridge.

Haas, Ernest (1968), *The Uniting of Europe*, Stanford University Press, Stanford.

Habermas, Jurgen (1988), *Legitimation Crisis*, Polity, Cambridge.

Halsey, A.H (1986), *Change in British Society*, OUP, London.

Hayward, Jack (1978) (ed), *Planning in Europe*, Croom Helm, London.

Healey, Denis (1990), The Time of My Life, Penguin, London.

Hennessy, Peter (1992), *Never Again: Britain 1945-51*, Jonathan Cape, London.

Hogan, Michael (1987), *The Marshall Plan: America, Britain and the Reconstruction of West Europe, 1947-52*, Cambridge University Press,

Cambridge.

Horne, Alistair (1988), *Macmillan 1894-56*, Macmillan, London.

Howarth and Cerny (1981) (eds), *Elites in France: Origins, Reproduction and Power*, Pinter, London.

Howe, Geoffrey (1990), 'Sovereignty and interdependence: Britain's place in the world', *International Affairs*, Vol.66, No.4, October 1990.

Ikenberry, John (1986), 'The State and Strategies of International Adjustment', *World Politics*, Vol.36, No.1.

Jervis, Robert (1976), *Perception and Misperception in International Politics*, Princeton University Press, New Jersey.

Johnson, Nevil (1977), *In Search of the Constitution: Reflections on State and Society in Britain*, Methuen, London.

Keohane, Robert and Nye, Joseph (1977), *Power and Interdependence*, Little Brown, Boston, Mass.

Kircheimer, O (1966), 'The Transformation of the West European Party Systems' in J. LaPalombara & Weiner (eds), *Political Parties and Political Development*, Princeton University Press, Princeton.

Kitzinger, Uwe (1973), *Diplomacy and Persuasion: How Britain joined the Common Market*, Thames and Hudson, London.

Kolodziej, Edward (1974), *French International Policy under De Gaulle and Pompidou*, Cornell University Press, Ithaca.

Lord, Christopher (1992), 'Sovereign or Confused? The Great Debate about British Entry to the European Community 20 Years On', *Journal of Common Market Studies*, Vol.XXX, No.4, December 1992.

Lord, Christopher (1993), *British Entry to the European Community Under the Heath Government of 1970-4*, Dartmouth, London.

Macrae. D (1968), *Parliament, Parties and Society in France 1946-1958*, Macmillan, London.

Marquand, David (1988), *The Unprincipled Society: New Demands and Old Politics*, Fontana, London.

Massigli, René (1978), *Une Comédie des Erreurs*, Plon, Paris.

Milward, Alan (1984), *The Reconstruction of West Europe*, Methuen, London.

Milward, Alan (1992), The *European Rescue of the Nation State*, University of California Press, Berkeley.

Monnet, Jean (1976), *Mémoires*, Fayard, Paris.

Moravscik, Andrew (1993), 'Preferences and Power in the European Community: A Liberal Intergovernmentalist Approach', *Journal of Common Market Studies*, Vol.31, No.4.

Morgan, Kenneth (1985), *Labour in Power 1945-51*, OUP, London.

Northedge, F.S (1973), *Descent from Power: British Foreign Policy, 1945-73*, Allen and Unwin, London.

Newton, S (1985), 'Britain, the Sterling Area and European Integration 1945-50', *Journal of Imperial and Commonwealth History*, Vol.13, pp 163-82.

Newton, S (1985), 'The 1949 Sterling Crisis and British Policy towards European Integration', *Review of International Studies*, Vol.11.

Pelling, Henry (1984), *The Labour Government 1945-51*, Macmillan, London.

Pimlott, Ben (1992), *Harold Wilson*, Harper and Collins, London.

Poidevin, Raymond (ed) (1986 (a)), *Histoire des Débuts de la Construction Européenne*, Bruylant, Bruxelles.

Poidevin, Raymond (1986), *Robert Schuman: Homme D'État*, Imprimerie Nationale, Paris.

Shuckburgh, Evelyn (1986), *Descent to Suez, Diaries 1951-6*, Weidenfeld and Nicolson, London.

Schwabe, Klaus (ed) (1988), Die Anfänge des Schuman-Plans 1950-1, Nomos-Verlag, Baden-Baden.

Seldon, Anthony (1981) *Churchill's Indian Summer: the Conservative Government, 1951-5*, Hodder and Stoughton, London.

Smith, M and Smith, S and White B (ed) (1988), *British Foreign Policy*, Unwin Hyman, London.

Stevenson, John (1984), *British Society 1914-45*, Pelican, London.

Strange, Susan (1971), *Sterling and British Policy*, OUP, London.

Taylor, A.J.P (1965), *English History 1914-1945*, OUP, London.

Wallace, William (1984), *Britain's Bilateral Relations within Western Europe*, Chatham House Paper No.23, RKP/RIIA, London.

Wallace, William (1986), 'What Price Independence? Sovereignty and Independence in British Politics', *International Affairs*, Vol.62, No.3.

Williams, P.M (ed) (1983), *The Diary of Hugh Gaitskell 1945-56*, Cape, London.

Young, John (1984), *Britain, France and the Unity of Europe, 1945-1951*, Leicester University Press.

Young, John (1988), *The Foreign Policy of Churchill's Peacetime Administration 1951-5*, Leicester University Press.

Young, John (1993), *Britain and European Unity, 1945-1992*, Macmillan, London.

Index

Acheson, Dean, 6-7, 16, 76-8, 103-5, 110-1, 115-7, 133, 167n.
Addison, Paul, 41n, 167n.
Adenauer, Konrad, 6, 16-7, 19, 20-2, 109, 113, 140, 143-4, 167n.
Alford, B.W.E., 167n.
Alsace-Lorraine, 113.
Argentina, 75.
Atlantic Alliance (see NATO).
Atlantic Council, 16, 18, 95, 108, 110-1, 116-7.
Attlee, Clement, 8-9, 11-2, 31, 46, 49-50, 66, 96, 104, 117, 125, 146.
Austin, Dennis, 65n, 167n.
Australia, 66, 74, 86.

Belgium, 57, 85.
Benelux, 8, 24, 33, 40, 85, 115, 131.
Bereitschaften, 109.
Berlin, 95, 109, 111, 115.
Berstein et al, 167n.

Bevin, Ernest, 2, 6-9, 14-6, 24, 28, 31-2, 37, 41, 49, 62, 66, 73-6, 78, 85-6, 88, 96-7, 99, 101, 104-5, 109, 111, 114-5, 126-31, 134, 138.
Bevin Plan, 78, 96-7.
Bidault, Georges, 6, 14, 18, 24, 130, 166.
Board of Trade, 6, 47, 56-7, 69, 71.
Bohlen, Charles, 78-9.
Boothby, Robert, 38, 73-4.
Bosuat, Gérard, 16n, 18n, 167n.
Bridges, Edward, 30, 125, 128.
Britain (see United Kingdom).
Bruce, David, 7, 82, 84.
Bullen, Roger and Pelly M.E, 6n, 40n, 49n, 111n, 113n, 124n, 127n, 135-6n, 139n, 147-8n, 162, 167n.
Bullock, Alan, 2n, 31n, 76n, 95n, 99n, 158n, 165, 167n.
Butt, D.M.B., 37, 43-4, 47, 102,

132, 135-6, 139, 141.

Cairncross, Alec, 14n, 43n, 56n, 167-8n
Camps, Miriam, 152n, 168n
Canada, 65, 74-5, 89, 95.
Ceylon, 76.
Channel Tunnel, 42.
Chiefs of Staff, 105, 113.
Churchill, Winston, 10, 36, 58, 62, 65, 67, 121, 147-8, 168, 170.
Clarke, Otto, 56.
Claude, Innis, 3n, 34n, 168n.
Coal Industry, 1-7, 9-10, 13, 16-20, 23-6, 33-4, 36-9, 43-51, 54-5, 57, 59, 64, 67-70, 75, 88-9, 95, 101-2, 105, 112-5, 121, 125-7, 129-37, 141, 143-5, 147-9, 152, 160, 162, 165, 167.
Coates, David, 158n, 168n.
Cold War, 5, 11, 95, 99, 123.
Commonwealth, 24, 31, 41, 44, 62-76, 78-81, 83-8, 96, 98, 124, 135-6, 147, 159, 163.
Conféderation Generale du Travail (CGT), 108.
Conservative Party, 1, 5, 10, 28, 41, 51, 54, 64-5, 70, 83, 121.
Containment doctrine, 77-80, 84, 96, 123.
Council of Europe, 2, 9, 28, 30, 33, 51, 64, 72, 85, 103, 129, 132, 148-50.
Council of Ministers (ECSC), 10, 16, 23, 29, 132-3, 149.
Cripps, Stafford, 8-9, 32, 37, 48-50, 129-32.
Customs Union, 20, 24, 38, 57, 68-9, 102.

Dalloz, Jacques, 18n, 168n.

Darwin, John, 71n, 168n.
Deutsch, Karl, 113n, 168n.
Dixon, Pierson, 33, 42, 66, 127, 148-50.
Dominions, 66, 68, 74.
Duchêne, François, 130n, 143n, 152n, 166n, 168n.

East Germany, 115.
Eden, Anthony, 33, 65, 67, 73-4, 81, 86, 95, 99, 147-50, 168n.
Eden Plan, 147-50.
European Coal and Steel Community (also see Schuman Plan), 19, 25, 43-6, 69, 89, 103-4, 114, 117, 129, 134-8, 141-2, 146-7, 149-50, 160-1.
European Defence Community, 38, 96, 103, 117, 149.
European Payments Union 2, 71, 85.
European Unity, 49, 51, 53, 66-7, 133.

Federation of British Industry, 43.
First World War, 21, 96.
Foreign Office, 2, 6, 11, 13, 18, 30, 33, 37-8, 40, 43, 47, 64, 73-4, 81, 87-8, 98-100, 102, 107-8, 111-2, 114, 123-4, 127-9, 133-6, 138-50.
Fourth Republic, 13, 41, 100, 108, 110.
France, 7-8, 11-20, 23-5, 33, 37-41, 52, 66, 77, 79, 82, 84, 89-91, 98-101, 103-5, 107-15, 124, 127-8, 130, 134, 138, 140, 142-3, 146, 158, 160-1, 166, 168.
Franco-German relationship, 2, 3, 6-7, 9, 11-3, 16-20, 21, 23-5, 33, 46, 50, 77, 79, 90-1, 105, 111-2, 117, 123-4, 127, 129-31, 139,

143-4, 146, 149.
Frankel, Joseph, 38n, 64n, 157n, 161n-4n, 168n.
Franks, Oliver, 76, 83, 87, 97, 107, 117, 123, 125.
Fritalux, 24, 57.
Fursdon, Edward, 168n.

Gainer, David, 111, 145-6.
Gaitskell, Hugh, 82, 112.
Gallagher, F.G.K., 38, 68, 150-1.
Gallup Opinion Polls, 38-9.
Gamble, Andrew, 161n, 168n.
George, Stephen, 168n.
Gilbert, Martin, 58n.
Gordon-Walker, Patrick, 69, 135.

Haas, Ernst, 33n, 168n.
Habermas, Jurgen, 3n, 168n.
Hall, Robert, 14, 30 32-3, 43-4, 46, 98-9, 127-9, 131, 136, 139, 141, 168n.
Hall-Patch, E, 30, 32-3, 98-9, 127-9, 131.
Halsey, A.H., 39n, 168n.
Harvey, Oliver, 13, 14, 17-8, 22, 24, 26, 37, 40, 87, 100-1, 105, 109, 111, 114, 126-7, 130-3, 137, 140, 144, 149.
Hayward, Jack, 161n, 168n.
Healey, Denis, 49, 72n, 168n.
Hennessy, Peter, 67n, 68n, 158n, 168n.
High Authority (ECSC), 1, 10, 12-3, 33-4, 102, 132-3, 136, 138, 140-1, 143.
Hill, Christopher, 64n.
Hitler, Adolf, 39, 66.
Hogan, Michael, 24n, 30n, 37n, 57n, 77-8n, 168n.
Hood, Lord, 38n, 140n, 151n.

Horne, Alistair, 2n, 169n.
House of Commons, 10, 36-7, 49, 65, 95, 133, 150.
Howe, Geoffrey, 42n, 169n.

International Authority of the Ruhr, 18, 144, 146.
Ikenberry, John, 163n, 169n.
Imperial Preference, 68-70.
India, 68, 74, 76.
Italy, 24, 40, 88, 98, 115, 161.

Jebb, Gladwyn, 2, 96-7, 104, 107, 138-9.
Jervis, Robert, 133n, 165n, 169n.
Johnson, Nevil, 38n, 169n.

Keohane, Robert and Nye, Joseph, 89n, 169n.
Kennan, George, 78-9.
Keynes, Maynard, 48, 160.
Kircheimer, O., 54n, 169n.
Kirkpatrick, Ivone, 99, 101-2, 108, 111, 114, 140, 143.
Kissinger, Henry, 12, 103.
Kolodziej, Edward, 63n, 169n.
Korea, 38, 80, 82, 95, 106-7, 109.

Labour Party, 1, 2, 5, 9-11, 28-31, 41, 43, 47-56, 66, 69, 70, 72, 82-3, 95, 104, 121, 130, 133-4, 137, 140, 145, 147-8, 159, 161.
Locke, John, 21.
Lord, Christopher, 35n, 86n, 169n.

Macrae, D., 110n, 169n.
Mallet, W., 87, 103, 109, 111, 115, 149.
Marquand, David, 35n, 160-1n, 169n.
Marshall Plan, 13, 20, 29, 85.

Massigli, René, 7-8n, 10n, 12-3n, 15n, 23-5n, 124n, 126n, 130n, 168n.
Middle East, 10.
Milward Alan, 20n, 24n, 49n, 56-7n, 85n, 157n, 160-1n.
Ministry of Defence, 6, 62, 108, 111, 123.
Ministry of Fuel and Power, 6.
Ministry of Supply, 6, 136, 146.
Moch, J, 110-1.
Monnet, Jean, 2, 6-9, 12-3, 15-24, 37, 43, 45, 78, 84, 87, 124, 127, 130-1, 134, 137-8, 149-50, 196n.
Moravcsik, Andrew, 8n, 35n, 169n.
Morgan, Kenneth, 8n, 10n, 48n, 54n, 71n, 104n, 169n.
Morrison, Herbert, 8, 22, 40-1, 49, 51, 76, 83, 87, 102, 108, 111, 117, 135, 140, 144-6.

National Coal Board, 49.
National Executive (Labour Party), 9, 48-9, 51, 95.
NATO (Atlantic Alliance), 10-1, 16, 18-9, 24-5, 78, 83, 89, 95-100, 102-13, 115-7, 122-4, 147, 150, 152, 162.
Netherlands, 10-11, 41.
New Statesman, 52-3.
New Zealand, 65-6, 74, 76, 86, 135.
Northedge, F.S., 162n, 170n.

OEEC (Organization of European Economic Co-operation), 20, 29, 32, 63, 72-3, 128, 132, 141.
Orwell, George, 39.

Pakistan, 76.

Parodi, A., 18.
Pelling, Henry, 39n, 170n.
Permanent Under Secretary's Committee (PUSC), 37, 73, 89, 98, 101-2, 124, 128, 134.
Petsche, Michel, 69, 128-30.
Phillips, Morgan, 104.
Pimlott, Ben, 56n, 170n.
Pitblado, David, 43, 47, 132-33, 135, 141-2.
Pleven, René, 38, 96, 98, 117.
Plowden, E., 43, 123, 135.
Poidevin, Raymond, 19n, 22n, 170n.

Quai D'Orsay, 12, 13.

Ruhr 14, 18, 20, 23, 53, 113, 116.

Saar, 19.
Scandinavia, 40, 52.
Schumacher, Kurt, 51, 109.
Schuman Plan (Also see European Coal and Steel Community), 1-6, 9-21, 23-5, 28, 33-9, 42-51, 54-5, 57, 62, 65-6, 67-72, 74, 76-9, 81, 83-4, 86, 88-92, 95-7, 99-103, 105, 109, 112-7, 122-5, 127-31, 136, 139, 140-7, 150, 157-62, 165.
Schuman, Robert, 1-26, 28, 30-1, 33-4, 36-9, 42-3, 44-52, 54-5, 57-8, 62, 65-72, 74, 76-9, 81, 83-4, 86, 88-9, 90-2, 95-103, 105, 109-10, 112-3, 114-7, 121-47, 149-51, 157-62, 165.
Second World War, 20, 63.
Seldon, Anthony, 170n.
Servan-Schreiber, J.J., 101.
Shinwell, E., 95, 105.
Shuckburgh, Evelyn, 66-7n, 86n, 170n.

Soviet Union (USSR), 63, 77, 96-7,
99, 100, 106, 111, 115-6, 124,
144.
Spaak, Paul-Henri, 31.
The Spectator, 36.
Spofford, General, 41, 117.
State Department, 17, 41, 78, 80,
86, 115-6.
Steel Industry, 1-7, 9-10, 13, 16-20,
23-6, 33-4, 36-9, 43-51, 54-5, 57-
9, 64, 67-70, 88-9, 95, 101-2,
105, 111-5, 121, 125-8, 129-37,
141, 143-9, 152, 161, 162, 165.
Sterling Area, 57, 67-8, 70, 73-4,
79, 86.
Stevenson, John, 39n, 170n.
Strang, Walter, 11, 47, 49, 87, 98,
103, 123-4, 126-7, 130.
Strange, Susan, 70n, 170n.
Sweden, 40, 44.
Switzerland, 40, 57.

Taylor, Paul, 55n, 170n.
The Times, 36, 38, 40-2, 90, 112,
136-7, 139, 163, 165.
Treasury, 6, 30, 43, 47-8, 128, 135,
141.
Treaty of Rome, 2, 29, 132, 151.
Truman, Harry, 58, 117.
Trades Union Congress, (TUC), 10,
48.

United Kingdom, 1-5, 7-17, 24-6,
28-36, 38-52, 55-8, 62-92, 95-6,
99-100, 102-3, 105, 107-8, 111-3,
115, 117, 121-42, 144-52, 157-62.
United States, 7, 11, 12, 16-7, 19,
20, 24-5, 41, 51, 62, 65-6, 70,
72-4, 76, 79-82, 86, 88-9, 91-2,
99-100, 103-8, 111, 116, 124,
129, 133, 144, 147, 149.

Versailles Treaty, 19.
Vichy regime, 100, 104.

Wallace, William, 42n, 170n.
West Germany, 12, 14-5, 19-20, 23-
5, 45, 57, 77, 90-1, 99, 102-9,
111-5, 136, 142-3, 146, 160, 165.
Westminster model, 30, 32, 34-5,
38, 42.
Whitehall, 6, 8, 45, 56, 69, 97, 132,
136, 162.
Williams, Philip, 82n, 112n.
Wilson, A.D., 18, 37, 56, 102, 133,
136, 138, 140, 142-5.

Young, John, 24n, 100n, 148n,
169n.
Younger, Kenneth, 13, 17-8, 26,
47, 97, 100, 104, 107, 115, 123-
4, 126-32, 134, 137-9, 144.